Making Self-Employment
Work for People with Disabilities

Making Self-Employment
Work for People with Disabilities

by

Cary Griffin

and

David Hammis

Griffin-Hammis Associates, LLC
Florence, Montana

·P A U L·H·
BROOKES
PUBLISHING C9 ®

Baltimore • London • Sydney

Paul H. Brookes Publishing Co.
Post Office Box 10624
Baltimore, Maryland 21285-0624

www.brookespublishing.com

Typeset by Integrated Publishing Solutions, Grand Rapids, Michigan.
Manufactured in the United States of America by
Victor Graphics, Baltimore, Maryland.

Tax laws, Social Security, Medicaid, and other social systems policies and laws change
over time. Therefore, the policy information presented cannot be used to make conclusive
determinations about taxes, social systems services eligibility, benefits eligibility, or
benefits payment amounts in individual cases. The suggestions in this book are not intended as a substitute for professional consultation. The authors and publisher disclaim
any liability arising directly or indirectly from the use of this book.

The stories in this book are based on the authors' experiences. For vignettes based on
actual people, individuals' names and identifying details have been changed to protect
their identities. Other vignettes are composite accounts that do not represent the lives
or experiences of specific individuals, and no implications should be inferred.

Library of Congress Cataloging-in-Publication Data

Griffin, Cary.
   Making self-employment work for people with disabilities / by Cary Griffin and David
  Hammis.
     p. cm.
  Includes bibliographical references and index.
  ISBN 1-55766-652-0
   1. People with disabilities—Employment—United States—Handbooks, manuals, etc.
2. Self-employed—United States. 3. New business enterprises—United States. 4. Small
business—United States—Management. I. Hammis, David. II. Title.

HD7256.U5G75 2003
658'.02'2'0874—dc21

                                                2003048040

British Library Cataloguing in Publication data are available from the British Library.

Contents

About the Authors

Cary Griffin, Senior Partner, Griffin-Hammis Associates, LLC, 5582 Klements Lane, Florence, Montana 59833; cgriffin@griffinhammis.com

In addition to serving as Senior Partner at Griffin-Hammis Associates, LLC, Cary Griffin is Director of Special Projects at the Rural Institute, The University of Montana. Cary is also former Director of an adult vocational program in southern Colorado, former Assistant Director of the Rocky Mountain Resource and Training Institute, and former Executive Director of the Center for Technical Assistance and Training in Colorado. Cary has written and managed more than $20 million in grants and contracts; is on the editorial boards for the *Journal of Vocational Rehabilitation* and the journal *Mental Retardation*; and has published extensively in the areas of leadership, organizational development, supported employment, and self-employment. Cary is a frequent keynote speaker and conference presenter; he consults internationally and can be found waving a bamboo fly rod on his days off in Montana.

David Hammis, Senior Partner, Griffin-Hammis Associates, LLC, 5582 Klements Lane, Florence, Montana 59833; dhammis@griffinhammis.com

In addition to serving as Senior Partner at Griffin-Hammis Associates, LLC, David Hammis maintains an ongoing relationship with the Rural Institute, The University of Montana, where he was Project Director for four employment and Social Security outreach training and technical assistance projects. He serves as Organizational Consultant for the Rural Institute's Rural Entrepreneurship and Self-Employment Expansion Design Project. In addition, Dave works with organizations nationally and internationally on benefits analysis, supported employment, supported entrepreneurial employment, and employment engineering.

Dave served as Project Engineer for Martin Marietta Aerospace before experiencing a significant disability and is the Past President of the Colorado Chapter of the Society of Manufacturing Engineers. He has worked in supported employment since 1988 and is personally responsible for the implementation of more than 250 Plans for Achieving Self-Support (PASS) that have led to employment, self-employment, and personal resources for people with disabilities. He has developed more than 175 jobs, including a considerable number of entrepreneurial successes for individuals with significant and multiple disabilities. In July 1996, Dave received the International Association for Persons in Supported Employment Professional of the Year Award for his "outstanding support and commitment to people with disabilities especially in the areas of Career Development and the use of Social Security Work Incentives."

Foreword

There is no longer a clear line between so-called conventional employment and self-employment. Because large companies hire and fire employees as the economy changes, hire part-time employees and temporary staff more often than in the past, and outsource significant portions of their work, the term *conventional employment* no longer has a clear definition. In response, workers often look for employment opportunities that allow greater control of their lives and their futures. Self-employment gives workers new options: a second income, full-time self-employment as part of a one- or two-person business, or small business ownership with several employees. In light of these changes, it is not surprising that people with disabilities consider the range of self-employment options when seeking possibilities for themselves.

In their work with people with disabilities who are seeking employment, Cary Griffin and Dave Hammis present self-employment as an option. Cary and Dave have seen that when people are educated and informed regarding their employment options, they will make the best decision for their future. For many years, Cary and Dave have worked with people with significant disabilities, many of whom have chosen and succeeded with self-employment. While working with organizations serving people with disabilities, as well as with the individuals pursuing employments, Cary and Dave have developed training and mentoring methods that have brought successful results across the country. *Making Self-Employment Work for People with Disabilities* shares the techniques and tools that have succeeded for them and can succeed for readers and the people they serve.

Cary and Dave have always shared their knowledge openly and freely by speaking, training, publishing articles, and personally working with individuals with significant disabilities. In this book, they continue that spirit of sharing. Equally important, they share the lessons that they have learned through their work. These lessons eradicate many assumptions and myths regarding employment for people with disabilities. The authors demonstrate how person-centered approaches break old patterns and stereotypes. Person-centered planning leads people to a community-based life with friends and family—a life in which people with disabilities can make informed decisions and direct their future.

Sound business planning and person-centered planning use many of the same methods. The similarities are what brought me, as a business person with long-term disabilities, to appreciate Cary and Dave's work so deeply. The person-centered approach is based on the reality that employment is simply what adults do! Whether employment is an easy goal to achieve or a significant challenge is irrelevant. You do what it takes, including bringing in community and business resources to help achieve the goal. This is also a basic business premise.

The person-centered approach brings together people who know and understand the needs and desires of the person with disabilities who is seeking employment. If self-employment is chosen, then it is based on what interests and excites the individual, as a person must care about and enjoy what he or she does

to maintain the business. The business also must match the skills of the individual and have a defined focus, which is another tenet of successful business development. Finally, the business must be self-sustainable for the long term, allowing it to become an ongoing part of the business and civic community.

Like most businesses, those run by people with disabilities require seed money and assistance to plan and start the business. They also need mentoring and technical assistance to make it through the problems and challenges that all businesses face during their first few years. When these factors come together, most self-employed individuals and small business owners with disabilities will succeed. This opportunity for long-term success is so important for people with disabilities, as it is often the only way for them to gain financial and social equity and to be viewed as competent citizens. Once a business is established, it is less susceptible to the changes in the business cycle than many of the more conventional jobs available for people with disabilities.

Self-employment does challenge the inventiveness of systems and human services professionals. Thinking like a business person requires a different point of view. *Making Self-Employment Work for People with Disabilities* gives human services professionals a significant "leg up" in this process. Cary and Dave have written from their professional perspective, which spans both the human services and small business worlds. This book combines best practices from both worlds. The business information and methods are written in a style that is clear and understandable for the nonbusiness reader.

Ironically, the greatest challenge for people with disabilities pursuing self-employment is dealing with the benefits that they receive from government programs. The chapters on financial issues for businesses elegantly delve into this topic. Dave's knowledge in this area is expansive. He is able to explain both potential pitfalls and opportunities in a logical manner, using examples that can be followed and used as models. Dave's comprehensive explanation of the Social Security Administration's Plan for Achieving Self-Support (PASS) describes this work incentive's advantages as a significant business funding resource; ways to use it most effectively; the differences in using the PASS if a person receives Supplemental Security Income (SSI), Social Security Disability Insurance (SSDI), or both; and many other secrets to successful use of this currently underutilized tool for self-employment success.

Self-employment for people with disabilities is both challenging and exciting. It is a positive challenge for people with disabilities who hope to have more income, become included in their communities, and improve the quality of their lives with family and friends. It is challenging to human services professionals who must move in this new direction, but the reward is achieving successful outcomes for their clients. Cary and Dave have made the challenges of self-employment for people with disabilities more achievable for all of us by sharing their knowledge and methods in *Making Self-Employment Work for People with Disabilities.*

Alice Weiss Doyel, M.S.
Author of *No More Job Interviews!*
Self-Employment Strategies for People with Disabilities
(Training Resource Network, 2000)

Preface

Making Self-Employment Work for People with Disabilities is presented in the most flexible and least prescriptive manner possible. Those seeking business ownership and those assisting people in starting businesses know or will shortly come to understand that the private enterprise option is the ultimate in non-linear experiences. Therefore, this guide is designed to present a framework flexible enough in its design to accommodate a myriad of business ideas and life circumstances. After serving as consultants on countless small business start-ups, we know that one size definitely does not fit all. Readers will have to adapt our suggested formats, customize the planning processes, and match their dreams and talents to the local economy.

This book is designed to guide the process of creating a small business that others will take seriously. We are not slaves to business planning, but we recognize that to support a venture, others need assurances and some level of formality. We also learned early on that people who start businesses need to focus on the future. This is true for knowing cash-flow demands, anticipating seasonal market influences, and planning Social Security Work Incentives (please note that 2002 benefits rates and rules are used throughout the book; for current information, go to http://www.ssa.gov/disability). If a disability hinders an individual's understanding of the future, his or her supporters must assist in charting the course. With a little forethought, anyone can own and operate a successful business.

Throughout this book, we emphasize the need for person-centered approaches. People who have experienced the drudgery of working at a job they dislike will instantly recognize that creating a business around the existence and exploitation of a market is a bad idea in the long run. Success generally stems from the love of one's labors, so we start there and create or discover the market as we meld customers with personal avocation. It is a balancing act for sure.

Many readers will have little experience with private enterprise. Again, this book emphasizes the need for a diverse assemblage of partners. In our own work and in our own small business, we benefit from the support of family and friends, local small business experts, trained consultants, and other business people offering such vital supports as accounting, marketing, and graphic design. Business ownership is the antithesis of isolation. Developing successful enterprises means rolling up one's sleeves and facilitating supports outside the traditional school and rehabilitation fields. The very act is liberating and instructive. In fact, in our intensive work on small businesses across the United States, we have discovered that many people working in transition and rehabilitation roles have personal dreams of business ownership. This secondary market for us once again reveals the nonlinear, unpredictable nature of for-profit enterprise. We trust that *Making Self-Employment Work for People with Disabilities* will help these latent-entrepreneurs find their calling—or at least supplement their human services paycheck.

Throughout the United States and the world, microenterprise continues to challenge predominant economic theory and thought. The growth of very

small businesses (generally with one to five employees) actually derives from the work of the Grameen Bank of Bangladesh. The Grameen Bank has helped spawn thousands of enterprises in Bangladesh, fueled the microbusiness movement across the world, and provided a foundation of possibilities that we drew on when beginning our work in this area. People with disabilities and people living in developing countries face similar circumstances. Poverty, a paucity of educational choices, lack of credit or personal equity, substandard health care and housing, stereotyping, and prejudice are shared experiences. Furthermore, even though self-employment ventures succeed in the United States at the remarkable rate of 79%, they are still seen as highly speculative and risky, especially for individuals with disabilities. There are more than 40 million Americans with disabilities facing an unemployment rate of almost 75%. Small business ownership seems to be a reasonable risk in the face of certain poverty, isolation, and dependence.

At another point in our careers, we might have considered the purpose of *Making Self-Employment Work for People with Disabilities* to be broad-scale rehabilitation and transition systems change. Certainly, we work every day with leaders who risk their careers making changes that improve lives a hundred fold. Yet, overall, the system either wears you out or waits you out. This book is designed for the individual and the small group who will make businesses happen one person at a time on a local level. This book's purpose is to change lives.

Acknowledgments

First and foremost, this book is the result of people trusting us and taking great risks. The many individuals with disabilities who entertained business ideas really wrote this volume, and their experiences are distilled here in what we hope is true to their courage to try something different.

Also, this book is the work of many, many people who explored ideas with us, challenged us, and did the hard work with us in the field. They include our colleagues at the Rural Institute at The University of Montana: Roger Shelley, Marsha Katz, Mike Flaherty, Nancy Maxson, Connie Lewis, Bob Snizek, Richard Kiefer-O'Donnell, Timm Vogelsberg, Jennifer Crouch, and Colleen Koch. Also included are the many colleagues, customers, and funders who took the risk of trusting us with their money and reputations: Tom Hayes and Lisa Newman at the Montana Job Training Partnership; Pamela Martin and Gayle Palumbo at the U.S. Department of Education, Rehabilitation Services Administration; Alex Kielty at the U.S. Department of Labor, Employment and Training Administration; Montana Vocational Rehabilitation; Paul Wehman, John Kregel, Vicki Brooke, Grant Revell, Mike Barcus, and everyone else at the Research and Training Center on Workplace Supports at Virginia Commonwealth University; Dave Roberts, Diana Beckley, and everyone else at the Region VII Community Rehabilitation Program–Regional Continuing Education Program at the University of Missouri; Kim Cordingly at the Job Accommodation Network; Betsy J. Kaufman at the Association of Small Business Development Centers; Carol Maus at AgrAbility in Washington, D.C.; Dennis Rizzo in New Jersey; Mary Strehlow and Linda Larson at Clark County Community Services in Vancouver, Washington; Molly Holsapple and Jo-Ann Sowers in Oregon; Steve Hall and Patty Cassidy in Colorado Springs, Colorado; Alice and Hoyt Doyel, Katherine Carol, and Tom Emmons in Denver, Colorado; Kathie Snow in Colorado; Rosalie Sheehy Cates at the Montana Community Development Corporation; Teri Goodwin and all of the staff at The Initiative in Seattle; Casey Jeszenka at the Small Business Development Center in Mangilao, Guam; Peggy Terhune, Dave West, and Johanna Kroth at The Arc of Stanly County, North Carolina; Doug Crandall and Nancy Brooks at Cobb County Community Services Board in Georgia; Ray Jensen in Seattle; Corey Smith and Joe Longcor in Michigan; Ray Marzoli at Work Incentives Policy at the Social Security Administration in Baltimore; Social Security Plan for Achieving Self-Support (PASS) specialists Vera Brodsky in Seattle, Roxanna Hunt in Colorado, Virena Riley in Cincinnati, Vicki Wilson and Timothy McEvoy in Kansas, and Sandra Beckley and Peter Prather in California; Neil Shim, Vocational Rehabilitation Director in Hawaii; Lisa Poteat at The Arc of North Carolina; Carol A. Beatty and Jackie Ring at The Arc of Howard County, Maryland; Brian Keith in New Hampshire; Carol H. Estes and Dave Matheis in Kentucky; Jopie Smith in California; Jennifer Jones and Ron Broome at the Alaska Works Initiative in Anchorage; Sheila Finkenbinder in Sitka, Alaska; Beth Kersey in Bethel, Alaska; John McClure at Western Washington University; Tammara Geary Freeman at

the Association for Persons in Supported Employment in Richmond, Virginia; Mike Callahan at Marc Gold & Associates; Robin Way and her colleagues at the Cerebral Palsy Association in Australia; and a thousand others who helped!

Finally, we thank our wives, Ellen Condon and Meg Hammis, who tolerate our travel schedules and offer us enviable support.

This book is dedicated
to the memory of Joe Schiappacasse,
our friend, colleague and brother of the angle.

He taught us more than we are
capable of understanding in this lifetime.

Chapter 1

Self-Employment as a Mainstream Approach to Adult Life

IMPORTANT TERMS IN THIS CHAPTER

Community rehabilitation programs (CRPs): Local rehabilitation agencies that generally offer sheltered employment, supported employment, service coordination, and other state-funded services to adults with disabilities. Most are funded primarily for individuals with developmental disabilities.

Small Business Administration (SBA): A federal agency that sponsors small business development programs throughout the United States. Offers free of charge technical assistance, financing, and information on enterprise development.

Small Business Development Centers (SBDCs): Centers in many U.S. communities that provide free assistance regarding business feasibility, business planning, marketing suggestions, financing, and management. SBDCs are part of the SBA.

Social Security Administration (SSA): The primary benefits system in the United States for people with disabilities. The SSA's most common benefits programs are Supplemental Security Income (SSI) and Social Security Disability Insurance (SSDI). The SSA also manages the Plan for Achieving Self-Support (PASS) program.

Vocational Rehabilitation (VR): A state and federally funded program charged with assisting eligible individuals with significant disabilities in finding employment. VR can and does support business development, vocational training, and college edu-

1

cation. VR offices are found in communities across every U.S. state and territory. Access to VR can also be obtained through local One-Stop Centers (see Workforce Investment Act).

Workforce Investment Act (WIA): This federal act created One-Stop Centers (also known as Workforce Development Centers) across the United States to serve all people seeking employment. VR and other disability organizations are collaborators in WIA, and it is another source of technical assistance and potential funding for wage jobs and self-employment.

Many people begin their working lives as teenagers. Delivering newspapers, mowing lawns, milking cows, preparing fast-food, washing cars, and baby-sitting exemplify the diversity of jobs traditionally assigned to youth to build character and a strong work ethic. Unfortunately, for most students with significant disabilities, this natural part of learning real-life skills and lessons, acculturating, and growing a work ethic is missing. Various legislation and legal decisions hold the potential for and promise of equal access to careers and substantive employment: the Education for All Handicapped Children Act of 1975 (PL 94-142); followed by the Individuals with Disabilities Education Act (IDEA) of 1990 (PL 101-476); and—supporting people with disabilities into adulthood—the Rehabilitation Act of 1973 (PL 93-112), the Workforce Investment Act (WIA) of 1998 (PL 105-220), the Americans with Disabilities Act (ADA) of 1990 (PL 101-336), and the *Olmstead v. LC* (1999) decision from the Supreme Court (Wehman, 2001). Still, most transition-age youth with significant disabilities graduate without paying jobs, and most adults with significant disabilities remain unemployed or severely underemployed throughout their lifetimes (U.S. Census Bureau, 2001). During the 1990s, a decade that witnessed one of the strongest economies in U.S. history, enrollments for sheltered workshops increased, and the number of special education students graduating into paid jobs remained agonizingly low (Butterworth, Gilmore, Kiernan, & Schalock, 1999; McGaughey, Kiernan, McNally, Gilmore, & Keith, 1994; Wehman, 2001).

This same time period witnessed the success of supported employment techniques, with more than 150,000 individuals in community jobs (Wehman & Kregel, 1998). These workers' disabilities were once considered too severe for the individuals to gain employment, but the techniques of offering ongoing workplace and personal supports, coupled with matching people with jobs they enjoy, eroded previous stereotypes in the rehabilitation professions and within the business community (Callahan & Garner, 1997; Griffin, Flaherty, et al., 2001; Wehman & Kregel, 1998). Self-employment, as described in this book, is the next logical step in the evolution of supported employment technology. Because all people who are self-employed use, create, and purchase a variety of supports—ranging from accounting services to sales representatives—owning a business meshes well with the American Dream and with the commitment of rehabilitation professionals, family members, friends, and neighbors to assist people with disabilities in achieving typical lives. Owning a business can be one of the least stigmatizing forms of employment for individuals with significant disabilities because the opportunity to gently rely on ongoing or time-limited rehabilitation services coexists with typically purchased business supports.

Self-employment is booming across the United States, with an estimated 20 million Americans owning home-based businesses. The self-employment rate is growing at more than 20% annually. Between 1990 and 1994, microenterprise (businesses employing one to five workers) generated 43% of all of the new jobs in the United States. Also, in the 1990s, 60% of microenterprises were owned by women, and these businesses created more jobs than all of the Fortune 500 companies combined (Access to Credit, 1998; Forrester, 1996; Friedman, 1996; Sirolli, 1999). This cultural and economic shift of taking individual opportunity, which appears to be largely unaffected by good or bad economic times, presents another promising career option to individuals with significant disabilities (Arnold, 1996; Brodsky, 2002; Griffin, 1999a, 1999b; Griffin & Hammis, 1996; Taylor & Wacker, 1997).

Approximately 2.5% (5,000 people) of VR successful closures are for self-employment, and the numbers are growing daily (Arnold, 1996). Numerous types of agencies (e.g., VR, developmental disabilities, mental health) in various states (e.g., Montana, Colorado, Kentucky, Maryland, New York, California) are exploring policy and funding mechanisms to increase self-employment opportunities. In 2001, Congress created the Office of Disability Employment Policy (ODEP) at the U.S. Department of Labor. ODEP encourages small business ownership through its guiding legislation, the WIA, and is funding special projects and training programs related to individuals with disabilities. The Rehabilitation Services Administration (RSA) within the U.S. Department of Education promotes self-employment as a reasonable outcome for state VR agencies and also is demonstrating various aspects of entrepreneurial ventures through training and grant programs.

Yet, to succeed, there must be a concerted and well-funded effort to train and retrain staff charged with supporting individuals who seek self-employment. Without this significant investment, community resources that exist to assist all citizens will be untapped, community rehabilitation agencies and VR counselors will be overtaxed due to the intensity and complexity of some business ventures, and consumers may be denied possible career advancement (Griffin & Hammis, 2001a; Shelley et al., 2002). It is also certain that if transition-age students are not expected to deserve more than just a plan, then what lies ahead for them is graduating into the dead-end of day activity centers, sheltered workshops, or adult services waiting lists (Butterworth et al., 1999). Self-employment, and perhaps graduating as the owner/operator of a small business, is a more positive option.

Self-employment is not for everyone. It is a personal choice that should be balanced by a variety of life circumstances, including financial position and funding, availability and quality of business and personal supports, and the viability of the business idea. Just as in supported employment, the driving ethics are that everyone is ready to work and that it is the responsibility of special education and rehabilitation professionals to provide or facilitate the supports that make success possible. In some cases, allowing the person to experiment with different career options is the greatest support available.

There appear to be certain indicators of success probability in self-employment, however. For instance, many small business owners learned their trade and understand the market because they worked for someone else first (Doyel,

2000). Still, because so many people with disabilities never get the chance to begin with a typical job, self-employment presents a unique opportunity to create an employment circumstance specifically tailored to their personal situation, degree of mobility, speed of production, stamina, health, and accommodation needs. Again, a person's disability should not determine his or her fitness for self-employment. Rather, each situation is assessed to point out the need for supports—such as financing, skills training in specific tasks, and tooling and/or assistive technology—in the same manner that any entrepreneur requires supports in areas of need. Typical business owners outsource accounting, marketing, subcomponent manufacturing, and other functions that they either cannot handle themselves or do not enjoy (Doyel, 2000).

EXAMPLES OF SUCCESSFUL INDIVIDUALS AND BUSINESSES

The authors and their colleagues across the country are privileged to work with numerous individual business owners whose stories illustrate the concepts and approaches to enterprise development found throughout this book. Consider, for example, Andrew—a middle-age gentleman who spent most of his life in institutions, workshops, and group homes. The authors and other staff at the University of Montana's Rural Institute, using the strengths-based approach, developed an inventory of positive attributes that included Andrew's friendly smile, his interesting sense of humor, and a personality that made those around him comfortable. Two noteworthy interests or strengths included his stuffed animal collection and his enjoyment of an existing volunteer position. As a volunteer at the local nature center, Andrew fed and groomed animals, interacted with other staff and volunteers (although he used little verbal language), and assisted with other chores.

The professionals in his life considered this gentleman "too disabled" to work, and although the nature center staff valued him as a volunteer, they did not have revenue for or an interest in hiring him. With Andrew's significant input, a proposal was developed for him to sell stuffed animals at the center. The proposal included assistance from the provider agency staff, who would manage his books and inventory, and called on the nature center staff to help with daily operations, such as money exchanges. The design of the business was not typical, and management of the business was different from most, but sales flourished and a strong partnership grew as the entrepreneur paid 10% of profits to the nature center for rent and minor assistance with the largely self-serve operation. Seven years later, the business expanded to sales of stuffed animals to other downtown stores. Andrew is now welcomed as a "regular" on Main Street, and is viewed as a success by the local developmental disability agency, which helped him move into his first apartment. In addition, because he has a bank account in the company's name, Andrew has amassed more than $8,000 in cash, well above the $2,000 limit for someone receiving SSI payments.

By taking a strengths-based approach (Callahan & Garner, 1997; Callahan & Nisbet, 1997; Griffin & Hammis, 1996), this business person's deficits largely disappeared, and his many attributes became apparent. Creativity, inventiveness, intuitive consideration of the tourist market, and ongoing and largely invisible supports that cost far less than the average day program led to success.

In rural North Carolina, a young man with autism constantly ran from his sheltered workshop. Using a person-centered approach to employment development, it was discovered that George was recognized in his family for his light touch when transplanting seedlings and for his infatuation with trucks and farm tractors. Seeing such equipment drive by is what prompted his running from the workshop. George was simply trying to catch a ride.

The team designed a job development plan targeting agricultural employment for George. As often happens, however, a chance meeting (with two brothers who owned a local farm) and an unsolicited donation from a greenhouse led to the establishment of George's business. He started a greenhouse next to the brothers' roadside fresh produce stand. After several licensing delays, "George's" opened its doors to supply specialty plants and vegetables to customers of the roadside stand and to start seedlings for the brothers' farm. George was once considered unemployable due to the severity of his disability and his "unacceptable" behavior. Today, he has an employment specialist who helps with production. In addition, George has rich natural supports from his family as well as from the two brothers who own the farm and teach him the trade using their experience and specific quality standards (they also give him occasional rides on their tractors). The business is projected to exceed its substantial profit projections for the first year by growing specialty food crops and poinsettias for the holiday market. Even if his income is less than projected, George has a rich and growing business relationship with two community members, meets dozens of customers weekly, is considered a talented entrepreneur by his family, and earns self-employment wages well beyond anything he earned in the workshop. Perhaps most surprising is George's impact as a role model. George's success inspired more than a dozen agency staff to discuss their own personal small business ideas with the authors. These frontline employees are gaining personal strength and taking risks because George is leading the way (Kroth, 2001).

Jennifer is 21 years old. She owns and operates Jennifer's Art Enterprises out of her parent's home in the Rocky Mountains. Three years ago, she was attending her local sheltered workshop. Like so many individuals with multiple significant disabilities leaving high school, Jennifer had virtually no choice in the matter: a sheltered workshop, a waiting list, or nothing. Seeing this as an unreasonable transition outcome after years in public schools, Jennifer's parents pulled together a team of people from the Rural Institute and the local developmental disability agency to form a person-centered plan. Jennifer, who loves to paint, started her own business, with management and sales assistance from her family and the developmental disability program staff. Family support is a common element in successful small business (Doyel, 2000; U.S. Department of Commerce, 2000) and is one of the most common, and often necessary, natural supports.

The business design is based on Jennifer using a sponge or rag dipped in watercolors and swirling it on a blank canvas. The result is a colorful background that is then purchased exclusively by a local well-known artist, who uses such backgrounds for various still lifes and landscapes. With the assistance of her family and the day program staff, Jennifer makes other products, too, including greeting cards. Jennifer is not getting rich, but she is earning money, contributing to her family's income, and continuing to participate in her community. Thinking creatively resulted in a unique business model, raised the expectations of all involved, and short-circuited an almost certain future of unemployment or enrollment in a sheltered workshop.

Edward is a young man in his late thirties living in a small town in the Northwest U.S. During most of his adult life, he worked for several glass installation businesses in his hometown of 25,000 people. His erratic behavior, caused by his disability, cost him those jobs, but not before he learned the ins and outs of the trade. As an employee and keen observer, Edward recognized lapses in customer service by his former employers, and he set out to start a business that accommodates the symptoms of his bipolar disorder and that addresses the needs of construction companies and homebuilders seeking high-quality windows and glass.

Edward's business idea was rejected by the state employment counselor. Yet, working with the local SBDC, as well as with the Rural Institute and the Montana Job Training Partnership through a U.S. Department of Labor–funded disability demonstration project, grant money was secured to launch the enterprise. The business started slowly, and finding customers was difficult. Costly local advertising reached few customers. Edward's budget was depleted after 6 months, but networking with local construction bosses in coffee shops around town soon brought a $40,000 order for windows, followed by another, and then another. With an initial investment of less than $20,000, Edward's business was grossing more than $100,000 per quarter after the first hard year, and it grossed roughly $750,000 in 2001. When the business changed from installation to showroom sales of custom windows, it faltered. However, it was saved by the visibility and personal sales calls of the owner. As in so many success stories, a family member (in this case, Edward's wife) provided support as the bookkeeper with a solid hold on the business's financial operations.

In these four examples, self-employment evolved as a natural option once a vocational profile of likes, dislikes, preferred environments, supports (needed and available), and existing and potential resources was developed. Desirable employment scenarios emanate from this person-centered planning process, which is detailed in Chapter 2. Self-employment is only one option and not always the best one. The decision to start a business must be based on the individual's dreams and desires, the ability to create or respond to market needs, and the availability of supports. Of course, the need for business supports is often used to discourage people with disabilities from pursuing self-employment.

Small business supports typically involve assistance with production or service delivery (operations), business planning, sales and marketing, and bookkeeping or accounting. These supports are commonly required for any business. As service dollars become more flexible and portable, personal control of resources becomes more widely accepted and leads to easier arrangement of business supports. At this point, creative leveraging of supports may be necessary. In Jennifer's situation, support came from an exclusive deal with the artist to create canvases. By developing an informal partnership with this artist, Jennifer generated revenue immediately; built her skills and reputation; and has been able, with family and agency support, to expand products. Jennifer still relies on sales of greeting cards, featuring her backgrounds and the artist's foreground paintings, for her primary revenue.

At the nature center, Andrew's business-within-a-business model worked best. This setup provided a steady stream of customers, who were drawn past the stuffed animals, and utilized existing employees to casually assist with daily business operations. Disability agency staff helped with the books and inventory. Numerous other business-within-a-business scenarios, including a small-engine repair shop and a copying business inside a rural health club, demonstrate the willingness of community businesses to partner with others who bring new revenue streams and customers to their door.

George's greenhouse is another business within a business that utilized disability agency support for production and bookkeeping while creating a symbiotic relationship with the farmers, who also trained to their specifications to guarantee the best possible goods for their roadside stand. George's success is integral to the farm's success. George, through his small business, has become a vital and contributing force in the local economic development movement—not someone seen only as a taxpayer burden or passive member of the community.

TYPICAL CONCERNS ABOUT SMALL BUSINESS AND DISABILITY

Implementing self-employment as an emerging technique with individuals with significant disabilities involves substantial attention to minimizing the fears of the prospective business owner (PBO), as well as those of the rehabilitation and local small business development professionals charged with assisting PBOs. The success rate of small business is surprisingly high, despite widely accepted beliefs to the contrary. The U.S. SBA reports that more than 79% of small businesses are still operating after the initial 5 years. In addition, the long-term trend in employment is away from major corporations to growing job opportunities in smaller firms (Miyares, 2002; SBA, 1996a, 1996b; U.S. Department of Commerce, 2000). Self-employment and small business are a defining characteristic of America's economic landscape and present a tremendous opportunity for those most challenged by the competitive labor market.

Still, many doubts remain regarding the viability of individuals with significant disabilities starting, operating, and managing businesses. The following concerns and questions are routinely raised when proposing small business development for and with individuals with significant disabilities.

Concern: Which types of assessments best determine whether self-employment is right for a particular individual?

Response: Formal paper-and-pencil tests; vocational evaluations; and assessments that measure interests, vocational skills, and traits or that suggest predictive validity in certain careers through psychometrics are neither particularly useful in nor advised for determining self-employment capacity. Person-centered evaluative approaches to identifying unique gifts, talents, learning styles, hopes and dreams, financial opportunities through Social Security benefits, family support, and other individualized inventories work best (Callahan & Garner, 1997; Griffin & Hammis, 1996). One successful format is presented in Chapter 2 and should be used in combination with the business feasibility testing outlined in Chapter 3.

Concern: If a person cannot read or write, how can he or she possibly be expected to operate a profitable business?

Response: Operating a small business is always a matter of degree. Although many small business owners perform most or all of the necessary functions, many others do not. Writing a business plan, for instance, is outside the expertise of many entrepreneurs, so SBDCs and a host of business consultants exist to assist in such matters. Literacy is not a prerequisite for business ownership. Inventiveness and support focused on accomplishing particular tasks are required. For instance, if someone cannot write but must complete invoices at the point-of-product sale, perhaps customers can fill out their own receipts; the owner can be guided by a graphic interface on a touch-screen computer; or an employee or business partner can manage these tasks.

Concern: How long should professionals support someone as a small business owner?

Response: Many systems are time limited, such as schools, WIA programs, and VR. When using these services, careful planning must be involved to accommodate necessary long-term supports through the business design (e.g., having a business partner, family member, or employee provide assistance), through purchase of business services afforded from sales (e.g., accounting, marketing), or through extended services available from states' general funds and/or Medicaid Waiver dollars used by developmental disability and mental health programs throughout the United States.

Concern: How much does a small business cost?

Response: Start-up costs for small business are as wide ranging as business ideas. Many microenterprises are started with little or no money and grow over time. Most small business in the United States cost less than $10,000 to start, and examples of businesses owned by people with disabilities show that the costs average approximately

$5,000 (Doyel, 2000; Newman, 2001). Ongoing support costs vary depending on the person and his or her disability, but these supports (e.g., transportation, medication, instructional assistance) are necessary even if a business is not started.

Concern: How does someone finance a small business?

Response: A host of revenue sources are available to finance a small business. As traditional developmental disability and mental health services funds become increasingly individualized or "portable," personal budgeting and control of individual rehabilitation and treatment money grows. In the near future, changes in state and federal policies will give individuals with disabilities more control over disability funds, and many people will be able to redirect their money away from traditional agencies and into their own hands through fiscal intermediaries or families. Individuals will be able to create a personal budget, using funding that once went directly to a service provider to buy the specific goods and services needed for success. For example, someone who generates $12,000 per year in state funding that goes to the sheltered workshop may be able to redirect that money directly into a personal plan for a job or business and to draw on those funds, just as the service provider would, for as long as needed.

Furthermore, both VR and the WIA programs support small business. Emerging demonstrations of Individual Training Accounts (ITAs) and intensive services funds from WIA providers are proof of the viability of enterprise development. VR funds, Tribal VR funds, and WIA funds also can be used together (if purchasing different items or services for the entrepreneur) and can be further blended with SSA Work Incentives and developmental disability, mental health, or other disability system funds to create a well-funded business start-up or expansion.

SSA Work Incentives have proven to be a tremendously flexible and lucrative business support fund for people (Griffin, Flaherty, et al., 2001; Hammis & Griffin, 2002; see also Chapter 6 for a detailed discussion of SSA Work Incentives). As the Ticket to Work program becomes available in all states by the end of 2003 through the Ticket to Work and Work Incentives Improvement Act (TWWIIA) of 1999, Social Security recipients will be eligible for a voucher redeemable through various approved vocational services. This voucher, or Ticket, is used to gain employment or to support a small business. The Ticket to Work program is a key component of President Bush's New Freedom Initiative allowing choices and opportunities for individuals with disabilities seeking long-term employment. In short, a Ticket is a voucher redeemable for assistance in finding a job through employment agencies across the United States.

There are also a host of loan and microloan programs available to PBOs. Local banks, SBDCs, and Tribal Business Information Centers (TBICs) are the best sources of information and access.

Concern: How long can a small business be expected to last?

Response: The tenure of small businesses varies considerably. Most businesses change over time, adapting to market shifts, customer preferences, the owner's health, and the presence of other opportunities. Many small business owners take on new products, move to new locations, or sell their businesses and use the profits to start new ventures, so longevity is largely a function of the business model and the owner's plans or opportunities.

Concern: Should families be involved in an individual's small business?

Response: Family support is evident in many small businesses. This is often a critical natural support and is traditional in the United States as well as in many other countries. Families can hire sons and daughters, make them partners in existing businesses, launch new enterprises with them, or loan or give them money to support a business. Many American families send their children without disabilities to college with savings that they had put away for 20 years. A family that has a child with a disability and can afford such expenditures should consider saving for a small business.

Concern: How small is too small for a business?

Response: A business should generate revenue for the owner and employees, if any. Typically, businesses grow in stages, as do earnings. A carefully planned approach should be used to generate money to live on without disqualifying the individual from the safety net of various benefits systems, such as Social Security and subsidized housing, until these resources are no longer required. Individuals facing unemployment or sheltered employment almost always earn more money in their businesses than the national average earned through sheltered work (Butterworth et al., 1999; McGaughey et al., 1994; Newman, 2001).

Concern: Can a business sustain interruptions when the owner has significant health problems or requires numerous breaks for medical and therapeutic treatments?

Response: A small business naturally contains the capacity to accommodate a host of personal needs. Some business owners close on Wednesday afternoons to allow for golf games; others close on Wednesday afternoons to attend physical therapy. However, a business with limited hours of operation may suffer significant financial setbacks, so having an employee or business partner who can carry on in one's absence is a wise support strategy.

Concern: Entrepreneurs are known to work 80 hours per week and to "do it all"—from sales to bookkeeping. How is an individual coming out of a special education resource classroom going to know how to do this?

Response: Although it is true that many business owners work long, hard hours, it is also true that many others do not. Profitable businesses allow owners to hire others to do much of the work, and many small businesses do not require 80 hours per week for operation. Still, the work can be challenging, especially to someone who has been deprived of a work ethic through unpaid "experiences" that devalue work and the worker, who has improper work supports, or who has been sheltered from typical expectations of career achievement. Starting a part-time or after-school business may be a worthwhile family activity that counteracts low expectations commonly afforded children with high support needs.

Concern: There are almost no jobs in rural America. How can a business survive in such a depressed environment?

Response: Despite the misconceptions, rural communities are rich in opportunity. People still buy goods and services locally, and products generated in rural areas can often be sold in more populated communities. The challenge remains matching a person's dreams and talents to a saleable idea. Taking a person-centered approach leverages the skills and passions of the individual and matches them to community needs. The person, not the market, however, always must come first to ensure commitment to the process. There are always unmet needs and uncompleted work in all communities. Matching a person who can do the work or fill the need with the customers is a challenge that is proving successful in rural communities worldwide (Griffin, Flaherty, et al., 2001; Sirolli, 1999).

Concern: Why not go to the sheltered workshop first to learn work and social skills?

Response: To paraphrase management consultant Don Blohowiak (1995), using a sheltered workshop to teach valued work and social skills might be like using a Ouija Board to improve family communication. Sheltered workshops were created to help people with disabilities gain employment, but only about 20% of individuals who enter a workshop leave it for a real job. Isolated settings, especially community facilities such as workshops, stigmatize people with disabilities and make them stand out as different and incompetent. These facilities and any other segregated models, be they recreational or educational, interrupt the typical flow of personal interchange and the activity common in communities and neighborhoods. Learning valued work and social skills occurs only in typical environments (Brown et al., 1979; Brown et al., 1987; Gretz, 1992; Hagner & DiLeo, 1993; O'Brien & Mount, 1991).

Concern: Many students and adults with disabilities appear unmotivated by money. How can they be expected to run a real business?

Response: Many students and adults with significant disabilities have not been exposed to family or professional expectations of career success. Bright futures are seldom anticipated by the medical personnel who advise parents of infants with disabilities, so dreams of children growing up to be firefighters, doctors, or other typical members of the community work force yield to the realities of speech-language and physical therapy schedules. Transition-age students, if they receive any inclusive vocational training, are typically exposed to entry-level jobs through unpaid work experience. Unpaid work experience can be especially helpful to students, families, and educators in discovering individual talents and passions. However, only having unpaid work opportunities is unnatural. Eliminating pay also can affect motivation; most youth who have paper routes, flip burgers at fast-food restaurants, babysit, or mow lawns expect to be paid and draw a critical connection between effort and reward. Furthermore, earnings in sheltered workshops average less than minimum wage, effectively breaking any behavioral connection between work and money (Butterworth et al., 1999; McGaughey et al., 1994). Creating opportunities to use personal talents, to explore various work environments, and to learn the connection between effort and pay is essential for all people.

Concern: The business community and business-related agencies, such as SBDCs, are not inviting to people with disabilities. How can they be persuaded to help?

Response: Most business development professionals have little exposure to individuals with disabilities. Nonetheless, they generally are welcoming, and if publicly funded, these agencies are obligated by law to assist these individuals. Seeking assistance does entail an educational process. It is wise to enter an SBDC, TBIC, or other program office with some ideas but without expectations for full service; these offices are underfunded and their staff are overworked. However, they are willing partners and are generally excited by the opportunity to start a new venture. The SBA's web site gives locations of local consultation services (see http://www.sba.gov/regions/states.html).

ADVANTAGES OF
SELF-EMPLOYMENT OVER WAGE EMPLOYMENT

Business ownership is on the rise across the United States, but most Americans continue to work for someone else. Those in the human services field also may be the least likely advocates for self-employment because of an attraction to the nonprofit work of public-sector employment—and perhaps because of a less recognized aversion to the competitiveness and unseemliness of the for-profit world. The human services field is a world of assisting, helping, and protecting, and the field sometimes views capitalists as cold, uncaring, and self-interested. All the same, the world of business affords individuals the economic civil rights that can leverage equitable participation in the greater community, and the status and self-determination that come from self-employment may prove liberating for many individuals. Self-employment provides a number of advantages over working for someone else:

1. The U.S. economic environment is allowing self-employment to grow substantially (Brodsky, 2002). Statistically, it is the largest market segment of new and expanding employment opportunities. With more than 80% of men and 54% of women with disabilities unemployed in the United States, the risk of attempting small business ownership is minimal compared with the possibilities of success (U.S. Census Bureau, 2001).

2. Self-employment offers the only substantial options available under the Social Security and Medicaid/Medicare systems to accumulate personal wealth and manage income in a way that is predictable and personally adjustable (Hammis & Griffin, 2002). Almost without exception, people with disabilities in the United States receive SSI and/or SSDI, as well as Medicaid or Medicare benefits. Under Medicaid and SSI regulations, an individual beneficiary cannot accumulate more than $2,000 in cash resources (i.e., total of all cash on hand and in checking accounts, savings accounts, stocks, bonds, and whole life insurance policies), unless the cash resources are sheltered in an irrevocable trust managed by someone else or in a PASS. However, a business owner receiving SSDI, SSI, Medicaid, or Medicare benefits can have unlimited funds in a small business checking account for legitimate operating expenses as defined by the Internal Revenue Service (IRS) and SSA rules as Property Essential for Self-Support (PESS). A small business owner can accumulate operating cash and other business capital resources and, thus, unlimited net worth in the business. This circumstance also creates the possibility of eventually selling the enterprise and using the proceeds to purchase a home, for instance. Self-employment creates an avenue for increasing individual wealth; wage employment has no comparable options. (See Chapter 6 for information on analyzing on Social Security income benefits.)

3. Self-employment offers individuals with disabilities who receive Social Security benefits a financial cushion (i.e., income for survival) during the business start-up phase and often throughout the life of the business. A

small business owner without a disability who has no other source of income as a backup must break even and provide survival income as well. Because most people with significant disabilities have SSI or SSDI benefits to cover daily living expenses, the business does not need to generate survival income; it simply has to reach the break-even point (see Chapter 7 for more information on break-even analysis).

Those in VR, WIA agencies (or One-Stop Centers), CRPs, school-to-work transition programs, and other employment services may go to SBDCs, TBICs, and the SBA for assistance with business plans. SBDCs and other small business agencies rarely write business plans, which is why technical training to special education staff, rehabilitation personnel, consumers, and family members is critical. It is important to note that developing cash-flow analyses and profit analyses requires a knowledge of Social Security and Medicaid/Medicare regulations, which SBDC and SBA advisors typically do not have.

The following example shows the importance of knowing Social Security and Medicaid/Medicare regulations. If the fixed cost to sell a product is $100 per month, the cost per item sold (cost of purchased wholesale product) is 50% of the selling price, and the selling price per item is $8.00, then the break-even point per year is $2,400 per year in sales or 300 items. Profit analysis shows that if $6,000 worth of items are sold (750 items in a year), then the profit is $1,800 per year or $150 per month. If the business owner receives SSI, however, which is reduced $1.00 for every $2.00 earned after the first $85, then the SSI monthly check is reduced by $32.50 per month or $390 per year. This $390 can be projected and SSI will reduce the owner's benefits each month based on these projections, or this amount can be paid back to SSI as an overpayment at the end of the year when the business taxes are filed. When projected, SSI reduces the check; if the cash flow is irregular due to seasonal sales or some other cause, then the owner may be unable to meet living expenses in some months. Discretionary net personal profits are reduced from $150 per month to $117.50 per month due to the interaction of the SSI system rules.

SBA and SBDC staff generally do not know these regulations and need technical consultation when projecting the interaction of SSI/SSDI checks and self-employment income. SSI does not balance net self-employment income on a month-by-month basis; instead, by regulation, the entire year must be divided by 12 months to perform the reduction calculations. This is a significant benefit to self-employment that is not present for wage employment, and it allows for significant fluctuations in income that do not affect benefits or Medicaid monthly.

4. Self-employed people with disabilities may have access to alternate sources of capital to build their business. Conventional small business loans and investors for business start-ups are difficult to acquire, often carry heavy interest rates, and can lead people into poverty with anxiety-causing debt. Banks prefer not to make small business loans unless substantial collateral is available. Obtaining a loan often requires that the business and business plan are well developed and show high growth potential. Wealthy individ-

ual investors and/or "angel investors" (those who invest in a business hoping to get a quick and substantial return on investment) are the exception rather than the rule.

5. Self-employment works for people with significant disabilities. Many think that self-employment is beyond the reach of people with disability labels. Understanding individuals in their home, community, and daily living contexts reveals opportunities for self-employment. Self-employment can closely match the small business owner's preferences, gifts, and unique contributions. Self-employment allows for the creation of a work opportunity designed specifically for someone who does not fit standard job description molds; at the same time, it respects context and natural supports for a unique, profitable, and viable form of community employment. Business ownership comes through a discovery process that lines up personal attributes, supports, dreams, talents, resources, and the marketplace.

6. Although approximately 150,000 individuals traditionally served by CRPs are now wage earners through supported employment, almost 400,000 people remain in day programs that need new avenues to address community employment (McGaughey et al., 1994; Wehman & Kregel, 1998). Self-employment offers people career advancement through increased wages and interaction with suppliers, customers, and mentors.

7. Self-employment offers individuals the opportunity to schedule their work day to accommodate their personal productivity levels, goals, symptom cycles, and schedules. Self-employment is a tremendous job accommodation, customized to unique circumstances, location, abilities, resources, and dreams (Griffin & Hammis, 2001a, 2001b; Shelley et al., 2002).

In sum, self-employment works for individuals with significant disabilities of all types—including traumatic brain injuries; sensory disabilities; autism, cerebral palsy, and other developmental disabilities; psychiatric disabilities; and physical impairments (Griffin & Hammis, 2001b; Newman, 2001). Self-employment even made sense for one man who has little or no verbal communication, rocked in his seat most of the day in a sheltered workshop, appeared unmotivated by money or coercive rewards, occasionally lashed out violently, and did not appear to value work. Such a description reflects a deficits-based frame of reference that leads many professionals and the community to assume that an individual is incapable of productive work. In fact, upon meeting this person, a new team focused on positive aspects discovered that he had strong interests, the ability to communicate things that were important to him, and a warm smile that would appeal to customers. Keying into these assets and ignoring the negative descriptors, the team supported him in starting a business that after 5 years continues to grow.

Self-employment is grounded in the belief that all people have strengths, interests, preferences, and an innate ability to perform work competently when offered choices, respect, support, hope, and opportunities. Abandoning stereotypes and taking a strengths-based, person-centered approach is a proven process in both supported employment and self-employment (Griffin & Hammis, 1996, 2001b; Sirolli, 1999).

BUSINESS PLANNING

Approximately 80% of successful small businesses in the United States do not have business plans. Yet, probably close to 100% of unsuccessful businesses did not have plans either. Business plans should never be the determining factor in supporting a business, but they are crucial if external funding is required (e.g., bank loans, microloan funds, funds from investors). The power of a business plan is that it presents the opportunity to think critically about the future needs of a business and an individual. It maps out and anticipates critical decision-making points; it allows the individual opportunities to think through his or her commitments; it clarifies when capital, equipment, labor, inventory, and various other resources will be needed; and it has the symbolic power of proving the individual's dedication to the venture. Perhaps most important is that the business plan presents an opportunity to pull together a team to research and write the plan, thereby laying the foundation for a supportive network of friends and colleagues available to help at various stages of development.

Many individuals requesting self-employment are unable to move beyond the early stages of business planning and feasibility testing. By policy and practice, VR counselors and WIA vendors are often discouraged to invest in meaningful feasibility studies or business plans. Self-employment is still viewed by many program administrators as risky, time consuming, and costly. Therefore, pressure is applied to counselors to get people into wage jobs quickly. Without the financial support that it takes to buy a business plan and feasibility study, the individual is frequently faced with choosing entry-level wage employment or no employment. As mentioned previously, even though some SBDCs will help people refine business plans and do feasibility studies, most have little expertise in understanding the interplay of disability benefits systems, the rehabilitation system, or the medical and psychological implications of disability. Frankly, most SBDCs are so understaffed that they cannot take a substantial role in writing a plan. Someone without writing skills certainly can own and operate a business, but without the capacity to write the plan, he or she may be doomed to unemployment.

In 2002, the SSA suggested that when PASS is used for self-employment, it should include a request for money to write a business plan. This is a significant step forward and illustrates the SSA's commitment to employment. Numerous VR offices also pay their vendors to develop feasibility studies and business plans while slowly minimizing the reliance on deficit-based vocational evaluations that repeatedly report that people need more training, when in reality, they need support.

Money

Perhaps the most controversial aspect of self-determination and self-employment is access to and control of money. The Montana Job Training Partnership (MJTP), the administrative unit charged with WIA implementation in Montana, partnered with the Rural Institute to design a demonstration project (funded through the U.S. Department of Labor) that illustrated the power of individualized funding and self-determination in self-employment. Since 1998, more than 200 individuals with disabilities have been served in Montana and Wyoming. Almost half of the participants developed a self-employment goal. The Montana/Wyoming Careers through Partnerships project utilized a series of trained vendors to handle money and provide some of the supports necessary for business development. The bulk of the money, however, went into training, equipment, inventory, and other consumer business needs. Average cash start-up costs were less than $5,000, with most small business owners earning approximately $8.00 per hour and working more than 30 hours per week. Most enterprises were founded in Montana, which is ranked among the lowest states for per capita earnings and productivity (Newman, 2001). Self-employment hours, wages, and costs rival those of wage employment; proved no more risky; offered a solution to needed job accommodations; and illustrated how numerous systems and communities can collaborate to solve the long-standing tragedy of rural unemployment.

Again, a team approach to business development was critical to the success of this project. The Rural Institute and MJTP worked closely with the various community service vendors (WIA operators, developmental disabilities and mental health agencies, centers for Independent Living, and local VR offices) and with entities such as the Montana Community Development Corporation in Missoula, which provided extensive technical support and feasibility advice. Long-term business supports often were required and available through select community rehabilitation providers, family members, and Rural Institute staff.

Lessons learned from the Montana/Wyoming Careers through Partnerships project guide new development and include the following:

- Most individuals know what they want to do, and customer choice and self-determination are the keys to success.

- Collaborative community-based supported employment practices provide formal and informal supports for working participants.

- Postemployment services are vital to job retention or career advancement.

- Self-employment is a viable option of employment, particularly in rural areas. Not only does self-employment allow individuals to work out of their homes, but it also often provides accommodations such as flexible work schedules and accessible work areas. Moreover, self-employment empowers individuals to establish partnerships that benefit their interests.

- Costs to individual programs are decreased when funds are leveraged from several sources, resulting in services to a greater number of participants. No-cost and/or low-cost services are available in every community.

- Very few participants have used funds for training, but many have used funds for postemployment services such as job coaching and financial support services (Newman, 2001).

Having financial resources available is critical for all businesses, but it is especially so for cash-poor individuals with disabilities. The Montana/Wyoming

Careers through Partnerships project demonstrated that people generally do not ask for more than they need and that what they need is minimal. If the money spent in an average year on evaluating and testing people to screen them out of services was used instead to support people's dreams, thousands of individuals could be earning a living today.

Another significant resource for cash, training, and support is SSA Work Incentives. Chapter 6 details the use of SSA Work Incentives such as PASS. Further information is available through the SSA (http://www.ssa.gov), through the Benefits Planning Assistance and Outreach program at Virginia Commonwealth University's Rehabilitation Research and Training Center on Workplace Supports (http://www.worksupport.com), and through a sampling of PASS plans that the Rural Institute's staff have written in their work across the United States (http://www.passplan.org).

Staff Competencies and Leadership Support

As with all new techniques, finding local champions is critical to success. In today's world of school-to-work transition and adult rehabilitation, there is much talk and some action regarding systems change, funding portability, individualized budgets, and person-centered approaches. However, also today, most individuals with significant disabilities never go to work (Butterworth et al., 1999; Wehman, 2001). Two enduring issues of self-employment for anyone are team assistance in developing a venture and long-term support for maintaining the effort. Although much of the support necessary is not costly and natural community supports can be leveraged for anyone, disability presents some unique challenges, costs, and adaptation needs. The critical roles of the special education and the adult rehabilitation systems cannot be overlooked and should indeed be transformed to focus on the individual instead of on the program or funding stream. The major barriers remain the lack of business skills of rehabilitation professionals and the hesitancy of schools, VR, and WIA to fund self-employment ventures, regardless of the success rate with typical citizens.

Providing the rehabilitation personnel tools that are necessary to evaluate business ideas is one part of the approach to assisting with small business development (Griffin, Flaherty, et al., 2001). In addition, numerous state agencies and federal entities are providing much-needed resources like rehabilitation and opportunities for special education professionals to attend seminars and take courses on business planning, feasibility, marketing and sales, SSA Work Incentives, and related topics that augment their decision-making skills. Also necessary is training and experience in building local teams, knowing communities and local resources, facilitating planning meetings, and respecting and supporting the dreams of people with significant disabilities. Critical avenues for organizational change and acceptance of self-employment as a community-referenced outcome include teaching good vocational profiling (instead of assessment); utilizing systematic instruction techniques to design production and operational approaches; and working with principals, teachers, classroom staff, CRP executive directors, finance directors, program managers, clinicians, and VR counselors to understand their roles in individuals' success (Griffin, 1999a, 1999b).

Systems change is needed that provides all of the major disability systems with support for changing from internally focused programs (rules, regulations, creating more and bigger funding streams) to community-referenced entities in true partnership with cities and towns. It is ironic that some rehabilitation systems are so driven by the demand for outcomes that risk taking is marginalized and excludes or seriously delays self-employment. The rehabilitation and school systems sometimes wear out (or "wait out") self-employment candidates, and these people either drop out of the system or accept wage employment as their only viable option.

Conversely, the developmental disability and mental health realms place so little emphasis on community employment outcomes that people with disabilities often spend their entire lives with few opportunities for employment. Even today, after years of supported employment funding, training, and pilot programs, these fields do not emphasize community employment and still rely on the failed job-readiness approaches that seldom fulfill the promise of achieving community employment. The answer lies somewhere between the school and rehabilitation systems' obsessive need for cost-effective and predictable outcomes and the complacency of segregated CRPs and day-treatment models.

Issues faced by people with disabilities are also of interest to communities, which historically solve problems for themselves (Etzioni, 1998; McKnight, 1995). Ernesto Sirolli (1999) adequately demonstrated in communities worldwide that person-centered self-employment works when teams rally around individuals and ideas, and numerous self-employment ventures by people with disabilities prove that microenterprise is a feasible avenue to economic fulfillment. Addressing the previously outlined issues streamlines the self-employment process and creates opportunities for success for individuals with disabilities, for the rehabilitation system, and for communities in need of economic development.

The following chapters of this book seek to help PBOs with disabilities, their families, and the dedicated professionals around them to achieve the following:

- Identify personal attributes, dreams, and opportunities that lead to the establishment of a lifelong career, whether through self-employment or wage employment

- Recognize that although some people are entrepreneurs with a strong spirit of enterprise that leads them to work tirelessly, most people simply want to earn a living—and self-employment is another method for approaching the labor market

- Realize that opportunity awaits anyone willing to rethink and reconceptualize products, services, and markets

- Use the many existing community services and supports that are tax supported and accessible under the law to anyone wanting to establish a business

- Embrace risk because, after all, a life of poverty, dependence, and isolation is truly the greatest risk of all

- Create a business and work environment that accentuates individual talent and accommodates personal needs linked to one's disability, transportation access, personality, family, or other life circumstances

Self-employment is new to many professionals in the human services, education, and rehabilitation fields. This book is designed to guide the development of small businesses. It is not the exhaustive source on all topics because so many local resources and people already exist to guide and nurture American citizens in these areas. The hard work of finding paying customers and satisfying them is the job of the owner and those providing support; however, reading this book carefully and completing its exercises allows people to conceptualize and plan an enterprise.

Chapter 2

Person-Centered Business Planning

IMPORTANT TERMS IN THIS CHAPTER

Business design team (BDT): A working collection of friends, colleagues, and experienced business people assembled to assist the PBO in formulating an enterprise idea, launching the business, and supporting the venture's growth.

Maps: A series of pictorial charts or written lists compiling important information about the PBO's life history, available and necessary personal and business supports, dreams and desires, talents, skills, and opportunities. Maps are used to guide the process of discovering potential business ideas and opportunities.

Person-centered business planning: A suggested format for business planning that seeks a fit between a person's talents and preferences and a viable business idea.

The business development literature contains references to business owner personality types, entrepreneurial assessments, and various checklists for determining a person's suitability as a business owner (Straughn & Chickadel, 1994; Sumner, 1999). Although there may be something akin to an entrepreneurial personality, owning a small business does not require testing to assess one's potential business character. The recommended approach, person-centered business planning, recognizes the need for business and personal supports. Simply put, person-centered business planning as developed by the authors is an inclusive process that seeks a fit between a person's talents and preferences and a viable business idea. Business ideas emanate from the individual's dreams and talents and are melded with a market that accepts the product or service. This approach focuses on supports and not on remediating deficits. Unlike traditional economic development approaches, this process starts with an individual's business idea and finds a market rather than first finding a market and then forcing people to produce a product or service that they may not be committed to or excited about.

Many people who want to start businesses already have ideas and a variety of resources to support them in their venture. Many others do not, however, and the following person-centered approach can be quite useful for refining a business direction. The process can be time consuming, but it does yield critical information for developing the business plan and for designing supports necessary for business success.

A few words of caution are required before ferreting out information. Some people's dreams and life circumstances are private, and it may not be appropriate for the assembled team to help design a business. During the group process, some ideas take on lives of their own and evolve. Most human services professionals know of people forced into jobs as department store greeters, for instance, because the individuals shake hands with everyone they see. Yet, handshaking may indicate a desire for human contact rather than a desire to meet strangers all week long. Therefore, the group process should be supplemented by extended periods of discussion and private discovery with the individual as well as his or her family, friends, and various supporters. Take some time to explore with those who are trying to understand their calling(s) in life, and value the knowledge and experience of the people who spend significant time with these PBOs.

Should the process yield no clear path, step back and consider a wage job as an opportunity for the individual to gain experience and make money. This is a natural means of discovering career paths, especially for transition-age students. Most successful business people learned about business by working for someone else first, so wage employment is certainly a reasonable outcome of person-centered business planning. For individuals with little or no work history, getting a job is a terrific first step to owning a small business. Yet, for many reasons, the job market locks out people with disabilities, so keep digging for clues about the individual that point in a business direction.

Finally, as part of the person-centered business planning process, visit workplaces where the dream makes sense: businesses owned or operated by people who probably have similar vocational motivations and can offer advice, suggestions, and encouragement. In other words, if the profile developed by the team reveals that the person wants to own a farm, then meet some farmers. Discuss with the farmers suggested processes for starting a farm, recommended specialty crops, possible financial concerns, ways to reach customers, and means for determining a farm's feasibility. People often support others who share their dream; they also know the business and can serve as mentors. Most people enjoy talking about their life's work, so engage them in conversation.

PRIMARY STEPS IN PERSON-CENTERED BUSINESS PLANNING

Person-centered business planning is a flexible, thoughtful, and action-oriented process that leads to business ideas and plans for individuals with significant disabilities. A person's disability is largely unimportant because it is the series of business ideas, contacts, supports, and actions taken that ultimately determines the individual's success. Disability is too often used as an excuse for why a person cannot work. All people can work and/or own a business when provided the proper supports. People are not unemployed because they have disabilities; people are unemployed because they do not have jobs. Many people believe that they are better off working for themselves or that they cannot easily enter the traditional labor market. For these individuals, self-employment makes sense. The business planning process that follows is based on various components of person-centered planning (Callahan & Nisbet, 1997; Forest & Pearpoint, 1992; Griffin & Hammis, 1996; Mount, 1987).

Identify a Key Support Person

Sometimes, the PBO acts as his or her own advocate and takes this role to better self-direct and guide the process. For individuals who have been excluded from society and may need assistance in getting connected to the business world, a rehabilitation professional such as a transition specialist, job developer, VR counselor, or service coordinator may be engaged. A family member also may serve quite effectively in this role and can offer supports that most people typically use in creating employment and a vision for the future. A current business owner or a mentor from the Service Corps of Retired Executives (SCORE), who can offer access to his or her peer network or business experience, may be recruited to advocate and support the PBO. Whoever takes on the responsibility of key support person is responsible for pulling together a preliminary BDT to help discover and customize business opportunities.

Develop a Positive Business Owner Profile

The BDT initially meets to review the individual's vocational progress and experience to date, discover the PBO's personal preferences, and bring to bear the team members' personal and professional relationships. An analysis of each member's past and present community connections and employment history creates potential contacts and insights that help clarify business goals and action steps. Maps or lists of various points of exploration (discussed later in this chapter) capture the information once those steps are reached.

Take Action

Too often, traditional special education and rehabilitation processes create barriers to transition, career, or business-ownership development by relegating consumers to menial or dead-end jobs. The person-centered business planning process proposed herein considers jobs and even owning very small businesses (e.g., running a lemonade stand) as experiential refinement of what is enjoyed vocationally and as stepping stones to a pleasurable career that is created through trial and error. When assisting someone else in realizing their career goals, it is important to remember that all of us have great latitude in how we select our careers. Furthermore, person-centered business planning looks beyond traditional models of support because these have proven largely unsuccessful or unsatisfactory to people with significant disabilities. Instead, those involved in person-centered business planning create community and job-site relationships that advance careers; use technology that increases competence and skill mastery; and utilize resources such as the SSA's PASS Work Incentive (see Chapter 6 for more details), which in several states can be directed by the consumer as personal budgets are. Most important, team members take action to create opportunity.

IN-DEPTH EXPLORATION OF THE PERSON-CENTERED BUSINESS PLANNING PROCESS

In conceptualizing a business, person-centered business planning functions as an inventive and inclusive process capable of exhibiting and utilizing the many talents of the PBO and the BDT. The unemployment rate is approximately 80% for individuals with the most significant disabilities who graduate from special education or are served by traditional CRPs (U.S. Census Bureau, 2001; Wehman, 2001). By fostering new relationships with families, small business owners and/or experts, and community members, the cycle of failure can be disrupted and new views of employability developed. During the 1990s, the authors assisted with dozens of business start-ups using this process. Person-centered business planning is not necessary for everyone; however, for individuals with significant disabilities and little work history, it has proven exceptionally successful, whereas typical approaches often result in unemployment (see Mount, 1994).

Traditional human services limit people's success because they	Person-centered approaches break these old patterns and stereotypes by
Tend to give power and decision making to professionals and others paid to manage the lives of people with disabilities	Recognizing, reinforcing, and utilizing the capacities and talents of individuals
Reinforce the idea, through segregation, that the community is unsafe and unwelcoming for people with significant disabilities	Building community membership by taking the training and education process into real business and community environments
Focus on disability and remediation rather than on capacity, contribution, competence, and individual desire	Listening to people's desire for real homes, jobs, friends, and futures
Create artificial measures of readiness that reinforce failure	Believing in the natural capacity of communities to assimilate all people

From Griffin, C., & Hammis, D. (1996). *Streetwise guide to person-centered career planning.* (pp. 2–3). Denver, CO: Center for Technical Assistance and Training; adapted by permission.

First Meeting of the Business Design Team

The person-centered business planning process is elegant in its simplicity. The first step involves assembling key people in the PBO's life. Again, this may begin with a few disability or special education professionals; family members; and friends from the neighborhood, classroom, or rehabilitation program. These people must meet the approval of the PBO, who is part of the selection process. Typically, the BDT includes four to eight people, all of whom pledge to act quickly and inventively in the best interest of and under the direction of the PBO.

The first meeting is usually the most vital and important, as the PBO's history, talents, and desires are revealed. The call to action also occurs at this time, with each BDT member taking on critical assignments. Career and business planning often fails because of a team's lack of commitment, solidarity, and innovation. Apparently, this results from far too many teams being composed of only traditional rehabilitation or special education staff, who operate well within their systems but have little experience engaging the local community as mentors and team members. The BDT's task is to set a course of action and then enlist help from community members, preferably business development professionals or community business owners. In most communities, local employers are among the most substantial contributors to charitable organizations. For instance, Kiwanis and Rotary service club members are predominately business people. These groups actively raise money for local nonprofit organizations such as homeless shelters and provide eyeglasses, wheelchairs, and other items for those in need. Groups such as the Muscular Dystrophy Association and Special Olympics are overwhelmingly supported through the work of community members who make their living in for-profit enterprises. Experience illustrates that when asked, these people will counsel others in joining the ranks of the self-employed.

Critical elements of the first business design team (BDT) meeting

---

Plan to meet for 2–4 hours.

Ensure that the PBO is the center of attention and in control.

Plan the logistics so that the meeting runs smoothly. Make certain that members have replied to their invitations, have flipcharts and markers ready to record vital information, and choose a comfortable location in the community (bank or SBDC conference rooms work well).

Keep the process positive, focused on outcomes, and action oriented.

Include people who are important to and supportive of the PBO.

Ensure that everyone contributes and takes responsibility for the outcomes.

Conclude the meeting by giving members written assignments that address business development actions.

From Griffin, C., & Hammis, D. (1996). *Streetwise guide to person-centered career planning.* (pp. 3–4). Denver, CO: Center for Technical Assistance and Training; adapted by permission.

Collecting Valuable Information

A variety of graphic maps or lists are used to identify key information during the first meeting. This process borrows heavily from the work of Michael Callahan (Callahan & Nisbet, 1997), Marsha Forest (Forest & Pearpoint, 1992), Beth Mount (1987), and others (Griffin & Hammis, 1996) and provides an interactive and revealing view of the PBO, the team members, and the community. This information is utilized to sculpt a preliminary action plan that is used in designing a business plan (see Chapter 4 for more details). The maps can be transferred to flipcharts for viewing and completion by the BDT. One highly recommended activity is to have some or all of the BDT members complete these maps for themselves either prior to or during the first meeting. These graphic data, when displayed to the whole team, dramatically illustrate the disparity between the lives of people without disabilities and the lives of those with disabilities. Most typical citizens can list hundreds of acquaintances, a strong employment history, educational opportunities, and an inventory of hobbies and interests, whereas, in the authors' experiences, most people with significant disabilities have been afforded few chances to meet others, work for pay, or explore their personal interests. This new baseline, the comparison of the PBO to those with typical lives, is a starting point from which the BDT begins to fill in gaps in the PBO's life. Such gaps include intimate relationships, a chance to have money in one's pocket, and control over decision making, as well as the opportunity to take "normal" risks like opening a small business.

The following subsections describe the various types of maps. Blank forms of suggested styles for the maps are provided in Appendix A at the end of the book.

Background Map

The Background Map exercise involves literally drawing a picture of the PBO's life up to the present. It focuses on key events in the person's life and reveals background information that may be vital to discerning existing community connections, situations to avoid, and dreams that can be reinforced through the proper associations and work life. A plan facilitator and/or the PBO draws a flowchart or set of symbols and writes critical dates and names on flipchart papers that are hung on walls, thereby creating a mural of the individual's life. Past experiences, critical events, and people often reveal the meaning behind the PBO's attitudes and expectations. Knowing the person's past and understanding his or her motivators helps the BDT offer encouragement and advice. In one such meeting, learning from James that his long-deceased father once worked for the state highway department helped his team understand his fascination with road construction. Upon learning this, the team was able to help James follow in his father's footsteps vocationally.

Places Map

The Places Map or list is designed to capture the places that the PBO frequents, finds pleasurable, or desires to visit. Typically, for individuals with the most significant disabilities, this map reveals that the person spends most of his or her time in a congregate living situation and in a sheltered day program or school environment. This being the case, experiential knowledge of real work, relationships, and learning are incredibly limited. The PBO's need for real-life experiences becomes a true goal for the BDT. This need should guide the development of the first in a series of jobs or microenterprises that eventually lead to or bloom into a desired career. The Places Map also helps expose the loneliness and isolation of people with disabilities and should guide the BDT in generating ideas and opportunities for community social interactions that will build the job seeker's social skills repertoire and relationship networks.

Remember, there is no need for "readiness" training. There are no entrance criteria for the community, and meaningful situations should be developed that add real-life experiences to the individual's personal repertoire (Brown et al., 1987; Griffin & Hammis, 2001a). If the PBO is still in school and has no work experience, then starting a weekend or after-school business may make sense. Or, a part-time weekend or after-school wage job may be the best way to refine business and career goals. Avoid unpaid work experiences, as these are not typical and further stigmatize and separate adolescents and adults with disabilities (even most adolescents have paying part-time jobs, not unpaid work experiences, as they grow up). Unpaid work experiences also teach individuals with disabilities that there is no reward for labor, thereby eroding the work ethic. Work by definition is paid, and most adults recall that as adolescents or teenagers, they simply obtained jobs delivering newspapers or washing cars. They might not have done this if these experiences were unpaid.

Dreams Map

The Dreams Map simply shows in words or pictures the PBO's desired accomplishments and experiences. In one instance, a young woman with a significant disability drew a woman's face on the paper. Because this young lady had almost no verbal language or other communication system, it took some time for the team to discover that she wanted to become a fashion model or an actress in television commercials. Although the family and staff at her rehabilitation agency knew she liked to sample cosmetics at the local department store, no one had ever linked this behavior with a career goal. Within 6 months of this meeting, a staff person with acting experience was hired, a professional portfolio was produced, and the individual's first commercial for a local car dealership was filmed. Dreams are important in establishing a course of action and in showing respect for individual aspirations. Having a dream is the same thing as having hope. Without hope, accomplishment is meaningless at best and unrealized at worst.

Relationships Map

A Relationships Map graphically records all people involved in the PBO's life. Typically, people with significant disabilities have very few unpaid companions in their lives. The greater the scarcity of supporters and friends, the more difficult escaping segregation will be. For an individual desiring many relationships, the BDT can consider enterprise development that brings the individual into contact with many customers and suppliers. The best advice for creating relationships is simply sharing environments on a routine basis with other people. Diverse community settings are best for incubating relationships. Even home-based businesses present numerous daily opportunities for community inclusion. Suppliers must be developed, customers served, bank accounts maintained, and so forth. All of these interactions dispel myths of the PBO's incompetence and increase his or her visibility throughout the commercial environment.

Preferences Map

The Preferences Map is one of the most critical. With additional discussion by those who know the person best, the PBO lists the specific activities and things that are most desirable, along with those that are least desirable. Typically, people want a job that pays well, friends, a home of their own, and free time. Undesirable items often include separation from family; loneliness; and a low-paying, tedious job.

Financial Map

The Financial Map lists all of the resources available to the PBO, and its completion helps build a personal budget for starting a business. This map also alerts the BDT to possible problems with earnings and benefits. A good Financial Map signals the need for outside accounting expertise on how to structure the business correctly, plan for taxes, and take advantage of SSA Work Incentives while avoiding the premature loss of benefits. The Financial Map is powerful because it points out available resources for starting a business that might otherwise be overlooked.

In the following example map, a personal budget shows the amount allocated from a state to a local program serving an individual with developmental disabilities, along with other possible sources of support that can be used to start and support a small business. Developing a personal budget graphically illustrates how much money is actually being allocated for this person's services.

In this sample personal budget, redirecting day-service dollars into the hands of the individual for just 1 year easily generates $15,000 for investment in a business (or wage job activities such as job development and work-site supports). Adding funds and technical support from the local SBDC, VR, and/or the Workforce Development Center as well as developing an SSA Work Incentive (PASS, in this example) leverages an additional $24,250. In most cases, individuals with developmental disabilities can also receive long-term funding for ongoing support, thereby providing a safety net in case the business fails. Small business start-ups often cost $5,000–$10,000; the extra funds will likely be necessary for ongoing supports, rehabilitation needs, and business expansion.

SBDCs do not provide funding, only limited services, so no dollar amount is factored in. In addition, the VR system is not an entitlement program. One must apply, be accepted, and then have a plan designed that approves funding. A similar situation applies to WIA programs, so these dollars cannot be guaranteed.

If the individual for whom the sample budget was developed stays in a segregated day program and earns only $55 per week (higher earnings than most people attending sheltered workshops actually make; Butterworth et al., 1999), the individual will earn $57,200 in wages over 20 years. The cost of a day program, at $13,000 per year for 20 years, will be $260,000. Even if the PBO starts a meager business that earns him or her only $6.00 per hour, 20 hours per week (well below what most businesses owned by people with disabilities actually generate; Newman, 2001), the earnings for 20 years would be $124,800, and it is doubtful the $13,000 support funding per year would be needed in full. Plus, the individual gains personal control, an identity separate from his or her disability, and the opportunity to engage in civic life.

Financial Map

People or agencies from which resources are currently available	Resources that I can use right now	Resources that can be developed for later use
Developmental disability day program funding	$13,000 annually	This $13,000 can pay for staff support, help with writing a business plan, and provide transportation
Job/business development from Vocational Rehabilitation (VR)		50 hours of small business development assistance at $40/hour = $2,000 and possible technical assistance
Job/business coaching	Developmental disability funding, plus money, can be procured from VR or the local WIA provider	70 hours of business support at $35/hour = $2,450 from the assigned developmental disabilities provider agency
Small business mentoring		Free from SBDC and/or SCORE
Plan for Achieving Self-Support (PASS)	Development can be obtained from the developmental disability provider or from a contracted benefits planner	I receive a relatively small monthly SSDI check of $550. My PASS is written for 36 months, so that totals $19,800.
Family support (if available)	$2,000	
The total support now available to me is $15,000 ($13,000 plus $2,000 from my family). With some development efforts (i.e., assistance with pulling these resources together into a plan), $15,000 plus $24,250 may be available, totaling $39,250.	$15,000 (some portion of the $13,000 allocation should be available long term based on individual need)	Funding from VR and job coaching ($2,000 and $2,450) plus PASS work incentive money ($19,800) totals $24,250

The previously discussed maps provide a graphical record that the BDT utilizes to begin business plan development. The next step in person-centered business planning involves developing a personal profile with the prospective business owner.

Business Owner Profile Development

A Business Owner Profile contains information that provides clues regarding the person's competencies, personal desires, and ambitions. The Profile might serve as the foundation of a résumé, a custom-fit business, or a clear employment path. The Profile is always developed in terms of the PBO's positive attributes, and brainstorming regarding "hidden" talents often results from the Profile's interactive development.

The Profile is not the result of formal testing or professional analysis. Such techniques tend to be deficit focused and pull the PBO back into the cycle of low expectations and unnecessary training that is hypothetically designed to help people "get ready." The Profile is instead a friendly examination of talents, positive attributes, and successes. The Profile is big on common sense and small on science. There is no standardized format (the related worksheet in Appendix A is provided merely as a starting point), there are no formal criteria, and professional jargon is discouraged. Family members may know of desires and talents that have not been witnessed and fostered in rehabilitation settings; therefore, family can offer tremendous insight when developing the Profile.

Initiating the Profile can be difficult. Having each BDT member complete the Business Owner Profile Worksheet (included in Appendix A) and share it with the other members can break the ice. People typically do not list their faults when creating a résumé or describing themselves to others. Once all members have made their presentations, they are ready to assist the PBO in thinking positively about his or her life.

Another process to get the BDT thinking positively is to role-play introducing the PBO to a local business owner or community leader. Have a couple members take turns introducing the PBO. Each person must identify at least six strong career characteristics that can be woven into the introduction (the following chart can be used for this exercise from Griffin & Hammis, 1996). The group discussion should focus on identifying these positive attributes, thereby setting the stage for Profile development and providing the initial language for a script to use with potential business supporters (e.g., SBDC staff, VR counselors).

Record at least six positive employment-related characteristics of the potential business owner:

1.   4.

2.   5.

3.   6.

Focusing intently on one person at a time allows the concentration of efforts and resources that are otherwise thinly spread and do little good for the masses of people with disabilities receiving long-term rehabilitation services. Each success breeds new ideas and workable techniques that make the next person and business a bit easier to support. Staying focused one person at a time reduces the risks to agencies and policy makers, slowly builds credibility one success at a time, allows time for learning from mistakes, and redirects what should be nonthreatening amounts of money a little at a time.

Chapter 3

Business Feasibility

IMPORTANT TERMS IN THIS CHAPTER

Business feasibility study: An assessment, through the use of research tools such as surveys or statistical analyses, regarding the likelihood of a business succeeding.

Marketing mix: The process of matching a product/service to specific customers by identifying the proper advertising, pricing, and availability.

Chapter 2 describes how the PBO and the BDT work together to unearth clues concerning personal and vocational attributes. In this chapter, the business idea is hatched, refined, and tested to maximize its chances for success. Throughout this book, the exercises ask the same or similar questions more than once. Redundancy is built into the process to completely scrutinize business ideas and ensure clarity concerning vital business planning elements. Also, the purpose of having the PBO and BDT work through these exercises is to refine the idea into a business focus and provide necessary personal and business supports. Once these supports are recognized, they can be arranged and structured to ensure that the person has a valued role in the business, that the person is doing the work that he or she desires, and that the business is generating income for the owner. For inspiration and guidance, the authors drew upon the many fine exercises in Straughn and Chickadel's (1994) *The New American Business System* and Sumner's (1999) *Business Plan Basics: NxLevel Guide for Micro-Entrepreneurs.* The authors further recommend that readers attend local microenterprise classes that use these small business guides.

REFINE THE BUSINESS IDEA

Typically, business feasibility for anyone begins with self-analysis. Many publications (e.g., Doyel, 2000; Griffin & Hammis, 2001a) and experts ask questions of the PBO such as

- Are you a self-starter?

- Do you get along with different kinds of people?

- Do you have a positive attitude?

- Do you enjoy making your own decisions?

- Do you enjoy competition?

- Do you exhibit self-control and willpower?

- Do you plan ahead?

- Do you get tasks done on time?

- Do you enjoy fast-paced, changing environments?

- Do you have high amounts of physical stamina and emotional energy?

- Can you work 80 or more hours a week?

- Are you prepared to invest your savings?

Although these questions all have some legitimacy for starting and operating a business, they can easily screen out people with significant disabilities. The problem rests with misconceptions about entrepreneurs. There is an almost mythical perception of the entrepreneur as an individual who single-handedly fights off customers with one hand while filling out loan applications with the other. He or she makes quick decisions, is in control, and never sleeps. In reality, most people who own businesses are self-employed, but they are not entrepreneurs according to the previously described characteristics. Self-employed people often do work hard, take personal financial risks, and have to make many decisions. People with significant disabilities are just as well equipped to run a small business as the next person, as long as support is available and affordable. Chapter 2 identifies some support needs and resources, and as the business idea evolves, paid supports—such as accounting, sales help, and marketing—are figured into the pricing of the company's goods and services. So instead of relying on personality testing, vocational evaluations, interest inventories, and other time and money wasters, this book takes the approach of determining how to offer inventive support in achieving business ownership. The issue, again, is one of support—not one of personality or readiness.

Most transition-age youth and adults with significant disabilities face a life of poverty and underemployment. Reliance on adult day programs has generated an employment rate of approximately 20% for people with significant disabilities. As noted previously, although it is a risk, investing only 1 year's worth of day programming funding to experiment with a business idea can reap a lifetime of rewards for a person with a disability.

There are more relevant and cost-effective questions to ask the PBO when refining a business idea:

- Does this business address a recognized need in the marketplace?

- Can this product/service be produced at a profit?

- Can this business realistically compete with other similar businesses?

- Does this business match your dreams and goals?

- Are you really interested in owning this business?

- How much time can you invest in operating this business?

- How much money can you invest in this business?

- Do you have, or can you afford, the necessary business and personal supports required to run this enterprise?

- Do you have, or can you acquire, the skills necessary to perform the parts of the business you wish to perform?

- How will this business affect your family?

These are the questions to ask of anyone who is considering starting a business. At this point, the PBO and BDT should use the information collected in Chapter 2 to discuss the idea of business ownership in general. As the specific enterprise idea becomes clear, the PBO and the BDT should keep returning to these core questions and the other exercises throughout this book to design a personally satisfying venture. Completing the Skills and Needed Supports chart (see Appendix A) can be helpful for further identifying and addressing business support needs.

After initially discussing these factors, the PBO should consider the following exercise for determining appealing aspects of and concerns about self-employment. Most people starting their own businesses will feel some anxiety, but communicating this feeling early allows the PBO and the BDT to begin support facilitation. For this exercise, the individual, with the team as needed, considers the various aspects of owning a particular business. First, the PBO records the things that appeal to him or her about owning a business. Then, the PBO records the things that concern him or her about owning a business. The team and the PBO then discuss the concerns and determine whether they can be remedied or accommodated or whether they pose serious threats to the PBO's running an enterprise. If the negatives far outnumber the positives, perhaps another means of employment is indicated. Again, it is normal to have concerns. The challenge for the PBO and the BDT is to creatively solve or circumvent these concerns.

Appealing aspects of self-employment:

Concerns about self-employment:

People/resources for exploring remedies to these concerns:

People/resources for exploring remedies to these concerns:

The next step for the PBO and the BDT is to explore, in more detail, the enterprise ideas developed through completing Chapter 2's brainstorming exercises and the Business Owner Profile Worksheet in Appendix A. It is especially important to include family members in this exercise as well, because family members are involved in the majority of successful American businesses. Attention to parents, siblings, and relatives (and their careers and business experience) can be crucial for getting good advice and support (SBA, 1996a, 1996b; U.S. Department of Commerce, 2000).

Most people have more than one business idea, and often it is difficult to select a course of action. The PBO and the BDT should complete a Business Concept Refinement Chart (see Appendix A) to refine the various ideas until one seems more reasonable than the others. Again, having the diverse experience of team members may prove essential for addressing each consideration.

A serious consideration in the preceding exercise relates to the uniqueness of the product/service being offered. Many businesses fail because they do not identify a true need of customers in the community. From the start, if people do not need or cannot afford or easily acquire the product, sales will suffer. Every business must address a real need or desire in the buying public or pull buyers from other similar products by offering a unique, value-added component. Opening another hamburger stand in a small community may be a bad idea. Yet, opening a hamburger stand that also sells beer may attract new customers and lure away customers from existing businesses that sell beer but not hamburgers. Or, maybe the other hamburger stands are only on one side of town. Opening one near a housing development across town might just be a good idea. The product is the same as everyone else's, but the location makes it more convenient. It is important to refine a business concept and match it to specific customers through targeted advertising, pricing, and availability. This approach is part of attending to the marketing mix, a concept that is described later in this chapter.

TEST THE BUSINESS IDEA

The information derived from the Business Concept Refinement Chart streamlines the business feasibility process. At this point, it is advisable to contact the local SBDC, TBIC, Women's Business Information Center (WBIC), or another local economic development entity and share the ideas with agency staff. Ask

for their advice. They know the local community, and they typically have extensive experience with business start-ups. Much of their advice and information is based on common sense, experience, and intuition honed after years of hearing business ideas. Nonetheless, do not be surprised if staff cannot fathom the idea of an individual with a significant disability owning and operating an enterprise. Much U.S. business education is based on the entrepreneurial model and is unthinkingly biased against people with disabilities or others with significant life challenges. Explain that this business is being planned with exceptional supports. What the PBO and BDT seek is an evaluation of the business idea, not an examination of the business owner.

The SBDC or other small business assistance entity can also recommend a variety of methods for testing the business idea. Testing is critical before investing too much time and money into the enterprise because in the current U.S. disability services system, people typically only get one or two chances to achieve success. There are so many people who need jobs and such meager resources that the system tolerates few failures. A bad business idea may make another attempt impossible within the disability and rehabilitation systems, so care must be taken when evaluating the business idea.

One common-sense, low-cost technique for testing business ideas comes from Rosalie Sheehy Cates, Executive Director of the Montana Community Development Corporation:

> Sell a few. Tell us how you did and what you learned. What did buyers think of the product; did they want more; would they pay more for it; should it be a different color or size; can you deliver it; is wholesale pricing available; is it as good as other similar products or services? (personal communication, March 1998)

Simply selling a few items or services and having a short discussion with customers can yield vital information. Of course, a lack of buyers might suggest that the product or service does not have a market, is overpriced, is considered of low quality, is being sold to the wrong people in the wrong place, or does not address a need. Although serious thought goes into the business analysis, actually selling an item before building an entire company around it makes sense.

Compare Business Information on the Internet

The Internet provides one of the best, cheapest, and easiest ways of comparing business ideas, exploring what others with similar ideas and businesses are doing, and linking with business owners worldwide. Not only are other existing businesses easy to find through a search engine (e.g., http://www.google.com), but also their pricing, product lines, terms of purchase and shipping, seasons of operation, advertising strategies, and other key business components are offered to the Internet researcher.

For instance, a search on the Internet for examples of dog grooming businesses revealed more than 260 dog grooming related sites. Exploring these sites revealed a variety of locations, specialty items, prices, and options—thus, a good sample of business models that PBOs can consider. Every business idea can be explored to reveal unique market niches, equipment and training opportunities, wholesale supply sources, technical expertise, and industry associations or trade groups that may offer valuable advice or even group health insurance. Most web sites supply telephone numbers and e-mail addresses. PBOs may want to call or write to the owners and ask for their advice.

Of course, local, state, and federal economic development assistance is available via the Internet as well. Local SBDCs are always listed, as are state SBA resources. A great site for finding government assistance for small business ideas and financing is http://www.firstgov.com; this is often the beginning point for determining available resources, regulations, and expertise. Other web sites, such as http://www.zapdata.com, offer market analysis research and are available at low or no cost. There are also on-line survey services, such as http://www.zoomerang.com, that allow the PBO to design a survey. To fill out such surveys, the PBO uses a personal e-mail list or one purchased from sources such as the local chamber of commerce or an industry trade group. The Arc of Stanly County, Albemarle, North Carolina, once used this service and a chamber of commerce e-mail list to poll local businesses about the potential need for paper-shredding services. Respondents scheduled shredding services before the business plan's feasibility testing was completed! The list of web sites in Appendix B may be useful for testing business ideas discerning feasibility by examining similar business plans, reading reports and research studies, checking regulations, finding financing, and so forth.

Conduct Telephone Surveys

Another way to test an idea is simply to ask potential customers what they think. Telemarketers often call prospective buyers to ask questions about buying products and services. Although telemarketing may annoy potential customers, a short survey that asks a person's opinion without giving a sales pitch is an effective and inexpensive way to obtain public opinion on a business idea. Large corporations spend millions of dollars on statistically correct surveys, but most small businesses launch successfully by asking small samples of customers very simple questions.

The first step in testing an idea is to determine whether the product/service will be sold at wholesale cost to other businesses or whether it will be sold to retail buyers. For a product that someone else will sell, like salsa sold at a grocery store, it makes sense for the PBO or an appropriate BDT member to call the store manager or buyer at work during business hours, not at home. If the business idea is a mobile dog washing venture, then it makes sense to call citizens in the early evening, asking first if they own a dog. A mobile dog wash would also be of potential interest to boarding kennels, veterinarians, pet stores, and the local humane society. Calling and/or making personal appointments to discuss interest in the mobile dog grooming business is a terrific way of getting information on the potential demand, pricing, and grooming options (e.g., wash; wash and pedicure; wash, pedicure, and hair trim). Caveats to keep in mind are that someone might try to steal the idea or want to hire the PBO as an employee. It is important to be ready for both possibilities. Being offered a job is not a terrible occurrence in many cases, but having someone take a business idea is. However, fear of this occurring is perhaps overstated, and most people are not in a position to simply drop what they are doing to start a new venture.

A telephone survey approach to retail mobile dog grooming might unfold as follows. First, the PBO determines the demographic profile of a likely consumer:

- Owns at least one dog

- May not have time to wash the dog

- May not have children who earn their allowance washing the dog

- Has a disposable income to afford the service

Second, if people who fit this description live in a particular part of town, the PBO searches the telephone book for telephone numbers of people in that area. He or she makes a list to record the answers so that data can be shared with the BDT. It is difficult to ascertain how many people must be called to get an accurate survey. The SBDC can help, or an Internet search for statistically valid samples may reveal some information. Yet, the BDT's common sense comes into play as well by determining that it is necessary to call enough people that a pattern of responses begins to form. Chances are that the PBO, or other members of the BDT who are assisting by making calls, will have discussions that challenge the business idea, improve it, or spark a new idea. The PBO and applicable BDT members should follow these leads if they are promising, rewrite or modify the questions to clarify the business idea, and return to the entire BDT with the concerns raised by the survey.

Although survey respondents should be asked the same questions, a conversational approach is much better than a rote, monotone interrogation. The telephone script might sound something like this:

"Good evening. I am developing a new business in town, and I am calling to get some advice. All I need is about 3 minutes of your time."

[Wait for acknowledgment. If the person is annoyed or busy, the PBO thanks the respondent and says good-bye. Otherwise, the PBO continues.]

"I am starting a mobile dog grooming business. Customers will make an appointment for their dog, and I will drive to their home and groom their dog in the rear of my van. My van is custom built and features a washing tub, hair dryers, pedicure equipment, and a full line of dog grooming products and shampoos. I graduated from the Belmont School of Dog Grooming last year and am licensed by the state health department to provide such services. I am wondering if you would use this business or if you have friends or family who might use it."

[The PBO records the response and follows up on questions that the respondent might have before continuing.]

"How often do you suppose you or your friends might use this service?"

[The PBO records the response.]

"Do you think that you would use the basic washing service, or would you prefer the full-service grooming?"

[The PBO records the response and pursues questions and comments in a friendly manner.]

"What day(s) of the weeks and times do you think would work best for you and your friends?"

[The PBO records the response.]

"I am thinking of charging $11.00 for the basic grooming. Does that sound reasonable to you?"

[The PBO records the response. The respondent may or may not agree with this price. The PBO does not argue about pricing but, rather, collects the information and makes decisions later. At this point more questions may be appropriate, but the 3-minute period is up. Unless the respondent continues to be enthusiastic, the PBO thanks the person for his or her time and says good night.]

This is simply a hypothetical scenario. There is no one correct way to approach the survey, although it is important to keep it simple, conversational, and friendly. The Telephone Survey Worskheet found in Appendix A can be used to design the survey and record responses.

Explore Wholesale Business Options

If the business design is based on wholesale sales as well—that is, dog grooming services to quantity buyers such as veterinarians and pet stores—then personal appointments should be arranged. During these visits, the PBO and the BDT determine the prospective client's service needs, preferred days and times for service, and so forth. Perhaps a veterinarian will offer to refer customers to the dog grooming business and display the business cards in his or her waiting room. In such a case, the PBO may pay a commission to the veterinarian. There are many ways to approach the price of services to those who decide to become wholesale dealers. Volume buyers should get better pricing than one-time users. After all, it costs less to groom 12 dogs in one location than to groom 12 dogs in 12 different locations. Pricing, promotion, and costing are discussed later in the book. At this point, it is crucial determine whether there is a market need for the product.

Conduct the Business on a Trial Basis

Another approach for testing feasibility is to set up the business on a trial basis if it can be operated without major licensing or equipment purchases. Say that a PBO wants to sell gourmet dog biscuits. This is an easy business to test on a trial basis. First, the PBO must apply for a retail sales tax license with the city or county if licensing is needed. Then, he or she needs to bake some treats at home and find a place to sell them. Perhaps the PBO could sell some biscuits wholesale to the local pet store and others from a rented kiosk at the mall or a booth at the county fair. Critical elements of this approach include the following.

1. Analyze the price of other similar products.
2. Find out how these similar products are packaged.

3. Determine how customers get these products.

4. Calculate expenses.

5. Sell the product/service on a trial basis to help refine the business model.

Advertise and Analyze the Response

Another way to test the market for a microenterprise is to advertise and await the response. Take the example of a lawn mowing business based on high-volume sales. Earl, the PBO, and his BDT decide that costs to consumers should be kept relatively low. Also, because travel time does not generate income (traveling significant distances between jobs raises costs while lowering gross revenue), the business design indicates that several lawns must be cut in the same neighborhood to reduce travel time. Earl can pitch a discount rate to customers in a specific neighborhood: They can sign up for weekly mowings throughout the summer for just $8.00 per week. Other lawn services charge $10.00 per week, but by limiting travel time and consolidating the work locations, Earl's business remains quite profitable. If it takes 30 minutes to mow an average lawn and Earl wants to work 6 hours per day, 5 days per week, then the optimal customer base is 12 lawns in the same neighborhood each day. With these numbers, gross earnings project at $96 per day, $480 per week, $1,920 per month, or $9,600 in a 5-month summer season (May through September).

Testing this business idea might involve calling around to secure lawn jobs or contacting property managers or real estate brokers to secure exclusive contracts for maintaining their properties. Another approach is simply designing a flier, canvassing neighborhoods to slip the fliers into mailboxes, and waiting for customers to call. If no one calls, then perhaps the price is too high or too low (some customers want high-quality service, not low prices) or prospective clients have children who mow the lawn to earn their allowances. The major problem with this passive approach to sales is that the reasons for not buying are not always apparent. For example, fliers distributed on a holiday weekend may end up in the trash when people return home to a full mailbox and sort their mail on Sunday night. Nonetheless, fliers and direct-mail advertising are effective means of testing business ideas and getting customers.

A flier's design should be clean and easy to read. The flier should also answer the basic questions of who, what, when, where, why, and how much. In the case of Earl's lawn service,

- The *who* is Earl's High Performance Lawn Care

- The *what* is lawn maintenance and edging

- The *when* is weekly during the summer season

- The *where* is the client's yard

- The *why* is multifaceted: Earl's provides the equipment, is cost-effective, and is professional, and the client never has to mow the lawn again

- The *how much* is clearly stated at $8.00 per week, with the option to pay by credit card

The flier should be printed on colored paper or on nice letterhead with an envelope. Intuition comes into play: What is the customer most likely to read? If the flier is a single piece of paper, the color should be bright enough to attract attention, and text should be limited and printed in large letters to reduce reading time. The following sample flier is easy to read and answers the critical questions.

EARL'S HIGH PERFORMANCE LAWN CARE
The Premier Lawn Care Service in Town

SUMMERTIME SPECIAL!!
Earl's grooms your lawn once a week for just $8.00

One call to Earl's and you'll never need to worry about lawn mowing or edge trimming again!!

Custom work and Spring/Fall clean up available by appointment

Earl's is fully licensed and bonded

Quality Guaranteed or Your Money Back!

Call or e-mail anytime
555-555-9181
Earl@Earlslawns.com

Visa/MasterCard Accepted

Sample flier for testing business feasibility.

CONCLUSION

Business feasibility is part science and part art. Most microenterprises rely on the opinions and experiences of friends, families, and assorted local experts. Starting a business does involve a certain degree of risk, but wage jobs also involve risk. Understanding that markets are diverse, that economic circumstances evolve, and that customer preferences change should forewarn the PBO and BDT that flexibility in the business model is preferred. In the world of commerce, companies and products come and go; they evolve, change, sell out, or move on. Planning and testing feasibility are essential, but the effort should match the size of the enterprise. Investing $1,000 in a feasibility study for a company that will gross $5,000 per year is probably not warranted; however, making a few telephone calls to potential customers, selling a couple dozen items at the county fair, or passing out fliers in selected neighborhoods are low-cost approaches to gauging market response. Producing a good product/service, having discussions with business experts, and developing a functional business plan are the best means of ensuring future success. Feasibility means making enough money to cover living expenses, having access to reliable suppliers, maintaining a cash flow that covers salaries and production costs, and establishing a support structure that keeps the business owner moving forward. Appendix B at the end of the book contains numerous business feasibility Internet resources, and the chapters that follow continue the process of growing a lasting enterprise.

Chapter 4

Building the Business Plan

IMPORTANT TERMS IN THIS CHAPTER

Break-even analysis: A determination of how many sales must be made before the costs of the business are paid. This relationship can also be reported in terms of how long (in months or years) a business must operate before paying off its debts and thereby showing a profit.

Business structure: Business organization for tax and management purposes, taking the form of sole proprietorships, partnerships, or corporations.

Cash-flow analysis: An analysis of cash needed for payroll, raw materials, and other business expenses compared with revenue received from customers. *Negative cash flow* means that money is coming in slowly or in smaller amounts than needed to pay the bills. *Positive cash flow* means that sales revenue exceeds expenses.

Fixed costs: Business expenses that generally do not change, regardless of sales volume. Rent, insurance, and vehicle payments are typical fixed costs.

Gross revenue: The sum of all income from sales.

Net revenue: The remaining income after paying all expenses related to making a product/delivering a service.

Variable costs: Business expenses that vary with sales. Raw materials are the most common variable expenses because if products are not sold, there is no need to purchase raw materials.

Business plans represent a desire to direct the operations of an enterprise in a systematic, predictable, and controllable manner. Most people recognize through common experience that human enterprise is chaotic and complex. Businesses are highly unpredictable but not simply in an anxiety-producing manner. With each new customer, the business is given an opportunity to grow, change, react, innovate, and profit. The same customer, if handled poorly, also brings the opportunity for failure. Business plans are not predictors of success but still play an essential role in making prospective business owners think about the future, gather important information, and create a sequential approach to the enterprise's growth.

The typical small business plan is a relatively simple document that lays out a very flexible course for opening, managing, and growing an enterprise. Business plans are powerful documents for many reasons. For those people wishing to borrow money or attract investors, a thorough and professional business plan is a must. For most people with significant disabilities, however, the plan serves to convince funders such as WIA agencies, VR offices, and the SSA that the business is feasible; is matched to the owner's interests, skills, supports, and target market; and logically depicts the steps and strategies for cash flow, marketing and sales, supplier relationships, production and/or service delivery, and sustained sales growth.

Furthermore, the process of writing a business plan helps uncover hidden flaws in the business idea, forces the writer(s) to look critically at each business concern, and helps identify critical tasks to complete and targets to reach prior to proceeding. The business plan can be overwhelming when considered in its entirety, but taking it step by step makes the task much easier and more understandable. Recommended steps include the following:

- Research similar businesses on the Internet and elsewhere.

- Consult the local SBDC.

- Visit other related businesses and interview their owners to gather experiential information.

- Consult other resources, particularly those by Doyel (2000), Straughn and Chickadel (1994), and Sumner (1999).

Financing, financial reports, and estimates are discussed in the following chapters; this chapter addresses the writing of the business plan. There is no one correct format for writing a business plan. The chapter includes basic questions PBOs are asked in order to complete the various sections required of most funders or lenders. At the least, these sections typically include an executive summary (or overview of the business plan), a financial projection, a description of the marketing approach, and an outline of proposed operations and management processes. Researching the questions posed in this chapter guides the PBO and BDT in collecting critical information to insert in a business plan format of the PBO's choosing. Traditionally, a business plan contains components in this order:

1. Executive summary or cover letter

2. Short business description

3. Brief discussion of the enterprise's management (which is always unique and specific to a particular area and, therefore, should be developed with local assistance)

4. Section on employees that describes recruitment, remuneration, and critical job descriptions

5. Section on operations and suppliers

6. Explanation of the marketing mix and sales strategy

7. Section on finances

Again, the Internet contains almost unlimited examples of business plans and formats. Researching these examples saves considerable writing time, but PBOs must remember that every business is unique, in terms of market and owner, and that others' ideas should not simply be copied.

BUSINESS PLANNING MAP

A Business Planning Map is provided for the PBO and BDT to use in developing the business plan. All businesses are different, with varying emphasis on the components, but this map provides a logical guide for developing the business model. Each section of the map is described, and information is provided on the critical elements that the business plan should include. Questions accompanying the information are provided to spark critical thought about the

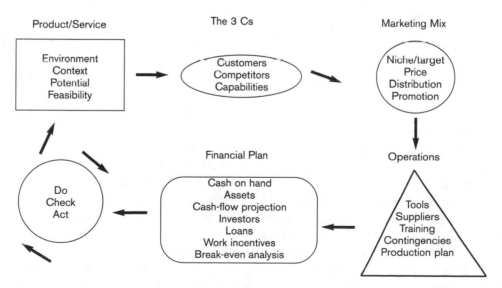

Business Planning Map. This map was created with the assistance and tremendous experience of Rosalie Sheehy Cates, Executive Director of the Montana Community Development Corporation (http://www.mtcdc.org). (From Griffin, C., & Hammis, D. [2002]. Jimbo's Jumbos: A primer on small business planning. *Journal of Vocational Rehabilitation, 17*[2], 92, adapted by permission.)

type of detail needed to write each section of the plan. It is important to note, however, that not all necessary information and questions are provided, nor are all of the questions here relevant to each business idea.

The Business Planning Map is a flowchart divided into five key areas: product/service, the 3 Cs, the marketing mix, operations, and the financial plan. When planning a business, all of these factors (and more that become apparent as exploration continues) should be discussed and recorded. The skeletal plan can then be used with financiers and rehabilitation funders to secure money, support, mentoring, and technical assistance. It is suggested that the PBO and members of the BDT consider the five business map elements distinct sections of the written business plan. Procedures are recommended for completing each section.

Product/Service

The PBO and BDT first write a precise statement describing the product/service and the location in which it will be offered. This statement includes information regarding the market environment and the reasons why the business will succeed in such a time and place. Next, the PBO and BDT provide an assessment of the person's situation: his or her assets and talents (e.g., family support, the availability of SSA Work Incentives, a passion for making the service or product), hopes and dreams, and (perhaps) disability and support needs. The plan writers should also include in the assessment a discussion of why this business makes sense to the PBO and those involved in the enterprise. The potential and feasibility examination digs deeper into the circumstances that appear to support this business idea, clarifies which tasks the PBO will undertake, and offers ideas on how the PBO sees the business growing or maintaining itself. This is an open discussion and recording process that clarifies the *who, what, when, where,* and *why* elements of the business, which are examined more closely as the map is followed.

Discussions of this sort occur within all new businesses, regardless of product/service offered. The PBO and the BDT should brainstorm a variety of business approaches, ask others in business for their opinions, and be flexible in meeting the needs of customers. Profitable and customer-friendly Southwest Airlines, for instance, only flies Boeing 737 aircraft. Doing so reduces the training costs for flight crews compared with other airlines that fly numerous aircraft models. Furthermore, proficiency in one type of plane's maintenance cuts down on training costs for mechanics. Stocking parts for only one jetliner model also holds down inventory costs. This allows savings to be passed on to the customer, which, in turn, helps the company remain competitive. This business decision has saved millions of dollars and generated income because of increased efficiency. Southwest Airlines could buy larger planes and expand to international markets, but its leadership wisely sticks to its market segment and core skills, thereby maintaining its customer focus and positive cash flow (Freiberg & Freiberg, 1996). Although Southwest's business was not started by individuals with disabilities, the same basic planning process is relevant for anyone starting a business.

The 3 Cs

The 3 Cs are the heart of planning, as they address customers, competitors, and capabilities. First, the PBO and BDT examine the potential *customers* of the business:

- Who are they?
- Where do they live?
- Why would they buy this product/service?
- Are they one-time clients, or will they want or need more of the product/service?
- Is price a consideration in their selection of a product/service?
- What quality of product/service do they expect?

   Next, the PBO and the BDT evaluate the *competitors:*

- Who is the competition?
- Will it be easy for another competitor to enter the market?
- Will the business compete on price, quality, or both?
- Can competitors be turned into partners or suppliers of component parts/services?
- What makes this product/service better than or different from the competition's?

   Finally, the PBO and the BDT summarize the *capabilities* of the business by posing a series of "what-if" questions, which emanate from the customers and competitors analyses. Take the Chapter 3 example of the PBO who wants to manufacture gourmet dog biscuits. Customers might include shoppers at the local PETsMART store. PETsMART already carries gourmet dog biscuits, so questions of capability include the following:

- Does PETsMART corporate policy allow the sale of local suppliers' products at individual PETsMART stores?
- If so, can the business meet the sales demand of PETsMART customers?
- Can the business attract the attention of PETsMART's corporate office and become its exclusive supplier of gourmet dog biscuits?
- Can these PETsMART customers be reached elsewhere, such as through local veterinarians, mail order catalogs, or web sites?
- Does PETsMART's current supplier of gourmet dog biscuits need assistance in meeting production demands?
- Do PETsMART customers use the Internet to purchase dog biscuits?
- Can the PBO purchase advertising space on the PETsMART corporate or local store web site?

Capability questions are practically endless; one leads to another. They are used to explore the myriad opportunities and threats facing the business. This questioning also points out potential problems or weaknesses in the initial business design, illustrates positive market trends, and reveals capacity needs (e.g., Internet sales require investments in computer equipment and Internet connections, the ability to accept credit-card payments, and space for shipping and inventory). Such information is generally collected during the feasibility study and is used extensively for this part of the written business plan.

Marketing Mix

As noted in Chapter 3, the marketing mix involves matching a product/service to specific customers by identifying the proper advertising, pricing, and availability. The written plan's marketing mix section builds on what the PBO and BDT have learned about customers, competitors, and capabilities. The niche or unique target market is determined by using the 3 Cs information. For instance, if research has revealed that most buyers of gourmet dog biscuits are upper-middle income professionals with children, then product distribution and promotion should perhaps focus on advertising and selling these biscuits where these customers are likely to find them, including upscale supermarkets, the Internet, and local veterinarians' offices. Determining likely customers can be time consuming but relatively easy. Some of the information is intuitive, some can be gleaned from marketing studies available through SBA and SBDC reports and archives, and some can be found in marketing publications or by talking with marketing professionals. Much of this research is common sense, such as selling products/services on a trial basis or using a survey (see Chapter 3). A few days or weeks of selling reveals some trends in the possible target customer. For more information on this topic, the book *Why We Buy: The Science of Shopping* (Underhill, 2000) is strongly recommended.

The price of goods and services is determined by more than simply the labor and materials used to make a product. Price should include overhead costs, such as salary and benefits, rent, legal fees, business licensing, insurance, shipping and handling, tooling and equipment, fringe benefits, communications, advertising, and depreciation. Pricing also has a psychological aspect. Sometimes buyers shop for bargains; at other times, they insist on name brands or high quality. Knowing the market helps determine the price. Some manufacturers offer the same product at various levels of quality. This is why cars come with optional equipment, televisions come in different sizes, and carpets come with different wear guarantees.

Distribution refers to where and how customers gain access to the product/service, and *promotion* refers to methods for attracting customers to the product/service (i.e., advertising and marketing). Distribution planning includes determining the physical boundaries of the sales territory, if any, and other aspects of putting the customer face-to-face with the product/service (e.g., shelf space for products or supplies, shipping and timely delivery). In terms of promotion, many small companies rely on word-of-mouth advertising about availability and quality of the service while some companies have large advertising budgets. Many companies—large and small—create web sites or buy advertising space on other company's web sites. Some buy newspaper advertisements or television and radio air time; others make public appearances or air infomercials. One start-up pizza delivery service in a college town offered a free pizza with the purchase of one at regular price—if the customer presented the delivery person with a torn-out yellow pages advertisement from a competing pizza delivery service. This strategy worked well for the company, as it gave college students what they wanted (quantity and low price) while eliminating its competitor's advertising (Kawasaki, 1995).

Operations

Operations is the technical aspect of producing the product/service. Many business owners believe that success relies on giving this component the most attention. In reality, the supporting aspects of marketing, cash flow, and competition can kill a truly great product. Although building a better widget is crucial, this component is only a piece of the equation. Devising the best process to create the product/service is based on factors like the numbers sold or guaranteed by a certain delivery date, payback analysis for labor-saving equipment, available manufacturing space, production skills, and work force availability.

Detailing the tools and equipment necessary for production or delivery is an essential piece of the business puzzle. If high-tech equipment is necessary, then its purchase and use must be planned for and figured into the cost of producing products/services. The PBO and BDT must explore possible suppliers and award orders based on volume discounts, freight charges, quantity discounts, quality, and product availability. Another cost that may need to be covered is training for the business owner and employees. Perhaps customer training will be necessary as well for proper and efficient use of a product. For instance, as a value-added customer service strategy, the makers of a do-it-yourself log cabin kit might consider providing customers with an instructional videotape detailing the steps of assembly.

Contingency plans are also necessary in the operations section. The PBO should know of alternate supplies in case a regular supplier is unable to deliver. If the busy season coincides with flu season and employees may be out sick, the PBO must ensure that adequate inventory is on hand to fulfill orders. He or she should also ensure that repair parts and mechanics are easily accessible when equipment breaks down. The PBO needs to make certain that adequate raw materials, workers, equipment, and shipping materials are on hand to meet the need if a product becomes instantly successful. Planning for such business circumstances is critical to success and illustrates the need for a comprehensive production plan and alternative plans based on potential upward or downward swings in sales. A production plan simply outlines the flow of the process, the people responsible for each activity, the time at which each activity begins and ends, and the quality checks that will occur along the way. Many people need a reminder of what gets done next, so they carry their production plans with them in their Day-Timers or Palm Pilots. For large manufacturers such as Ford Motor Company, entire corporate divisions manage the logistics of production.

Operational designs for small businesses are difficult to develop because every product/service is fairly unique. Moreover, each PBO's methods and standards vary, so personnel management strategies are largely personal. Added to this are the challenges and accommodations related to a person's disability. Furthermore, the need for local, specific assistance is critical, underscoring that the PBO must have access to local business supports, mentors, and rehabilitation or education personnel who can serve as consultants.

Financial Plan

Generally, the financial portion is the most critically constructed and managed portion of the business plan. Small businesses regularly suffer from cash shortfalls, which is typically considered negative but can a be a great opening for discussing a partnership with an existing small business in need of capital.

Business Structures

Before launching a sole proprietorship, the PBO should consider forming a limited liability company (LLC) with an existing business that can leverage the PBO's resources. (An LLC also can be constructed as a business within a business, as discussed later in this chapter.) Under a partnership, the existing business might be able to provide the supports that the new entrepreneur needs most, such as supervision and training, retail space, transportation, a ready customer base, and mentorship. Many business owners get started by learning the trade from someone else, so this is a natural method of career and business development.

The following example of a potential partnership involves Tyler, who is interested in photography. Tyler wants to learn the trade, wants to expand his photographic skills, and can generate approximately $20,000 in funds from a PASS. In this scenario, Tyler meets with Juanita, a local photographer who operates a small retail storefront and has agreed to serve as a host business owner. Tyler and Juanita explore what the host business needs to increase profits. Assuming that the business will benefit from increased retail inventory, the two parties write an agreement establishing the partnership. With assistance from the local SBDC to fine-tune the arrangement, they follow the terms set out by their local secretary of state. In this case, Tyler agrees to invest $20,000 in new digital cameras and to receive payments in proportion to the investment and retail markup. Juanita can arrange to take a percentage of the profits or simply acknowledge that by augmenting her inventory, she has increased customer traffic through the store, thereby expanding potential sales of related equipment and photographic services.

In such situations, the new partner with a disability may or may not work in the store. In most cases, working in the store is not essential when establishing a partnership based on a return on investment. However, working there is preferable. If the PBO does work in the place of business—for instance, if it is decided that Tyler will run the cash register and the 1-hour photo processor—the partnership agreement should be written to reflect payments to a partner for those tasks as well.

The point is to structure the business to meet the needs of the consumer and to reap the benefits of a variety of natural supports. The primary types of legal business structures include

- *Sole proprietorships:* The owner and the business are the same in a sole proprietorship. Business and personal tax returns are filed together. Roughly 75% of all U.S. small businesses operate as sole proprietorships (Ketchum, 1998). The advantages to sole proprietorship is that it is simple and inexpensive to start and allows for maximum control by the owner. The disadvantages include personal legal liability and the limited ability to raise capital from investors.

- *Partnerships:* This is a business with more than one owner; it divides profits and losses among partners. The advantages include the spreading of risk and the incorporation of more experience and capital from the various partners. Disadvantages include personality conflicts and disagreements over strategy and money.

- *Limited liability companies (LLC):* This option, a form of partnership and the fastest growing company structure in the United States, allows for the reduced personal liability of a corporation but with the tax advantages of a partnership. The advantages include liability protection and no double taxation (paying company and personal income taxes). The disadvantages include variability of tax and liability benefits from state to state and the sometimes high cost of start-up.

- *Incorporation:* This is a likely choice for companies with employees. Attorney costs and licensing fees can be substantial. Advantages include the protection of personal assets if the company fails or is sued. Disadvantages are the filing fees and potentially high taxes. There are two variations on corporate structure as well. The first is the S Corporation. S Corporations are identified under the IRS subchapter S. They feature limits on personal liability and eliminate double taxation. However, S Corporations have to pay taxes on some fringe benefits, have limits on retirement benefits, and are restricted to a total of 35 investors. The other type of corporation of interest is the C Corporation, which is taxed under the regular corporate income tax rules. C Corporations provide good liability protection and allow for the sale of stock to raise capital, and ownership is easily transferred. Yet, C Corporations are subject to dual taxation, involve a high degree of regulation and paperwork, and can have high start-up costs because of legal fees and registration costs.

Information on the advantages and disadvantages of each can be explained by the local SBDC, and most bookstores carry guides about these models. The proper licensing of the business is important for anticipating investors, taxes, payroll, governance, and management models.

Cash-Flow Analysis

The best structure for a business becomes more clear once the financial analysis and the business plan are drafted. To complete a draft of the cash-flow analysis, the PBO first determines how much on-hand cash can be used to support the business in its critical start-up phase and beyond. Assets such as capital equipment and machinery to produce the product/service are assigned a value. In this portion of the plan, the PBO also considers property that can be sold or used as collateral.

The cash-flow projection is performed to anticipate how much capital is necessary for at least the first year and when the capital is needed to fulfill customer orders. A cash-flow projection can be simple or complex, but it must include the cost of producing the goods and services; the projected accounts receivable; the purchase of supplies throughout the production cycle; and the cost of payroll, taxes, and all associated costs. The analysis indicates how much money is required to run the business as well as when and from what sources infusions of cash can be expected. If lenders are involved, the cash-flow analysis may cover the entire length of the loan. However, owners of many small business start-ups who do not seek external cash look only 1–2 years into the future.

The cash-flow analysis helps the PBO identify the need for loans, investors, and partners. It also provides a glimpse of an often unclear future and may prompt a revision of manufacturing methods, modification of the product line, or a change in marketing strategy to attract more buyers in a specific demographic range. It might even indicate that the business should be launched ahead of schedule. The cash-flow analysis is an educated guess, but it is critical for planning a smooth production cycle and anticipating possible peaks and valleys in income and expenses.

A significant source of business capital can often be generated for the PBO through use of a PASS. An individual's PASS can pay for vehicles, production equipment, training, special clothing (e.g., uniforms), and advertising. The PASS program represents a loan-free approach to self-financing that can also be used in combination with funds from other sources such as VR and Department of Labor programs. Chapter 6 details the use of PASS and other SSA Work Incentives for the small business owner.

Break-Even Analysis

The break-even analysis is closely tied to the cash-flow analysis. It is another tool for analyzing the amount of money invested by the owner and others compared with projected revenue from sales. A typical break-even analysis predicts the date that business profits will pay off the investment.

Say that the young operators of a corner lemonade stand spend $2.00 on cups, $4.00 on lemonade mix, and $1.00 on poster board for their sign. Their total investment, not counting the value of their time, is $7.00. They plan to sell lemonade for $.50 a cup. To pay off their debt ($7.00), they will have to sell 14 cups of lemonade ($7.00/$.50 = 14 cups). Therefore, 14 cups is their break-even point. After that, all sales are pure profit (their self-employment wages) until they buy more supplies, at which time they need to break even again.

Some break-even analyses use a variety of scenarios to represent best- and worst-case payoff dates. For instance, one plan proposed a business within a business at a nature center (see Chapter 1). The initial break-even analysis used a fixed cost projection of $100 per month ($1,200 per year) for business rent. There were no advertising or other costs. It also used an average stuffed animal sale of $8.00, with a wholesale product cost of $4.00 per stuffed animal, or 50% of the sales price. The plan noted that for Andrew, the PBO, to break even, 300 stuffed animals per year would have to be sold at $8.00 each, resulting in $2,400 in sales. The $2,400 would then pay the yearly rent of $1,200 and the $1,200 inventory cost (i.e., the product cost of the 300 stuffed animals at $4.00 each).

As noted in Chapter 1, Andrew had significant disabilities. The business proposal was based on the host nature center's agreeing to receive a 10% payment on all gross sales in return for business space. In this scenario, the break-even point is exceeded with every sale. The profit risk was based on sales volume. A large volume of sales translated into a high business rent; a low volume of sales meant that the business owner paid almost nothing for business rent. Therefore, if Andrew sold 10 stuffed animals at $8.00 each in one month, the cost per sale would be $4.80 (the wholesale product cost of $4.00 plus and additional $.80 for the 10% of gross sales for business rent). The nature center would receive $8.00 for business rent that month, and Andrew would earn $32.00 ($3.20 profit per sale). The manager of the nature center loved the business idea and plan and presented the idea to the board of directors, which unanimously approved it.

The break-even analysis is a relatively simple tool that helps refine a prospective small business idea quickly. Often, after someone proposes a business idea, the next series of general cost and pricing questions leads to a quick analysis of how many products need to be sold to break even on annual costs. It also shows how much profit is generated after the break-even point. The basic questions to develop a simple break-even analysis are

1. What are the fixed costs per month or year, including rent, advertising, utilities, and insurance? (Fixed costs are those that remain largely unchanged regardless of sales or production.)

2. What are the variable costs per product/service sold, including inventory costs and commissions per unit or service sold? (Variable costs increase or decrease with sales/production. The assumption is that if a company sells handkerchiefs but no one buys them, no fabric needs to be purchased.)

3. From the previous two questions, a rough break-even analysis develops, illustrating the point at which sales cover the fixed and variable costs per product sold. Chapter 7 includes a chart that illustrates the break-even analysis graphically.

All of the previously described components eventually merge into a business plan that guides development of the enterprise, helps secure support and funding, and offers a step-by-step approach to growing the business. This approach organizes and simplifies the steps that the business owner takes to launch and operate the enterprise. Taken day to day and one step at a time, a logical sequence of actions becomes clear for everyone involved. The following example involving Max illustrates the evolution of a business from dream to reality.

MAX'S STORY

Max is an 18-year-old student attending special education classes and living in a community of 20,000 people. He has had several in-school jobs and one summer job at a car wash. Max's person-centered plan recognizes that he enjoys socializing, likes selling things, is an early riser, and likes money. He will likely graduate from high school in the next 2 years. Max's parents want him to have a full-time job or be a business owner by graduation. With help from his special education teacher, Max signed up for VR, which agreed to help him, and applied for SSI and Medicaid. Max just started receiving a monthly SSI check of $545, the SSI rate for 2002.

The school, with the support of VR, is providing an employment specialist to assist Max in finding a job or starting a business. His parents are also helping by attending free evening classes on starting a small business at the local SBDC. At one of the classes, Max and his father met Angelica. She had just started a coffeehouse on the corner of Main and State Streets in the center of town. The coffeehouse occupies a vacant retail space that needed extensive renovations. Hoping to attract the growing crowd of people who commute to jobs in the city 45 minutes away, Angelica also had a drive-up window installed to provide quick service. Although Angelica's business is based on quick customer turnover at the drive-up window, it also provides a safe and comfortable oasis for walk-ins. She has outfitted the coffeehouse with books, magazines, daily newspapers, paintings and photographs from local artists (for sale, of course), overstuffed chairs, and pleasant music. She features gourmet coffee roasting, custom blends, and a full variety of espresso drinks.

Angelica put her life's savings into the coffeehouse. Financially, she is just getting by as her business slowly grows. During the SBDC class, she mentioned that cash flow was a constant problem. She has two part-time employees who work with her from 6:30 A.M. until 11:00 A.M., during the coffee rush and clean-up period. She stays open until noon, then goes to her home studio to work on pottery. She wants to expand the coffeehouse product line but cannot afford fixtures or staff because her credit is exhausted. Angelica is looking for an investor, although she does not realize it yet.

Later on at home, Max and his parents discuss business opportunities at the coffeehouse because Max likes people, enjoys getting up early, and loves selling things. Max and his parents decide to invite Angelica to lunch. They make the following proposal. Max will purchase a portable, refrigerated bagel cart and install it in the coffeehouse. If the bagels do not sell, then Max can take the cart elsewhere. Max will also bring a self-serve customer table to set up alongside the cart so that customers can prepare bagels to their liking. In addition, he will purchase a production toaster and work table to be placed behind the cart. Max will work from 6:45 A.M. to 9:30 A.M. each day. After picking up several dozen bagels at a bakery and condiments at the grocery store (cream cheese, jam, peanut butter, and butter), Max's father will drop him off at the coffeehouse. Max's employment specialist will meet Max at the coffeehouse and provide support until he learns the business and his co-workers (the coffeehouse staff) become accustomed to helping out during very busy times. All sales will be rung up on the cash register at the coffee counter. Max will receive the profits from his sales, less $150 per month rent and 10% of gross based on cash register receipts. Should customers want bagels after 9:30 A.M., the coffeehouse staff will prepare them and credit Max with the sales.

Angelica likes this idea because it will bring in new customers who want food, it saves her from buying expensive refrigerated display cases and toasters, and it allows her to add an employee without actually paying wages or incurring worker's compensation expenses. Because Max will operate as a sole proprietor, he will not need worker's comp. His wheelchair will not be an issue because Angelica followed the code of the Americans with Disabilities Act when remodeling her store.

This concept of a business within a business provides support for Max because

- Sales are rung up on one cash register

- The coffeehouse offers free advertising

- Max avoids the hassles of setting up a retail business alone

- Max receives mentoring supports from Angelica and her staff

- Max can set aside his earnings in a PASS and grow the business even larger, perhaps adding employees and multiple locations

- Max is considered a business owner with a network of customers and suppliers who rely on him and know him as a contributing member of the economic community

Max and his parents decide to implement the business idea. They need to request financial support from VR. A business plan is the mechanism for convincing this agency to "invest." Angelica is involved in the preliminary business design conversations. She shares her knowledge of the market and influences the plan based on her business needs as well.

Max and his parents remember that the business plan is a professional document, a marketing tool. They know that it must look neat and be free of grammatical and spelling errors. (The PBO can get assistance and advice from the local SBDC, purchase the services of a business plan writer, or use a PASS or VR money to pay for a business plan writer to develop the concept.) They put the executive summary on company letterhead and print the document on quality paper. Starting with the executive summary, Bagels to the Max is launched.

Max's business plan was developed on the basis of three sources. First, examples from other similar enterprises were found on the Internet and through the SBDC. Second, the Business Planning Map flowchart, discussed previously in this chapter, was implemented. Third, the following aspects were considered in Max's business plan.

Bagels to the Max
P.O. Box 345
Lynnwood, CO 80101
555-555-5555

March 1, 2003

Mr. Tom Smith, CRC
Colorado Vocational Rehabilitation
1444 Cottonwood Drive
Lynnwood, CO 80101

Re: Request for Services and Supports

Dear Mr. Smith:

Following our meeting last week, my team and I put together the final elements of my business plan. This letter serves as the executive summary, and the full plan is attached. Please review this proposal to receive Vocational Rehabilitation (VR) services and supports, and forward any questions to me at the telephone number above. I look forward to speaking with you soon.

Bagels to the Max will be organized as a sole proprietorship under the IRS code and the rules of Colorado's secretary of state. Bagels to the Max is a business-within-a-business model designed to ensure a steady and reliable customer flow Monday through Friday. The host business is Angelica's Coffeehouse on the corner of Main and State Streets. The proprietor, Angelica Austin, has been involved in designing my business concept. Her coffeehouse is a recent addition to the local marketplace; has a growing reputation for high-quality service and products; has two part-time staff, plus the owner; has had a positive cash flow for the past 3 months; will provide me with ongoing extended supports; will provide business assistance, inventory control, and accounting services for a small fee; and is located in a fully accessible storefront. This business matches the vocational profile that I developed with my teacher, family, and employment specialist.

My team's business feasibility study involved surveying more than 100 coffee customers at Angelica's Coffeehouse; discussing sales volume with the local bakery that will provide bagels at wholesale; and thoroughly searching the Internet for marketing and sales information about similar businesses. Because Bagels to the Max will be located in the coffeehouse, more than 150 customers per day could potentially purchase bagels. Casey Locke at the Small Business Development Center (SBDC) has reviewed this plan and considers it highly feasible. He can be reached at 555-555-5551 if you have any questions.

Currently, there is no other gourmet coffeehouse in town. The nearest espresso stand is 5 miles down Route 297 on the way to the city. This business does not sell bagels. My major competition would come from fast-food outlets, such as McDonald's, or local convenience stores. My service will be unique, however, because I will toast fresh bagels (various plain, sweet, and savory varieties) that complement the high-quality coffee drinks offered at Angelica's Coffeehouse.

My parents plan to provide long-term supports; the school will serve me for at least another year; and Angelica and her staff will offer ongoing business supports. I am also convinced that as I meet people in the store, my network of business and personal associates will guarantee me lasting success.
   I request your consideration of the following items for my business:

• Mobile bagel display and refrigeration cart (maple finish) from Unico Industries	$3,000.00
• Commercial "Electro-Drive" toaster	$300.00
• Customer service table (maple finish)	$110.00
• Job coaching for the summer season (25 hours at $40 per hour)	$1,000.00
Total request	**$4,410.00**

My family, the host business, and my school are providing extensive business supports and job coaching throughout the start-up and at least through the next school year. Note that I also will be holding profits in a business bank account, allowed under the Social Security Act as Property Essential For Self Support (PESS), to expand and replace equipment as necessary. I will also develop a Plan for Achieving Self-Support (PASS), possibly to buy a delivery van or mobile bagel service once the first business phase is successful and I have saved enough money to shelter in a PASS.

Thank you again for your ongoing support and advice. The business is ready to go, and with your agency's support, I know that it will be a success.

Sincerely,

Max Barkley
Owner, Bagels to the Max
cc: Angelica Austin

Business Plan

1. Primary product/service

The primary product/service is selling high-quality bagels quickly as a sole proprietor located within the "host" business, Angelica's Coffeehouse.

Details: Currently, Bagels to the Max plans to offer plain bagels, sweet bagels (blueberry, cranberry, chocolate chip), and savory bagels (cheese, onion, sesame seed). It has an exclusive purchase arrangement with Valley View Bakery for assorted bagels at $4.50 per dozen regardless of flavor or variety.

2. Business goals

Short-term goals include

- Learn the best possible methods for attracting and serving customers
- Create a profitable enterprise that helps Max achieve financial freedom and gives him recognition as a business owner in the community
- Increase operating hours from 13.75 per week to 30 hours within 12 months

Long-term goals include

- Increase sales to allow the hiring of several employees
- Expand to mobile sales or other fixed locations

3. Support

Max will be assisted in learning the business and managing operations to ensure a profitable venture by the following people: Angelica and her staff at the host business; Max's teacher; Casey Locke, Max's self-employment specialist at the SBDC; and Max's family.

4. Other complementary products/services

A.   Initially, Bagels to the Max will offer grape and strawberry jam packets, cream cheese packets, peanut butter packets, and pats of butter at the customer self-service table.

B.   Within 1 year, Bagels to the Max will add custom gourmet low-fat and regular cream cheese mixes (chive, pineapple, garlic, sun-dried tomato).

C.   Within 1 year, Bagels to the Max will offer a toasted bagel with melted cheese.

D.   Within 2 years, Angelica's Coffeehouse will offer sandwiches, a venture in which Bagels to the Max will be a partner.

E.   Within 4 years, Bagels to the Max will add a mobile bagel and bakery delivery (in collaboration with Valley View Bakery).

F.   Once sandwiches are offered by Angelica's Coffeehouse, and if Max's PASS allows the business to buy a van and the business will support a driver/delivery employee, Bagels to the Max will provide lunch delivery service.

5. How each complementary product/service listed in #4 adds value

A. Provides greater choice and satisfaction to customers; value-added service
B. Provides greater choice and satisfaction to customers; value-added service
C. Provides greater choice and satisfaction to customers; value-added service
D. Provides greater choice and satisfaction to customers; value-added service
E. Expands the market share and increases convenience for customer
F. Expands the market share and increases convenience for customer

6. What is the anticipated market position for the primary product/service (i.e., high quality/high price, moderate quality/low price)? Are you seeking an upscale, an average, or a discount-seeking buyer? Explain.

The host business is based on high quality, quick turnaround, and moderately high cost for convenience. Most customers are heading to work and want coffee and a quick breakfast. By designing the business to complement Angelica's core coffee business, the host enterprise offers additional products to customers at minimal investment. Angelica's Coffeehouse, like most small businesses, is undercapitalized and can benefit from having a complementary business attached.

Customers who come to the coffeehouse to meet colleagues or to relax are also satisfied with high-quality goods and an environment that never rushes them. Just as Starbucks created a "third place" environment outside of home and the office, Angelica's Coffeehouse is a haven from work and daily stresses. It is relaxed and relaxing—a place where friends can meet, talk, and enjoy each other.

Gourmet bagels fit in perfectly as a fast, easy, and inexpensive indulgence. They are comfort food for the morning rush and the long commute to the city. They also fit with lingering over a cup of fine coffee during a morning break.

7. Business/work hours

The business will be set up beginning at 6:45 A.M., after bagels and condiments are purchased at the bakery and grocery store. During the rest of this school year, Max will work until 9:30 A.M. daily so that he can return to school after serving the morning customer rush. Beginning this summer, Max plans to work from 6:00 A.M. until noon Monday through Friday.

8. Who is the likely buyer (e.g., younger/older, male/female, wealthy/restricted income)? Where would the buyer look for this product/service? Explain.

The customer demographic for Angelica's Coffeehouse is mixed, but the predominant buyers are young professionals. Drive-up customers generally commute to city jobs, while fixed-site customers are employed locally. According to Angelica, the age range for more than 70% of customers is early twenties to late fifties, and a growing college student population is evident mid-morning. Max and Angelica believe that it is possible to capture the lunch crowd by extending hours until 1:30 P.M. in the coming year.

There seems to be a fairly even mix of male and female customers. Most customers appear to have discretionary income. Offering moderately high priced, high-quality brewed coffee with one free refill is attracting college students who come to talk and study. This gives the shop a busy and successful atmosphere but may crowd out paying customers when lunch or increased breakfast items are added later.

9. Will the buyer need to purchase this product/service more than once? How often? How does this affect the marketing approach, packaging, and volume discounts (e.g., a lawn mowing service gives a $10 discount to customers who sign up for six mowings)? Explain your strategy.

According to an Angelica's Coffeehouse customer survey, 75% of customers return regularly. It is believed that customers who do not return found the prices too high or were traveling through town (e.g., tourists, business people). Angelica's Coffeehouse has begun a Coffee Club that offers free drinks and discounts after the customer makes a certain number of purchases. At present, no such plan is in place or anticipated for Bagels to the Max. Our pricing is reasonable and in line with surveys of bakeries and restaurants in the area. Bagels to the Max pays $4.50 per dozen for bagels. We sell bagels with choice of cream cheese, butter, jam, and peanut butter for $1.75 each. Projected monthly expenses follow in the answer to #10.

10. Expected wages/pay. Explain the basis for this calculation or forecast.

• Wages (Max), calculated at $7.00 per hour for 13.75 hours per week times 4 weeks	$385.00
• Rent (includes utilities, insurance, marketing, and accounting/ bookkeeping services)	$150.00
• Depreciation/amortization (5-year replacement on $3,410 in equipment)	$56.83
• Miscellaneous expenses (e.g., condiments)	$50.00
Total monthly expenses	**$641.83**

Based on anticipated bagel sales of a modest 60 bagels per day (5 dozen) and assuming that operating hours are not increased, gross revenues equal $2,310 per month ($1.75 x 60 x 22 days worked on average per month) or $27,720 per year. Angelica's Coffeehouse receives10% of gross sales (estimated at $231.00), which brings net receipts for Bagels to the Max to $2,079 monthly or $24,948 annually.

Based on sales of 110 dozen per month, the per unit cost of a bagel to Max is the sum of all costs: $641.83 plus Angelica's 10% of the gross at $231, which equals $872.83 divided by the 110 dozen bagels. This results in $7.93 for the average unit cost of bagels. When the cost of $4.50 for a dozen bagels is added, the cost is $12.43 per dozen bagels sold ($7.93 plus $4.50 equals $12.43). Dividing $12.43 by 12 reveals that each bagel costs $1.04 to sell. With a sales price of

$1.75, the net profit per bagel is $.71. Thus, selling a projected 1,320 bagels with a $.71 profit generates $937.20 net profit per month or $11,246.40 per year. Plus, Max would also have wage earnings of $4,620. Each month, Bagels to the Max will also set aside 20% of net profit for income taxes. If sales are off peak, enough profit margin exists to lower prices and still make profits. Weekly sales calculations will support price changes in consultation with Angelica.

11. How will you know if your product/service is over- or underpriced? What do similar products/services sell for at other businesses?

Because 150 potential buyers patronize Angelica's Coffeehouse daily, selling to 30% of traffic is considered reasonable according to retail food studies and the SBDC. One goal of the business will be to increase sales through better signage and possibly a greater variety of bagels and toppings. Angelica will also run "pairings" specials such as "Buy an espresso and receive a bagel for $1.00." On these sales, Angelica will waive the 10% fee on gross profit. This discounted pricing should influence the buying patterns of the customers and increase the likelihood that in the future, the customer will purchase bagels at regular prices.

Bagels to the Max will also monitor local retail bagel sales to align prices and assess ongoing or new competition in the market. Trends in bagel sales will come from trade magazines; Internet searches; and ongoing discussions with the bakery, Angelica, and customers.

12. Where will you sell this product/service (e.g., other people's stores, your own store, door to door, in magazines, over the Internet?). List specific outlets.

As noted previously, this is a business within a business. The host business acts as a magnet, attracting customers. Bagels to the Max adds value to the host. Eventually, mobile bagel sales will be developed, along with delivery services.

13. How will the product be packaged? What will it look like? Explain.

At the recommendation of the SBDC, the business conducted a Five Senses Exercise, along with Angelica and her staff, as the retail space is shared. This study involves anticipating what the owners and customers desire in a coffeehouse environment and then addresses the sensory concerns regarding when customers encounter the bagel stand.

What should customers see?

Bagels to the Max will display a variety of fresh bagels in straight rows under the glass display lid of the cart. The menu selections will be obvious and in plain sight. Cream cheese, jam, butter, peanut butter, and plastic knives will be within easy sight and reach at the customer self-service counter. The bagels will be toasted on the toaster conveyor in full view of the customers and served in a custom-printed Bagels to the Max bag or on a decorative paper plate (part of the 10% fee to Angelica). The

work area will be maintained spotlessly by Max's and Angelica's crew. The price of bagels and the daily selection will be plainly posted at the bagel counter. Angelica will hand draw the sign every morning while she is preparing the sign for the coffee-house's daily specials.

What should customers hear?

Overhead speakers will broadcast popular music soft enough so that orders can be heard clearly. Max will greet each customer with "Good morning! What can I get for you today?" Once the customer is served, Max will gently remind him or her to pay at the coffee counter. He closes by saying, "Thank you. Have a great day."

What should customers taste?

Each morning, Max will prepare fresh samples and display these bite-size bits next to their flavor labels on the display case. Only fresh gourmet bagels will be offered for retail. Day-old bagels will be discounted and sold in bags of six for $4.50. Customers will also have their choice of various fresh, high-quality condiments.

What should customers feel?

All bagels will be quick-toasted so that they are crisp on the outside with a smooth inside. The bagel will be served warm, and condiment portions will be large enough to satisfy customers. Customers will never feel rushed: Bagel orders will be staged to occur while customers are awaiting their coffee order in a spacious waiting area that also has stools. Bagels to the Max will be a relaxing but speedy experience.

What should customers smell?

The predominant smell will be fresh roasted coffee beans and brewing coffee, punctuated by toasted bagels of various flavors. The air inside will be moist, warm, and rich with flavor.

14. Will each package contain multiple products? Will the product(s) be bundled with other complementary products from your company? Will you bundle complementary products from other companies? Explain.

Bagels to the Max anticipates that most customers will only order one bagel at a time; however, the previously described pairing and loss-leader events will likely occur throughout the year. Also, day-old bagels will be sold per half dozen.

15. What image do you seek for this product/service? That is, is it convenient for customers? Is it cheaper than similar services offered by other businesses? Does it add value to or complement another product/service that the customer is likely to use? Are you pledging high-quality customer service? Does it have "snob appeal," or is it for the "do-it-yourselfer"? Explain.

Angelica's Coffeehouse insists that Bagels to the Max "enhances" and adds value to coffee sales. Therefore, the business is designed with the understanding that only the highest quality bagels will be sold but that price will be monitored to ensure that

cost does not drive customers to one of the local fast-food vendors. Also, in keeping with Angelica's business model, the bagel service will be "seamless." In other words, Bagels to the Max must remain convenient for the customer. To do this, Bagels to the Max will retain employment specialist and family support for the first phase of operations, and Angelica will provide co-worker support to ensure that speed and service are maintained. Max will be supported in ways that always highlight his many competencies.

Any on-site support people (e.g., employment specialists, family members) will always appear to be working *for* Max and not *with* Max. They will wear attire that fits with that of the coffeehouse employees. Generally, this includes clean jeans and T-shirts. The dress code is very open, but all clothing must be clean and free from rips, holes, or tears.

All health and safety regulations will be addressed and monitored. Cleanliness measures will be exceeded.

16. Does this service complement another company's service? What makes your service better? Does the opportunity exist to bundle this service with the product/service of another company? Explain.

As explained previously in this business plan, Bagels to the Max complements the host business, Angelica's Coffeehouse, by solving its undercapitalization problem, providing a value-added service, and contributing to fixed income through rent payments.

17. What is the overall promotional strategy for your product/service? What "look" or image do you want?

The host business will undertake primary advertising through print advertisements and by hosting art shows and special events. Angelica's Coffeehouse will consistently list bagels as a primary product available to drive-up and in-store customers.

18. How will you use advertising? Is this a major part of your marketing strategy? Which advertising outlets will you use? How often will you advertise?

A. Print advertising (newspapers, yellow pages): Once operations are stabilized within approximately 6 months, Bagels to the Max and Angelica's Coffeehouse will share costs for trial product bundles and loss leaders (e.g., buy one bagel, get the second for half off; buy two premium coffee drinks, get one bagel for $.50 off). Bagels to the Max will possibly also offer buy one, get one free coupons or per dozen sales via $1.00-off coupons available in the local entertainment newspaper.

B. Direct mail: N/A

C. Television: Angelica's Coffeehouse sponsors both the local public television station and local access programming, so the business is mentioned on air. As part of this strategy, the availability of Bagels to the Max will be made clear in all future sponsorship/advertising. This will be a component of Max's monthly 10% gross revenue payment to Angelica.

D. Radio: N/A except for special events. For instance, on-air advertisements for new artist showings will mention Angelica's Coffeehouse. Sample advertising copy for such an event might read, "On Friday night, new local artist Carol Chambers will be exhibiting her landscape watercolors. The event is hosted by Angelica's Coffeehouse, featuring Bagels to the Max." On such evenings, as appropriate, Bagels to the Max will offer desserts (e.g., cookies, pie, cake) by special arrangement with the bakery that supplies the bagels. In the future, radio advertisements may be placed for the morning drive time. The purpose of advertising in this time slot would be to attract new customers and, once a lunch menu is offered, to "plant the seed" that commuters should plan now to have a relaxing lunch at Angelica's Coffeehouse with a bagel or sandwich from Bagels to the Max.

E. Word of mouth: This type of advertising is critical to all small businesses. It is anticipated that the hospitality, speed, and quality of service will attract new customers and keep repeat customers.

F. Business cards and brochures: Bagels to the Max business cards will feature the business name; Max's name; and the address, telephone number, and fax number of Angelica's Coffeehouse.

G. Novelties: Bagels to the Max will carry two styles of travel mugs with the Bagels to the Max logo on one side and the Angelica's Coffeehouse logo on the other. Angelica has designed a logo for Bagels to the Max that complements the existing Angelica's Coffeehouse logo. Mugs will be sold at only a 5% markup to entice buyers and spread advertising passively.

H. Signage: Angelica's Coffeehouse will add Bagels to the Max to its window signage at no cost. Daily specials will be posted behind the coffee counter and at the bagel case. A menu board will list daily flavors and prices. The bagel cart will feature large lettering, supplied by the cart manufacturer as part of the sale price, that reads "Bagels to the Max."

I. Classified advertising: N/A

J. Telemarketing: N/A

K. Press releases and public service announcements (PSAs): Angelica will write a press release to announce the grand opening of Bagels to the Max. Max's disabilities will play no role whatsoever in the release or in any advertising. Consent will not be given to mention Max's disabilities in human interest stories printed in local papers or presented via other media outlets.

L. Sales staff: All sales staff will dress as mentioned previously. Having counter employees wear Bagels to the Max T-shirts is being considered for the future. (Selling such T-shirts to customers is also being considered for the future.)

M. Other: N/A

19. How will you measure the effectiveness of your promotions?

Sales of coffee mugs will indicate their promotional value and people's affiliation with Bagels to the Max and Angelica's Coffeehouse. Coupon receipts, when such specials are offered, will be an indicator of promotional success.

Because promotion of Bagels to the Max largely depends on the success of Angelica's Coffeehouse, Bagels to the Max will work to support Angelica's culture and climate and should benefit from increased drive-up and walk-in customers.

20. How much do you propose to spend monthly on marketing and advertising? How will you know if it is enough or too much?

The 10% of gross sales allocated monthly to Angelica's Coffeehouse covers basic advertising. Advertising campaigns such as selling promotional items should be self-sustaining through sales of these novelty items. According to the agreement with Angelica, at least one print advertisement per week will mention Bagels to the Max; store signage will highlight Bagels to the Max or the availability of Max's products; and special events at the coffeehouse, which are scheduled at least monthly, will feature Bagels to the Max.

21. Other issues of product, price, place, and promotion

It is anticipated that as the business matures, delivery services and expansion to other locations will help keep Bagels to the Max in the public eye.

This sample has been provided to exemplify considerations to address in a business plan. It is recommended that the PBO and BDT record the answers to the relevant preceding questions in a word-processing document. Then, they can simply paste the language into a new document and add some transition statements, and the narrative portion of the plan will be complete. (Chapter 7 details financial statements to include in the business plan.) The business plan template found in Appendix A serves as a guide. It is important to remember that not all businesses or plans are alike and that the PBO and BDT should not be restrained by this one suggested format. They should be certain to comprehensively address the uniqueness of the particular business being considered. As noted previously, operation and management of a business is almost always unique and specific to the business owner. Therefore, developing this portion of a business plan requires significant individualized effort, study and understanding of management principles associated with the specific business and of personnel legalities in the state of operation, and hands-on advice from local experts, such as SCORE or SBDC members or a personal mentor.

Chapter 5

Marketing and Sales Tactics

IMPORTANT TERMS IN THIS CHAPTER

Business to business (B2B): Business to business enterprises are designed to sell only to other companies and not to the general buying public. These are also known as *supplier companies* because they supply other businesses with essential products or services.

Customer demographics: Key identifying characteristics of potential customers, such as their income level, age, gender, educational attainment, hobbies, and so forth. These demographics are used to develop marketing and sales approaches that reach particular people. Products/services are also modified to meet the needs of specific groups (e.g., minivans are marketed toward growing families; sports cars are targeted toward singles).

Marketing: The act of creating or revealing a need for a product/service in the customer's mind.

Sales: Providing the means and the opportunity for a customer to purchase a product/service.

The exchange of goods and services between a business and the customer is the most critical of all commercial relationships. Marketing and sales are natural and mandatory elements of all businesses and must be seriously addressed by all enterprises. If no one buys the product/service, the business does not survive. No matter how well conceived or well located an enterprise, a business owner's most crucial support is the paying customer. Attracting customers is the function of marketing; closing the deal and trading the product/service for cash compose sales. Marketing is the magnet that pulls in buyers, whereas making sales is the act of commercial exchange.

MARKETING ESSENTIALS

Most small businesses have a limited amount of resources for marketing. Developing and launching a marketing campaign can be quite expensive. However, small businesses generally do not need the marketing reach of large corporations like General Motors or Microsoft. Most can establish a brand in the mind of customers with reasonable effort and expense. One of a business owner's first actions must be to identify the target market. This is accomplished at least briefly in the business plan but requires ongoing attention as the business is launched and grows. A common mistake is thinking that everyone is a potential customer for the company's chocolate chip cookies or desktop publishing business. The fact is that even the most successful businesses usually only attract a small percentage of a community's population or of a market. By identifying those most likely to want and need an enterprise's products/services, the marketing and sales campaigns can be specifically designed to appeal to those customers. This activity takes time, but for many small businesses, it ends up saving time and money by focusing effort on only the most likely customers.

The PBO and the BDT should complete the Market Positioning Worksheet (see Appendix A) when developing the marketing approach. The worksheet is designed to refine the demographic character of both primary and secondary customers. A primary customer is most likely to purchase the product/service based on his or her situation, needs, and attitudes. A secondary customer uses the product/service for a different reason or with less intensity than a primary customer. Identifying these customers allows the business to target specific marketing, products, and services at particular consumer groups. For instance, in Chapter 4's example of Bagels to the Max, the primary customer is an individual on the way to work who buys a cup of espresso and a bagel to go. A secondary customer is perhaps a manager who buys two dozen bagels for his staff every Friday morning as an end-of-the-week treat. The primary customer probably has different needs than the secondary consumer. The primary customer wants a high-quality, fast, and reasonably priced breakfast. The secondary customer is likely more concerned with a variety of flavors, the convenience of a sturdy box or bag, and an assortment of cream cheese flavors. A little research can reveal the unique needs of the customer. Although one company cannot always cater to the unique needs of every possible customer, this research helps the proprietor design a business and marketing effort that satisfies many consumer needs. The worksheet also contains a section on marketing for B2B companies; many small businesses are B2B because they wholesale their products to retailers.

After completing the Market Positioning Worksheet, the PBO and BDT should talk to others and brainstorm about how customer and competitor characteristics might influence the company's sales and marketing approach and about which new products/services might add value for the customer. Although a marketing approach is developed before the business opens, it is advisable to continually refine and evaluate the opportunities for new approaches as the competitive environment and the enterprise evolve. The following completed worksheet for Bagels to the Max reveals the value of gathering such information.

Market Positioning Worksheet

Customer demographics or identifiers	Primary customer	Secondary customer(s)
Location of the customers (e.g., city, county, particular part of town, cyberspace)	Commuters on their way to work. Some will use the drive-up window; others will stop in briefly. Many are in cars, so product should be easy to eat and not too messy.	Buyers of one or two dozen for special occasions/office treats. College students who want a snack while studying or relaxing. The occasional crowd attending an art show held at the coffeehouse. Tourists or others traveling through town.
Age range	Working adults who are looking for convenience and quality. Children are not a serious customer base, although offering a peanut butter and jelly bagel might be a good breakfast choice for them. Consider selling bagel-based bag lunches for children as the business grows.	Working adults who want value and selection and college students who want value. Consider placing coupons in the college newspaper and having a coffee and bagel "happy hour" to bring in customers during slow business hours (from 10:00 A.M. until noon).
Male or female?	Both	Both. Consider adding stuffed chairs to create a welcoming study environment for college students. Also consider whether students (who generally only spend a little money) staying will inhibit higher paying customers.
Income level (e.g., low, middle, high)	Varies, but primarily individuals with expendable income who can also afford a $3.00 cup of coffee.	People who buy a dozen bagels for the office probably have a middle-income level. Students generally have a low-income level. Selling one bagel at a high price to a commuter may generate more profit than selling five bagels at low cost.
Educational level	Educated individuals who understand value and quality and possibly seek status.	Educated
Career type ("white collar," "blue collar")	Largely professional. Expect to be served promptly and treated with respect. Seek quality.	Mixed
Marital status	Mixed. Customers with children may be in a rush to get to work after dropping off their children at school. Consider how to be an "oasis" during the morning rush. Offer speed and convenience. Consider marketing bagels as a "guilty pleasure."	Mixed
Has children?	See "Marital Status" category.	Generally, no.

Market Positioning Worksheet

Customer demographics or identifiers	Primary customer	Secondary customer(s)
Pet owner?	N/A, although consider having dog treats available at the drive-up window.	N/A
Hobbies/interests	N/A	Some will be attracted to the art shows.
Religious/political traits	N/A	Perhaps a bit liberal or even counter culture (college students).
Do potential customers know that they have a need for this product/service?	Absolutely	Absolutely
Do potential customers need your product/service but not know it?	Some buyers may think that ordering a bagel will take too long; advertising should dispel this notion.	Some customers may not know that bagels are available by the dozen; advertising should dispel this notion.
Marketing for Business to Business (B2B) Companies		
Type of business to supply	N/A	N/A, although in the long term, Bagels to the Max could set up delivery accounts to cater meetings and special events for other companies.
Specific businesses to supply	N/A	N/A
Size of business revenue	N/A	N/A

Market Positioning Worksheet

Customer demographics or identifiers	Primary customer	Secondary customer(s)
Number of employees	N/A	N/A
Location(s)	N/A	N/A
Other descriptors	N/A	N/A

Sources of Marketing Research Data List the pertinent "whos", "whats", "whens", and/or "wheres" discovered from each category.	
Similar businesses	1. The Valley Bakery 2. Called a bagel shop in the city and talked with the owner about her business. 3.
Related web sites	1. Checked http://www.wholebagel.com to learn some history as well as marketing approaches and current business trends. 2. Searched for "bagels" on an Internet search engine and discovered many stores nationwide. Have started e-mailing them to ask for pointers. 3. Bought a book on small business at http://www.amazon.com.
Yellow pages and business directories at the public library	1. Several yellow-pages listings for restaurants with drive-throughs; most are for lunch and dinner. 2. Local fast-food restaurants like McDonald's and Burger King are open for breakfast, but Bagels to the Max can emphasize the health aspects of its whole grain flour and natural ingredients. 3.
Newspaper business section, classified advertisements, and display advertisements	1. The business editor at the local paper agreed to run a special article on Bagels to the Max. 2. Some companies listed on http://www.wholebagel.com sell generic marketing posters and signs about bagels; however, Bagels to the Max can make its own signs for less money. 3. The college newspaper will mention Bagels to the Max; it will also sell advertising/coupon space for $100 per edition. 4. The best forms of advertising may be word of mouth and window signs at the coffeehouse.

Market Positioning Worksheet

Sources of Marketing Research Data List the pertinent "whos", "whats", "whens", and/or "wheres" discovered from each category.	
Chamber of commerce and/or local economic development office	1. If Bagels to the Max joins the local chamber of commerce, it will be featured in the upcoming chamber of commerce newsletter. Annual dues are $75.00 unless Bagels to the Max can use Angelica's membership. 2. 3.
Small Business Development Center (SBDC), local business incubator, and/or Small Business Administration (SBA) programs	1. The SBDC is helping with marketing and sales. It recommends high quality and convenience as primary tactics. In a small town, customers will hear about a new product quickly. It is important to concentrate developing smooth business operations before spending a lot of time and money on advertising. 2. 3.
Business and trade schools	1. N/A 2. 3.
Bankers, investors, and/or financial advisors	1. N/A 2. 3.
The state's Secretary of State office, Internal Revenue Service, and the state department of revenue	1. N/A 2. 3.
Vocational Rehabilitation (VR)/One-Stop Centers, employment security, and/or community rehabilitation programs (CRPs)	1. VR counselor has been very helpful in offering marketing ideas, is making fliers, and is encouraging other agencies to buy bagels from Bagels to the Max. 2. 3.

Market Positioning Worksheet

Sources of Marketing Research Data List the pertinent "whos", "whats", "whens", and/or "wheres" discovered from each category.	
Census data and U.S. Department of Labor and/or U.S. Department of Commerce reports	1. Census reports say that people are continuing to move here but work in the city, so the market will grow if commuters can be convinced that they need coffee and a bagel for their drive to work. 2. 3.
Industry associations	1. Cannot currently afford the dues to join the National Alliance of Bagel Retailers, but consider joining next year–their conference might provide some additional business ideas. 2. 3.
Other sources of information	1. Angelica has sales experience and has been very helpful. 2. A salesman friend of the family is helping generate customer service ideas. 3.

From Griffin, C., Hammis, D., Katz, M., Sperry, C., Flaherty, M., Shelley, R., Snizek, B., & Maxson, N. (2001). *Making the road by taking it: Team and individual exercises for self employment training* (pp. 37–41). Missoula, MT: The Rural Institute, The University of Montana; adapted by permission.

As the previous example illustrates, completing the Market Positioning Worksheet leads to new ideas; the refinement of the business model; and, most of all, the targeting of particular market segments or customers. Once specific customers are identified, the marketing and advertising strategy is designed. In the case of Bagels to the Max, phase-ins of new products and services, such as bag lunches, appear possible. Yet, Max has received business advice stressing that satisfying drive-through customers must be the priority until he achieves a reputation for speed, value, and quality. Taking on too many business variants too quickly distracts an owner from the core business and permanently harms the customer base.

MARKETING AND ADVERTISING APPROACHES FOR SMALL BUSINESSES

Most small businesses both market and sell their product/service. Marketing creates the consumer's need for a product/service while selling satisfies that need. Of course, the two activities are closely linked, but a good marketing strategy usually makes selling easier. Because people generally enjoy buying things, the challenge is reaching customers with a message that motivates them to act. Determining who the customer is and what the customer needs is part of the previous marketing exercise. Marketing capitalizes on needs and offers solutions to various customer problems.

Business owners should always ask, "Why does the customer need this product/service?" The answers help define the marketing approach. For instance, Honda sells cars. On a marketing level, however, the company deals in transportation—helping people get from Point A to Point B. On a psychological level, Honda appeals to customers who want to look smart for buying such a reliable and efficient car. On a practical level, Honda appeals to buyers who value reliability and resale value. Yet, Honda also increases its profits by offering high-price options, such as sunroofs, CD players, and global positioning systems built into the dashboard. Honda quality sells itself, with the assistance of its sales staff, but marketing through various forms of advertising—and the all-important word-of-mouth from satisfied customers—is priceless. The lesson is that marketing can appeal to many different buyers on multiple levels and that having a quality product that generates a high degree of customer satisfaction is critical. This is especially important for small businesses, which tend to have limited advertising budgets.

Another example of a defined marketing approach is McDonald's. Better food is available at many other restaurants. However, McDonald's advertises consistency (all Big Macs taste the same), value for the dollar, cleanliness, and speed or convenience. Of course, McDonald's does market its food as being delicious, but the company's image remains the same. One of its past slogans was "You deserve a break today" (which emphasizes a carefree experience), not "You deserve the best darn food on the planet." McDonald's remains true to its customer demographic: people in a hurry who want tasty food at a reasonable price.

Wal-Mart is another store with customer-focused marketing. Wal-Mart carries quality items, although not the highest quality items, at a reasonable price. Its advertisements portray Wal-Mart employees as friendly and helpful. The store's advertising theme is clear and direct: "Always low prices!" Wal-Mart offers a superior selection and caters to working-class Americans who want value for their money.

The Home Depot also created a niche and became a market leader. It offers the "do-it-yourselfer" good products at good prices in a friendly environment. The store is especially welcoming to women, who were often ignored in small-town hardware stores because home repair and remodeling was considered the work of husbands and fathers. The Home Depot recognized the buying power and influence of women and created a store that openly offers technical advice and assistance to all customers. The Home Depot markets self-confidence, and its selection and reasonable pricing help sales, too (Underhill, 2000).

The 4 Ps: Product, Price, Place, and Promotion

Most small businesses are successful because of the focus on core competencies. The cabinet maker down the block delivers high-quality products on time. The local restaurant serves a good breakfast 24 hours per day, just like its sign says. The local used car dealer carries a small selection of high-quality ve-

hicles that local drivers need, stands behind the quality of his cars, and has a quick and competent mechanic. No amount of marketing savvy can make up for a bad product/service, so proprietors must pay attention to quality. Designing the marketing approach starts with the actual product and addresses the other three "Ps": price, place, and promotion (Mariotti, 2000; Zyman, 1999).

Product

The product/service must either satisfy or create a customer need. For example, with the increase in single-parent homes and working mothers, technological advances in microwave technology were used to develop the microwave oven. Until it was marketed, people did not know that they had use for such a contraption. By the end of the 20th century, however, most families owned a microwave oven because of the product's speed, convenience, and reasonable price.

It is important to ensure that a potential business satisfies or creates a need. The PBO and BDT benefit from recording this need in descriptive terms.

This product/service satisfies or creates the following need:

Price

An old saying in marketing claims that "there is a buyer at every price." The issue becomes whether there are enough buyers at a particular price. Pricing is psychological in that many customers equate price with quality, so low price actually drives some customers away. K-Mart is an example of a company based on low-cost goods that attracts customers with few dollars to spend and drives away customers looking for quality and lasting value. Conversely, Rolls Royce only sells a few very expensive cars each year. By selling a small number of its product, the company and the customer maintain status. Rolls Royce cars are high priced because the company hand-builds them. In addition, the company caters to a few select buyers and, therefore, charges a premium price to stay in business. Furthermore, the company's products are of superior quality and actually increase in value over the years, as opposed to most automobiles.

The trick to pricing is to produce goods that are affordable to the customer and that generate profits for the company. Common pricing strategies that companies use include "skimming," or maintaining a high retail price while selling limited items (e.g., Rolls Royce), and "discounting," or offering low prices but making profits by selling large numbers of items per customer (e.g., Wal-Mart). The PBO and BDT should determine the appropriate pricing strategy for the potential product/service.

Strategy for pricing the product/service:

Place

The product/service needs to be sold where there is customer demand and access. In other words, manufacturing snowshoes in Florida necessitates a retail outlet in a location where it snows. Some business owners sell their products out of their homes. This works if local zoning laws allow businesses to be operated out of private homes (typically referred to as a "light-residential area") and if customers are willing to drive to the homes. Most products, however, are sold at the point of production (e.g., produce at a roadside stand) or in retail space. Lipton brand soup mix is sold on grocery store shelves. Marketing is used to attract shoppers to the soup aisle, but the grocery store owner first had to be "sold" on the idea of providing shelf space. Lipton pays a percentage of sales to the store owner. If Lipton soup mix does not sell, the store loses revenue and likely drops the product. Anyone producing a product that needs retail space must factor buying shelf space into the cost per unit.

Another approach to finding a place for a product is the use of a sales representative. Commonly called "sales reps," these people are based in most large cites and work throughout the country. They typically operate on a percentage of sales basis and generally specialize in specific product types. For instance, a small business that rebuilds lawn mower engines and is located in a town of 500 people is faced with a very small market. To stay in business, the company needs access to a broader base of customers. A sales rep who travels around to hardware stores could be useful in setting up accounts across the country. A hardware store could then offer rebuilt engines or could service its customers by shipping broken lawn mowers to the rebuilder.

Sales reps also specialize in food products, novelties like pens and key chains, industrial machinery, and almost anything that is sold retail or wholesale. Service businesses use sales reps, too. For example, talent agents for actors and models serve the same purpose: someone selling another person's products or services. Before hiring a sales rep, the business owner needs to obtain letters of reference from the representative's satisfied customers. In addition, a legal contract must be negotiated that clearly states the costs associated with the relationship, performance expectations, and critical timelines for related activities. Local SBDCs or businesses in similar markets can assist PBOs interested in identifying potential sales representatives.

The Internet presents another approach to product placement. Although many people think that having a web page will draw in customers, it is not that simple. First, the Internet is crowded, with millions of web sites offering goods for sale. Search engine use does not guarantee that customers will find your web site. Customers often have to know about the web site through advertising, and advertising should offer up-to-date product information. A business web site must also meet the customer's needs and be easy to use, and it helps if the site accepts credit cards. Perhaps the best use of web sites is as an advertising tool that shows the business is sophisticated and current. Web sites are often great as a value-added service as well. For instance, a company that retails a product may maintain a web site to list detailed warranty information, stream instructional videos, and provide optional accessories that can be purchased on line.

Internet sales can also occur through on-line auction houses such as eBay, which attracts more than 6 million buyers daily. Items can be auctioned for a small fee, and the seller does not have to maintain a web site or look for customers. There are some tricks to selling via on-line auctions. Learning how to use key wording for a product description allows sellers to draw in customers quickly and make sales. Sellers who post products on an auction web site but also maintain a web site to sell products independently can add a simple line to the auction description (e.g., "If you are interested in other similar items, please see my web site at http://www.morestuff.com").

The issue of place is critical to the small business owner because customers determine the success of any business. If customers cannot reach the product/service, the company does not succeed. The business plan addresses this topic both in the marketing and in the distribution sections (see Chapter 4). Distribution is a particular challenge facing small, and especially rural, companies. It is no small task and demands any PBO's attention.

Strategy for placing the product/service:

Promotion

Advertising and publicity inform customers who can use the product/service to satisfy a need. Not all promotion is done with an extensive advertising budget and the use of signs, commercials, or display advertisements. Many small businesses rely on word of mouth and their visible location to draw in customers. The quality, desirability, and apparent value of a product/service bring in first-time and repeat customers. Sticking to the core competency is critical for the new business, so this should be the first consideration in any marketing approach.

Of course, most businesses need to "get the word" out in multiple ways. Radio and television advertising are good options, but they are expensive, and the saturation levels needed to reach and affect the buying behavior of customers can be prohibitive. In one instance, a small business owner purchased several thousand dollars of radio advertising in a small, isolated mountain town only to discover that without a rush hour, few people were in their cars or in range of the station long enough to hear his commercials. Another business owner was able to limit such advertising expenses by getting a local television station to make a full-blown commercial for her as a public service announcement because she donates a portion of her profits to research on a particular developmental disability.

Print advertising is also effective and includes the use of local newspapers, classified advertisements, fact sheets, brochures, fliers on public bulletin boards, and signs. All of these generate interest and can be of tremendous help in advertising a business. Many local newspapers gladly run stories on new businesses in the business section. Many newspapers and radio or television stations may also want to run human interest stories because a person with a disability is opening a business. This certainly can be valuable publicity, but it can also mean that the disability—not the business—will be emphasized. In advance of the interview, the business owner and the BDT should let the interviewer know that the focus of the story is the new business and the product/service offered.

Another way to prevent the cute human interest story is to write press releases about the business regarding a store opening or expansion. Newspapers generally welcome well-written releases, and their editors can provide guidelines for composing and submitting them. The same press releases can also be used for chamber of commerce newsletters and in the announcements section of the company's web site.

Achievable through many different methods, promotion and advertising are ongoing, common-sense activities. The PBO and DBT can use the following list to help guide the marketing design.

1. Advertising does not have to be expensive. There are many opportunities for free or inexpensive advertising. Relationship marketing is founded on the idea that personal contacts help grow small businesses quite effectively.

2. Advertising is useless if a product/service is inferior. Business owners must pay attention to the operation of their business; make certain that the product/service meets the customer's expectations; and practice good customer service, essentially by asking, "How would I want to be treated?"

3. One "big-bang" marketing event or campaign generally is not enough to sustain and grow a business. Most marketing relies on long-term repetition to gain customers. It is estimated that a person has to experience an advertisement 7–20 times before investigating or buying a product (Gerson, 1994).

4. There is no single right way to market or advertise. Different approaches reach different buyers. Some low-cost experimentation might prove successful for certain businesses.

5. Advertising is not a replacement for hard work. Running any business can be difficult. Advertising helps bring in customers, but it does not satisfy them—that remains the job of the company.

6. Advertising may not attract new customers. Sometimes promotion is important simply for holding on to old customers—that is, for reminding them that they still need a service/product. This is especially true of "preventive" businesses such as house painters, oil change shops, or dental clinics.

7. Advertising seeks to solve a problem. Customers need a product/service for many reasons; typically, to fill a need. Grocery stores feed the family, gas stations feed the car, office supply stores feed the copy machine, churches feed the soul, and high-end sports car dealerships feed the ego.

8. Promotion never ends. Although few things are more annoying than someone "selling" every minute of the day, advertising needs to be ingrained in the business culture. Opportunities are everywhere, but if the business owner does not pay attention, sales are lost. This is why community and professional networking is so important. Developing a network of friends, colleagues, suppliers, and customers provides a ready source of support, income, and ideas for new products and improved customer service.

The Business Promotion Matrix lists a number of commonly used methods for promoting products and services. A sample Business Promotion Matrix follows for Bagels to the Max, the company discussed in Chapter 4. Completing this matrix required Max and his BDT to consider each method of promotion

Business Promotion Matrix

Promotion type	Description	Timing	Cost/benefit
Business cards	Yes. Will be displayed on the service counter at Angelica's Coffeehouse and will be given out in other environments. Symbolic of a real company.	Immediately.	Inexpensive way to convey business ownership and contact information. Also shows business operating hours.
Brochure	No.	Probably never.	Companies rarely need this expense.
Fliers for public bulletin boards	Yes. Put these up around town to announce the grand opening and the speed and convenience of getting a bagel with one's coffee.	Immediately.	Cheap and easy way to advertise. Many places require that fliers be approved before they are posted, so the owner gets the opportunity to meet another business owner/manager about the business.
Newspaper coupons	Yes. Will place in the college newspaper to attract students during downtime at the coffeehouse.	Soon, once the core business is operating smoothly.	Students may not spend a lot but make the place look busy. Might discourage the lunch crowd if a lunch service is later offered. Angelica will decide.
Yellow pages advertisement	Yes.	Immediately.	Paying Angelica to add the bagel shop to her large display ad (sharing the cost is an advantage of being within another business).
Personal sales calls	No door-to-door sales. Will greet customers from the counter and continue to practice welcoming and thanking routine.	Immediately.	Presenting a good and friendly appearance is important, regardless of the sales venue.
Direct mail	No. Maybe later when and if delivery service is added.	Later.	Can be effective in spreading the word about new services and products and can be inexpensive.
Telemarketing	No.	Probably never.	Can be annoying to potential customers.
Web page	No.	Maybe later.	If delivery service is added, people could send orders via e-mail—very efficient.
Internet auction	No.	N/A	N/A
Storefront window signs	Yes.	Immediately.	Angelica has added artwork and "Bagels to the Max" to the windows and the drive-up menu board.
Good customer discount club	Yes.	Later.	Once the core business is operating smoothly, a customer card will be added (buy 11 prepared bagels and 12th one is free). Pricing may need to be modified to afford this.
Radio advertisements	Maybe.	Later.	Most existing customers commute, so they (and new customers) can be reached by radio advertisements. Need to generate more working capital first.

Business Promotion Matrix

Promotion type	Description	Timing	Cost/benefit
Radio interviews	Yes.	Immediately.	Have a taped interview scheduled for the local public affairs spot in 2 weeks. Will also get on two city radio stations next month to discus the business.
Press releases	Yes.	Immediately.	Angelica, the SBDC manager, and Max created it. Will be in the local paper next week and the chamber of commerce newsletter next month.
Civic group membership	Yes.	Immediately.	Joined the chamber of commerce with Angelica; split the cost. May join its small business group that meets Tuesday evenings. Good connections!
Television advertisements	No.	Later.	Too expensive right now.
Infomercial	No.	N/A	N/A
Public access television	Yes.	Soon.	The college has a public access station, which will do a human interest story on the business. Have already discussed focusing on the bagel business, not the disability.
Human interest story	See previous reply regarding public access television.	See previous reply.	See previous reply.
E-mail advertising and coupons	Not right now. Perhaps later as the business grows.	Probably never.	E-mail advertising and coupons can be inexpensive and effective tools, but attention must be focused on the other methods for now until business operations mature a bit.
Novelties	Yes.	Soon.	Working to add "Bagels to the Max" to the Angelica's Coffeehouse company T-shirts. Staff wear the shirts, and they will be sold for $12 each as well. Will also add logo to the coffee mugs too. No need right now for other novelties (e.g., pens, key chains).
Logo	Yes.	Soon.	Angelica is designing it to fit with the coffeehouse logo; it will go on the T-shirts, coffee mugs, Bagels to the Max business cards, and so forth.
Presentations at house of worship	Yes.	Soon.	Not yet scheduled but a possibility.
Other:	N/A	N/A	N/A

("Promotion type" column), consider how it could be personalized or customized to fit this particular business ("Description" column), determine when such an approach might be best used ("Timing" column), and whether this approach was cost-effective ("Cost/benefit" column). It should be noted that in the example, some promotional items were not considered good risks (e.g., brochures) and others were staged for later use (e.g., radio advertising). When starting or expanding a business, it is suggested that business owners and BDTs use a similar process, completing the blank Business Promotion Matrix in Appendix A to determine when they will launch their promotional campaign.

SALES

Selling is a difficult but necessary task. The "used car salesman" image sometimes overshadows the thoughtful approach that is necessary to assist customers in getting what they need and desire. One successful sales strategy is to sell without selling. Many people worldwide enjoy Coke and/or Pepsi. No sales force goes from house to house, knocking on doors and asking the residents to try a sample. Both companies sell their products by ensuring that they are firmly planted in the consumer's mind. The companies sell on many levels and use sophisticated marketing, advertising, and distribution strategies. Coke and Pepsi machines are conveniently located in many places throughout the world. The machines themselves are product billboards. Print advertisements in magazines, television commercials, radio advertisements, store displays, special sales, and contests all reinforce the message that when people get thirsty, they need a Coke or Pepsi. The companies have sales teams, but these teams do not approach the end user. Instead, their job is to distribute the product so the end user can find it. Sales teams sell to grocery stores and secure locations for vending machines. Advertising, not sales, brings customers to the product, which is very accessible.

Most small businesses never have or need the expensive and extensive marketing and distribution programs that large corporations have. Yet, all large corporations began as small companies and grew to billion-dollar enterprises by creating a useful product/service that was priced right for the customer. Being successful in any size business demands that customers buy the product/service, and that takes sales savvy.

Sales approaches in retail businesses (i.e., running a store-based operation) and in service operations differ. For example, a store is a set location, so atmosphere and physical accessibility can create a positive environment for customers. One approach to crafting a positive, customer-friendly environment is to perform the Five Senses Exercise, previously mentioned in the Chapter 4 example of Max's business plan. This exercise works for service companies but is more appropriate for retail or office locations that customers visit. Using the information gathered from brainstorming sessions about the retail or office environment allows customers to buy and reduces the need to coerce or sell to them. The exercise can begin with broad generalizations but should eventually lead to concrete and specific actions for the business. The complete example of the exercise for Bagels to the Max follows.

Five Senses Exercise

Sense	Description	Importance
What should customers see?	On the outside, there will be friendly signs welcoming customers. The drive-through lane and window will be clearly marked. Menus will be posted on the windows and at the drive-through. Large letters will be used to make the drive-through menu legible through a rolled-up car window on cold mornings. Inside the bagel shop, customers will have an unobstructed path to the menu board and to the ordering counter. They will see smiling staff who greet them happily. All staff will wear name tags with first names in large letters. Customers will see Max hard at work fulfilling bagel orders. Customers will clearly see a nice selection of flavored bagels, cream cheeses, and spreads. The tip jar and the prices for a single bagel or a dozen bagels will be prominent.	Bagels to the Max is an integral part of Angelica's Coffeehouse. Bagels to the Max has to fit in and complement the coffeehouse but also has to attract customers. Buying a bagel to go with one's coffee needs to be convenient, fast, and affordable. Customers will want quality and choice, and they want to know that first thing in the morning someone is glad to see them. The store and drive-through must look welcoming to ensure repeat business! Staff name tags are important because the marketing approach is based on a long-term relationship—that is, on getting to know the customers.
What should customers feel?	Customers want to feel welcome above all else. This will be accomplished by making it easy to buy coffee and a bagel. Operations will be fine tuned, with no wasted steps. This will improve customer satisfaction because the transaction will be quick but the customer will not feel hurried. For those who wish to linger, there will be chairs, magazines, and low-cost coffee refills (in Angelica's Coffeehouse). The customer will not be made to wait or to feel rushed or crowded.	Customers on their way to work do not want to feel any more harried. Angelica's Coffeehouse and Bagels to the Max will work together to provide an oasis in the morning, but one that allows customers to speed through if that's their need (i.e., provide the no-hassle breakfast).
What should customers hear?	Drive-through and walk-in customers will be greeted by the staff serving them with a bright "Good morning! How may I help you?" Returning customers might be asked how they are doing, how they liked the bagel flavor that they tried the other day, and so forth. Staff will never pry into a customer's private life; rather, they will allow the customer to openly converse if desired. Lively music will be playing at a pleasant level in the background.	Customers will feel welcomed but never interrogated. Staff will not ask questions like "Are you married?" "Did you hear the joke about the two guys from South Dakota?" and "Why do you eat so many bagels?" Customers can buy bagels from other businesses, so they have made a conscious choice to patronize Bagels to the Max. Thus, customers want to know that their business is appreciated.

Five Senses Exercise

Sense	Description	Importance
What should customers hear? *(continued)*	In an attempt to determine the atmosphere to establish, music selections will range from popular to classical to reggae. Customers will never hear staff shouting or complaining! Customers will hear staff communicating to get orders out and thanking patrons for their business. If a customer is ever dissatisfied, Max (and his employees, when they are brought on) will act immediately to correct the situation. The customer is always right!	
What should customers taste?	Customers will taste the best bagels possible. All bagels will be guaranteed fresh; customers will be able to return any bagel that does not meet their expectations. Sample plates will be displayed on the countertops along with small bowls of flavored cream cheese for dipping. Next to the samples will be a sign that reads, "Take some to work with you!" to spur sales by the dozen.	Sampling will allow the customers to take control of the situation; they will be able to make more informed buying decisions. Sampling also creates a "buzz" at the counter and draws in more people while they wait for their specialty coffees to be prepared; it gives waiting customers something to do and will boost sales.
What should customers smell?	The warming lights and the toaster will mix the fresh-baked smell of bagels with the coffee aroma, making the entire retail area inviting and warm. The toaster will NEVER be set at a level high enough to burn a bagel. The aromatic cinnamon bagels and cream cheeses will be allowed to breathe, while the garlic and onion bagels may need to be closed inside the display case.	The fresh coffee smell will highlight the bagel aroma. Coffee roasting will coincide with the morning rush to further entice and welcome customers.

It is recommended that business owners and BDTs complete the Five Senses Exercise because it gives business owners concrete ways to attract and retain customers (see Appendix A for a blank version of the exercise). Again, setting up the right welcoming environment allows businesses to sell without "selling," but there is no one right way to perform the exercise. For instance, some companies might invite customers in to help decide what other customers will want to see, feel, hear, taste, and smell.

The Five Senses Exercise can also be used for Internet sales—conceptually, of course, as not all of the senses are engaged on line. For instance, if someone sells jewelry on eBay, bidders are more apt to be interested if they can see a picture of the item and read the seller's shipping cost and return policy. Bidders might also want to know if the seller has similar items or will help them find the perfect anniversary gift for their spouse. All of these customer service/ value-added components support the activity of sales, and offering such value-added information on line takes little time or effort.

Television commercials and radio advertisements, web sites, and toll-free telephone lines help pull customers toward a business, but sales is often a person-to-person event. Businesses that rely on face-to-face or personal types of selling must refine their approach, identify their customers through purchased mailing lists or market research (as noted Chapters 3 and 4), and practice their sales style. Almost no one enjoys an encounter with a slick salesperson, primarily because the customer feels like an unappreciated target of deception. The salesperson needs to make a good first impression. Having a coach (perhaps a family member or mentor from the local SCORE office) help with this can boost self-confidence and make sales a bit easier for those who shy away from asking for someone's business. Creating a 20-second introduction is a helpful exercise for overcoming the anticipation of a chamber of commerce luncheon or public gathering in which the business owner is beginning a relationship-building campaign. The PBO and BDT should write out a simple introduction for the PBO that is friendly, informational, and leads others into conversation. The PBO should practice his or her introduction but also remember that conversation is both talking and listening. Listening is the key skill of great salespeople; they allow customers or acquaintances (who are also potential customers) to talk themselves into buying the product/service. First, though, customers or acquaintances need to know who they are meeting.

The 20-Second Introduction contains a few critical elements. Basically, the introduction communicates the person's name, the name of his or her company, and what he or she does with the business. Max's introduction for his first after-hours chamber of commerce business event is as follows:

"Hi, I'm Max. I own Bagels to the Max. It's located inside Angelica's Coffeehouse. We just opened! Here's my business card."

Max's 20-Second Introduction is simple and to the point, as it should be. The following two spaces are provided to explore scripts for a 20-Second Introduction.

20-Second Introduction #1

20-Second Introduction #2

The PBO might also want to practice asking the other person his or her name and business, although these prompts are rarely necessary. Business owners with disabilities often require coaching or support with carrying the conversation past the introduction. Individualized supports are critical. For instance, a business owner who uses augmentative and alternative communication might preprogram conversations and have a partner help. Someone with speech difficulties can do the same.

Developing a "sales pitch" can be difficult, so practicing with friends and mentors is crucial. Use of a Features and Benefits Analysis can streamline the process. This is a common tool that reveals the script for a sales call or the "copy" (i.e., wording) for a print, television, or radio advertisement (Gerson, 1994; Griffin, Hammis, et al., 2001). A *feature* describes a particular aspect of a product/service; a *benefit* is the result of using the product/service. For example, features of a high-pressure, self-service car wash include high-pressure sprayers for removing dirt and road salts from the customer's car. The benefits are low cost, self-service, and extended life of one's automobile. When the business owner attends a Kiwanis meeting, she can tell the other members that her new car wash has high-pressure spray wands that customers themselves use at low cost to clean road grime and corrosive salts from the finish and undercarriage of their expensive vehicles.

The following Features and Benefits Analysis completed for Bagels to the Max (see Appendix A for a blank copy) yields company information that Max can use when he

- Answers customer questions

- Suggests that customers buy a dozen bagels for their office mates

- Designs his sales coupons

- Gives radio and public access television interviews

- Answers questions at chamber of commerce meetings or church presentations

- Decides to expand his business to include delivery services

Every business is different, so sales approaches must be customized to complement the product/service, targeted customer, location, and market niche. Nonetheless, it is important that business owners and/or their salespeople follow some general guidelines.

Successful Sales Strategies

1. *Preparation is crucial.* Anyone selling a product/service must know its features and benefits and how those specific characteristics will satisfy

Features and Benefits Analysis

Features	Benefit(s) to customers
Fast service	Gets them on the road to work without delay
High quality	Provides early-morning energy through nutritious and wholesome food
Great taste	Is good *and* good for you Comes in several flavors to satisfy the need for variety Is an exciting alternative to toast or cereal
Convenience	Drive-through allows customers to get a bagel and coffee for the drive to work
Reasonable cost	Provides a quality bagel at a reasonable price Is cheaper and healthier than a fast-food breakfast sandwich
Building community	Allows patronage of a locally owned company, so purchases help neighbors
Features that might be added later to improve business	**Potential benefit(s) to customers**
Free delivery to nearby businesses	Would provide on-site treats for office workers and other businesses Would be convenient, reasonably priced, and always fresh for the best flavor Would not require people to leave their store or office to buy bagels
Bagel sandwiches for lunch	Would expand opportunities for customers to buy a good, reasonably priced meal from a conveniently located restaurant
Bagel sandwiches as part of bag lunches	Could be a solution for busy parents: Before dropping off their children at school, parents might pick up a bag lunch consisting of a peanut butter and jelly bagel, gourmet cookie, and piece of fresh fruit
N/A	N/A

the needs of the customer. The salesperson must also understand the needs of the customer and be prepared to meet these needs.

2. *Selling is personal.* Customers want to know that salespeople and business owners care. This is not about intimacy. Rather, it entails listening to the customer before telling him or her how the product/service fulfills a need or solves a problem.

3. *Listening is more important than talking.* If the salesperson does not hear what the customer needs and wants, then he or she is liable to offer the wrong product/service, thereby injuring the opportunity for a lasting relationship.

4. *Prospecting is an ongoing process.* Although Coke and Pepsi "pull in" customers through advertising and product placement, many companies must rely on meeting and greeting new potential buyers. Building a network of friends, suppliers, and business associates is crucial to finding new customers. Studying information on the Internet, attending meetings, and being active in the community are ways to research and identify prospects.

5. *Initial contacts can make or break a customer relationship.* Salespeople should beware of interfering. For instance, a dishware salesperson should not call on a restaurant owner during the lunch rush. In fact, sales calls made without prior contact (i.e., "cold calls") are seldom appreciated. In general, a "warm call" approach is greeted more favorably. A call is "warmed up" by sending the prospective customer a letter of introduction, meeting the person at a social gathering and following up later with a telephone call, or sending the individual product literature that prominently displays convenient contact information (e.g., toll-free telephone number, e-mail address).

6. *Use leave-behinds.* Businesses should have written materials that explain the function, features, benefits, and cost of their products/services. Known as "leave-behinds" in the sales profession, these materials act as passive sellers. People enjoy reading about or seeing pictures of products/services in which they are interested. Leave-behinds like fact sheets, brochures, or even short videotapes or CDs give customers time to make buying decisions without feeling pressured or inconvenienced.

7. *Be prepared to handle objections.* Customers who are new to a product/ service may doubt its viability or value. Allow customers to decide by providing information that addresses their fear of buying. Such information includes endorsements from other customers, product testing results, cost/benefit analyses, or simple taste tests (e.g., for Bagels to the Max).

8. *Allow customers to say no.* Sometimes a customer simply does not need or want a product/service. The salesperson should be respectful and polite because trying to force a sale may cut off a prospect forever. If the salesperson walks away and promises to be in touch later, the customer is re-

lieved from making a decision that he or she wants to avoid and will likely remember the salesperson's graciousness later.

9. *Add-ons—or accessories to the product/service—are important.* Once a customer agrees to buy a product/service, it is a good time to offer a value-added service or item. For instance, when a customer decides to buy a new car, the salesperson will ask the buyer if he or she wants to purchase an extended warranty.

10. *Stay in touch.* No sale is ever final. Salespeople should call customers and ask how they are enjoying their recently purchased product/service. For Bagels to the Max, asking repeat customers about their previously purchased bagel gives customers an opportunity to compliment Max or to make suggestions. Ongoing contact with customers shows that their business is deemed important to the company.

11. *Follow up.* If a customer asks a question to which a salesperson does not know the answer, the salesperson should find the answer and get back in touch with the customer. If a customer has a problem regarding price or delivery time, the salesperson should contact the customer immediately to avoid unpleasant disputes. Such actions help maintain the relationship.

12. *Be a gracious guest.* Sales calls typically occur in someone else's environment. The salesperson should be a good guest, arriving promptly and being sociable but businesslike.

13. *Be concise.* Friendly talk is important for loosening up the situation but should be kept to the minimum. Customers are busy, and salespeople should respect that.

14. *Exhibit proper appearance and personal behavior.* Salespeople must be neat and clean and should dress respectfully and appropriately. An individual selling banking services should dress as people in the banking environment do. A person selling auto parts may dress a bit nicer than those who work in an automotive store but certainly should not wear a three-piece suit. An individual on a sales call should not smoke, drink alcohol, tell dirty jokes, discuss politics or religion, or exceed the set meeting time (unless the customer makes it clear that he or she wants to hear more).

15. *Ask for a referral.* Even if a sale is not made, the salesperson should ask the prospect for the name and telephone number of someone who might be interested in the product/service. Word of mouth and referral sales are critical in all businesses.

16. *Be kind.* Individuals should not attempt to make sales by complaining about, slandering, or attacking a competing company or product. The item being sold should be allowed to stand on its own. Customers are smart and will buy what is best for them. Resorting to attacks offends or frightens customers, so emphasis should be placed on the qualities of the product/service being sold.

17. *Use good personal management.* Salespeople should keep appointments, record orders immediately, manage their time effectively, and avoid missing deadlines.

18. *Provide customer service.* The company must ensure that billing and accounting services support sales, deliveries are timely and arrive as promised, telephones are answered in a kind and courteous manner, and warranties and guarantees are honored with minimal customer frustration. A salesperson should never promise something that the company cannot deliver.

19. *Know the product/service.* If possible, an individual should use the product/service before selling it. He or she should study specifications, quality discounts, manufacturer's recommendations for use, guarantee information, and delivery times. Many small businesses make and sell the product/service and know it inside out. This is a terrific benefit because their salespeople can answer most questions and speak from the heart.

20. *Get busy.* Selling is hard and often scary work. The best way to sell is simply to jump in, make calls, write letters, and meet people. It is recommended that a salesperson set a quota of calls to make per day or week, keep a file of prospects to call back by a certain date, and identify where his or her sales process is weak and get help fixing it (Bivins, 1994; Griffin, Hammis, et al., 2001; Straughn & Chickadel, 1994; Underhill, 2000; Zyman, 1999).

Marketing and sales are critical to all businesses. Some marketing and sales approaches pull in the customer (e.g., those used for grocery stores or professional sporting events), while others push the customer to make a decision (e.g., those used at automobile dealerships or lawyers' offices). Both approaches work for the respective product/service. Because no product/service sells itself, reaching enough customers to stay profitable is accomplished through advertising, promotion, sales, and distribution. As enterprises become established, it is critical to satisfy existing customers' needs with consistent service. Yet, it is also important for companies to attract new customers through novel promotional methods and/or products. Enterprises stay healthy by satisfying long-term customers and by capturing new ones; marketing and sales make this possible.

Chapter 6

Small Business and Social Security Income Benefits Analysis

IMPORTANT TERMS IN THIS CHAPTER

Accrual accounting method: A business accounting and bookkeeping approach that accounts for income for when it is earned, billed, or due, which may not be when income actually is received, and accounts for expenses when they are incurred, which may not be when the actual payments for the expenses are made.

Blind Work Expenses (BWE): An SSI work incentive used to exclude work-related expenses for blind individuals in monthly SSI check reduction calculations. If someone is blind when the SSA determines his or her SSI eligibility and payment amount, the SSA does not count any earned income used to meet expenses in earning the income. Monthly SSI cash benefits are reduced roughly $1.00 for every $2.00 earned based on gross wages or net earnings from self-employment (NESE) for anyone receiving SSI each month. If someone earns $800 per month, then he or she will receive roughly $400 less from SSI each month due to his or her $800 of earned income. If an SSI recipient who is eligible for BWE earns $800 per month and spends $400 per month for cab rides to and from work, then the SSA will not reduce his or her SSI check by $400. He or she will be able to claim BWE of $400.

Cash accounting method: A business accounting and bookkeeping approach that tracks and records income when received and expenses when paid.

Constructive receipt of income: Restriction that requires a small business owner to take payment and record income if a customer has available funds to pay for a product/service. The intent of this restriction is to prevent small business owners from "stalling" payments to show lower income during a business year.

Impairment Related Work Expenses (IRWE): An SSI and SSDI work incentive that excludes expenses that are directly related to the individual's impairment and necessary for work. Both SSI recipients and SSDI beneficiaries can claim IRWE. With the IRWE work incentive, the SSA deducts the cost of items and services that a person with a disability needs to be able to work (e.g., attendant care services, medical devices). The SSA may deduct these expenses when determining whether the individual continues to be eligible for SSDI. The IRWE work incentive can also be used by someone who receives SSI. Doing so allows this person to receive increased SSI cash benefits each month that he or she can work.

Net Earnings from Self-Employment (NESE): NESE results from subtracting all IRS-allowed business expenses from the gross product/service sales of a small business. NESE are computed prior to paying federal taxes. Thus, NESE are the taxable income from self-employment, not wages.

Plan for Achieving Self-Support (PASS): An SSI-only work incentive. A PASS is not an SSDI work incentive; however, SSDI monthly income may, in some situations, be set aside monthly in a PASS account so that individuals receiving SSDI income become eligible for SSI also and therefore can use a PASS. With an SSA-approved PASS, a PBO may set aside income and/or resources over a reasonable time that will enable him or her to reach a work goal and become more financially self-supporting. The PBO then can use the income and resources that are set aside to obtain occupational training or education, to purchase occupational equipment, or to establish a business. The SSA does not count the income and resources that are set aside under a PASS when deciding SSI eligibility and payment amount.

Property Essential to Self-Support (PESS): A resource exclusion that applies to SSI recipients. PESS excludes resources such as business equipment, property, and unlimited business cash resources in a small business account that are used in the operations of a small business. Business-related resources excluded under PESS policies are not included in SSI's and Medicaid's personal resource limits.

1619(b): 1619(b) allows an SSI recipient's Medicaid coverage to continue even if his or her earnings (along with other income) exceed the limit for an SSI cash payment. 1619(b) applies to SSI recipients only.

Social Security Administration (SSA): The primary benefit system in the United States for individuals with disabilities. The SSA's most common benefit programs are Supplemental Security Income (SSI) and Social Security Disability Insurance (SSDI). The SSA also manages the PASS program.

Social Security Disability Insurance (SSDI): The SSDI program is authorized under Title II of the Social Security Act. SSDI is an SSA benefit program that pays monthly cash benefits to individuals with disabilities. It is based on an individual's payment into the Social Security trust fund from earnings and Social Security taxes collected throughout his or her lifetime work.

Supplemental Security Income (SSI): The SSI program is authorized under Title XVI of the Social Security Act. SSI is an SSA benefit program that pays monthly cash benefits to individuals with disabilities based on economic need and disability.

Substantial Gainful Activity (SGA): SGA is evaluated by the SSA and refers to the work activity of people who claim or receive disability benefits under SSDI and/or claim benefits because of a disability (other than blindness) under SSI. SGA only applies to SSI during *initial* SSI eligibility determination. With SSDI, the SSA uses earning guidelines to evaluate work activity. The SSA then decides whether the work activity is SGA and whether the worker is still legally considered to have a disability. Although this is one test used to decide if someone has a disability, it is a critical threshold in disability evaluation.

Unincurred business expenses: Self-employed business support given at no cost, such as equipment purchased by the state VR agency, to a business owner receiving SSDI. Unincurred business expenses do not apply to SSI recipients. The cost of the support given to the business owner is deducted from net earnings to determine whether the owner's earnings exceed SGA.

Unpaid help: Assistance given at no cost to a business owner receiving SSDI, which any other business owner would be required to purchase as a business labor expense. Examples include relatives, friends, or professionals performing business-related tasks for free. Unpaid help does not apply to SSI. The fair labor cost of the assistance given to the business owner is deducted from net earnings to determine whether the owner's earnings exceed SGA.

Vocational Rehabilitation (VR): A state and federally funded program charged with assisting eligible individuals with significant disabilities in finding employment. VR can and does support business development, vocational training, and college education. VR offices are found in communities across every U.S. state and territory. Access to VR can also be obtained through local One-Stop Centers (see Workforce Investment Act).

Workforce Investment Act (WIA): This federal act created One-Stop Centers (also known as Workforce Development Centers) across the United States to serve all people seeking employment. VR and other disability organizations are collaborators with WIA, and it is another source of technical assistance and potential funding for wage jobs and self-employment.

This chapter presents the core Social Security self-employment policies. It also emphasizes the importance of developing a benefits analysis for a PBO receiving SSI and/or SSDI. All of this information is critical to consider when planning and executing small business applications. Chapter 6 builds on Bagels to the Max, the small business example used throughout this book, by creating a benefits analysis for Max and his small business plan. The final portion of this chapter addresses and expands on the analysis of SSI/SSDI benefits planning issues and opportunities that are associated with small business ownership.

OVERVIEW OF SELF-EMPLOYMENT AND SOCIAL SECURITY CONCERNS

Approximately 8,300,000 people with disabilities ages 18–64 receive SSI and/or SSDI cash disability benefits each month (see the SSA's Annual Statistical Supplement for 2000). Potential and existing small business owners who receive SSA cash disability benefits (i.e., monthly SSI or SSDI) must understand and plan for the effect of self-employment earnings on their benefits. This is a critical component throughout the process of planning, starting, and operating a small business.

Importance of Preparing a Benefits Analysis

Small business owners with disabilities who receive SSI and/or SSDI benefits from the SSA must account for a series of critical factors. SSI and SSDI policies and laws regarding self-employment differ from those for regular wage employment. Self-employment income generally affects Medicaid, Medicare, Section 8 housing, food stamps, and other support programs. In some cases, significant new gains occur as a result of small business earnings and resource exclusions. In other cases, small business earnings that are not planned for can lead to substantial losses. Preparing a small business benefits analysis, or examining how a small business will affect the business owner's benefits, is a very important initial step in the processes of developing a small business and identifying ongoing support needed for long-term business success.

Numerous individuals with disabilities depend on some form of SSI and/or SSDI benefits, including Medicare and Medicaid, for daily living and work supports. Careful attention must be paid to how a small business interacts with each person's benefits because many people with disabilities rely heavily on their benefits to provide necessary supports. Unfortunately, there is no single solution, as each person is different and each business and SSI/SSDI benefits "package" is unique. The initial section of this chapter provides relevant information on preparing a useful and accurate benefits analysis for a small business owner with a disability. The final section of this chapter provides benefits planning and implementation methods for starting and operating a business.

Coordinating with Business Planning Activities

Ideally, a disability benefits analysis is integrated throughout various business planning activities. Often, the opposite is true. A business idea is developed; a business plan is written; SBA counseling is provided; and, finally, the impacts on benefits are considered—if considered at all. This lack of concern results in part from the mistaken notion that wages and self-employment income are the same thing and operate under the same policies and laws. Another misconception is that such information is too complicated to understand ahead of time and that everything will work out when the SSA, Medicaid, Section 8 housing, and other systems are informed of the small business and its activities. It is hoped that this chapter dispels these "myths" and shows that benefits information for self-employment is accessible, very useful, and important to understand.

Cash Flow Analysis Impacts

One benefit for a small business owner with a disability receiving SSI is that if the business owner was living on his or her small SSI monthly check ($545, per the 2002 SSI rate) before starting the business, the continued receipt of SSI each month offers a potential economic cushion. However, once SSI is notified that the business exists, SSI requests a prediction of self-employment income for each year of operation. If the business owner predicts $685 per month in NESE, his or her $545 SSI check will be reduced by $300 per month or $3,600 per year. If the business is cyclical—with uneven cash flow and sales, both of which are fairly common, and insufficient start-up funds—there may be months in which the business and/or the owner cannot recover from the monthly deficit of $300 in SSI income.

1. A PBO living on the 2002 federal rate of $545 SSI per month before starting a business has the following monthly income:

    Total living income = $545 per month

2. This PBO is about to launch her business and projects $685 NESE per month. As a result, income and SSI check reductions apply:

    The $545 monthly SSI is reduced by $300 monthly because of NESE projections of $685 monthly and the following SSI check reduction formula:

    (NESE − $85)/2 = ($685 − $85)/2 = $600/2 = $300 less SSI each month

    In turn, $545 SSI − $300 = $245 SSI received by the PBO

    The SSI Check reduction formula of (NESE − $85)/2 is based on an SSI policy where an SSI recipient's monthly SSI check is reduced $1.00 for every $2.00 earned after excluding the first $85 of earnings each month. The $85 exclusion is actually a combination of a $20 general income exclusion and a $65 "earned" income exclusion. In an SSI and NESE only situation (no SSDI nor other unearned income), the $65 and $20 exclusions are combined to result in an $85 income exclusion, before dividing by two. Dividing by two then accounts for the $1.00 SSI check reduction for every $2.00 earned each month.

    Therefore, assuming that the PBO earns exactly $685 NESE per month from her new business, she will have a total monthly income of $685 NESE + $245 SSI = $930 total income per month.

A cash flow issue related to this analysis is that the PBO predicts $685 NESE for each month of the year. This may well be an accurate *average* NESE prediction for the year but not reflect *actual sales and NESE* that occur every month. As often the case during business start-ups, this PBO may not reach the 12 month yearly average of $685 NESE per month for many months and, in fact, may not have any NESE in the first few months of the business start-up. However, by law, SSI has to calculate and then implement SSI check reductions based on the yearly NESE projection of $685 per month as an average monthly amount reported to SSI by the PBO. SSI will reduce her SSI check according to the income predicted for the entire year, regardless of whether the PBO actually has income in the first few months of her business start-up. With no NESE in the first few months, this PBO would only have the reduced $245 SSI for living expenses.

Cash flow analyses need to account for Social Security benefits. Often, general practice small business advisors do not know how or why such income is affected. Therefore, they do not include benefits information in cash flow projections for small business owners receiving Social Security benefits. SSDI, for example, is an all-or-nothing check each month. If someone who was receiving a $900 SSDI check monthly loses that income by not considering SSDI policies and laws, it could be difficult to recover from the unexpected loss of $900 per month and to develop a successful small business. Some people receive both SSI and SSDI each month, which doubles possible complications—especially if no benefits planning is conducted. The good news is that these issues are relatively easy to anticipate if time is taken up front to develop a sound benefits analysis.

Break-Even Point Impacts

It is important to note that SSI and SSDI also significantly alter a small business's break-even point, or the amount in sales that yields enough income to cover expenses. Not all break-even analyses incorporate the owner's salary, or "draw," but it is recommended that SSI and/or SSDI beneficiaries highlight the potential impact on benefits while "breaking even" on operating costs. For example, the number of hours worked to break even are crucial to SSDI beneficiaries due to monthly hour restrictions on SSDI check receipt. Addressing this issue after SSI/SSDI impacts have occurred can result in overpayments to the SSA and, at times, the complete loss of the SSI or SSDI needed for daily living costs.

Business Start-Up Funding Impacts

SSI and SSDI hold potential for additional business start-up funding through PASS, a work incentive from the SSA. A PASS does not work for every small business. When a PASS can be used, SSA policy allows PASS monthly business start-up support funds to last at least 18 months—and potentially longer. Again, a benefits analysis in the early stages of business planning provides critical information on the applicability of using a PASS and substantially alters the approach to securing start-up funding for a small business.

Medicare and/or Medicaid Impacts

Regarding health care coverage and long-term living supports, Medicare and Medicaid can provide substantial opportunities for small business owners with disabilities. Yet, both also can be critical issues if SSI or SSDI is lost unexpectedly without associated benefits planning. Self-employment holds a unique possibility for wealth accumulation in the SSI and Medicaid systems through PESS, another SSA work incentive. This policy allows a small business owner who receives SSI and/or Medicaid benefits to have unlimited liquid cash funds in a small business account and unlimited small business resources and property. Such opportunities do not exist in regular wage employment. A single person employed in a wage job must have less than $2,000 in liquid cash resources if he or she is to receive SSI.

Other Support Program Impacts

Small business owners with disabilities are often involved in a wide array of support programs beyond SSI, SSDI, Medicare, and Medicaid, including programs such as Section 8 housing, home- and community-based Medicaid waiver funding, food stamps, supported living funding and other programs unique to veterans (some for children of veterans with disabilities), annuities from insurance accident funds, and possibly some welfare assistance. Each program tends to account for self-employment in roughly the same manner as Social Security and Medicaid, but this varies from state to state based on different policies and internal operating approaches. For instance, in some states, food stamp consideration is based on a monthly accounting of gross small business sales and NESE per month, with each month's NESE fluctuations reported. Conversely, SSI income is distributed on the basis of yearly NESE divided by 12, resulting in the previously noted SSI check reductions. Again, it must be stressed that not planning for the impact of self-employment on support programs can cause tremendous financial difficulties for an individual with a disability.

For years, small business activities, even minor computer or bookkeeping tasks, could not occur in a Section 8 residence. As of 2002, however, exceptions in Section 8 small business policies allowed parents receiving welfare to operate child care businesses out of Section 8 housing in some situations. Also, Section 8 rental policies as of 2002 allowed small business activities to be operated out of a tenant-based apartment if the apartment is primarily used for housing and incidentally used for legal profit-making activities. It should be noted that some Section 8 rental contracts may still list the older restrictions, requiring the PBO to inform local Section 8 housing staff of the policy changes.

UNDERSTANDING SELF-EMPLOYMENT INCOME AND SOCIAL SECURITY BENEFITS

Gross Income versus Net Earnings from Self-Employment

Self-employed people with disabilities and people who assist them commonly confuse gross sales or gross earnings with gross wages. NESE, not gross sales, are the earnings that must be reported to the SSA, Medicaid, food stamps, and Section 8 housing programs. Thus, it is important to provide agencies with the correct amounts to prevent negative effects on benefits. Traditional employment support personnel report all income as gross wage earnings (which must be reported to the SSA based on gross wages, not net, monthly amounts). As a result, when a small business is developed, it often automatically reports gross self-employment income to the SSA (as if it constituted gross wages) instead of reporting NESE.

The SSA understands small business and self-employment and treats self-employment basically the same way that the IRS does. Gross sales from a small business are not the measurable and taxable self-employment income given to the IRS or to the SSA; instead, NESE are reported to both agencies.

Supplemental Security Income

Say that a business sells $10,000 in products/services in a year and has $7,000 in business expenses that are allowed by the IRS. The NESE (prior to the owner's draw and taxes) is $3,000. The SSA and the IRS consider the NESE of $3,000 the owner's income for the year.

Continuing with this example and applying it to an SSI recipient, the owner would be subject to the standard $1.00 reduction in SSI each month for every $2.00 earned each month, after the first $85 of net self-employment earnings in a month. (Note: The $85 exclusion may not always apply, but for the purposes of this chapter, it is fair to use the entire $85 per month income exclusion as an example.) Therefore, the SSI check reduction would be based on $250 per month, which is derived from $3,000 per year in NESE divided by 12 months. SSI would apply the formula ($250 − $85)/2, resulting in an $82.50 SSI check reduction each month or $990 less SSI for the entire year. Had $10,000 yearly gross sales, or $833 per month, been reported as NESE or mistakenly reported as gross wages, the owner's SSI check would have been reduced by ($833 − $85)/2 = $374 each month for a total yearly SSI reduction of $4,488.

SSA's policy is to apply their check reduction formulas on the total yearly NESE reported or predicted, not on an actual monthly basis. Therefore, some important gains occur over wage reporting through which wages, by policy, are adjusted on an exact monthly basis. Leveling of SSI monthly check amounts can be a substantial bonus in self-employment compared with the impact of monthly highs and lows on wage income reporting. For instance, wages often fluctuate monthly for people working with wage jobs due to 5-week paycheck months or vacations, sick time, or various pay-period approaches used by employers. People who have their SSI checks adjusted monthly from wages reported to SSI find that SSI check amounts vary widely and that income often is not corrected by SSI in a timely manner. As a result, they end up owing the SSA money for SSI overpayments. Wage workers who receive SSI often experience a high level of frustration with SSI's constant letters and monthly check adjustments when they report their wages to SSI. However, small business owners who receive SSI report their income as a yearly figure. As a result, they receive the same amount of SSI each month and only one yearly letter from SSI about their income projections. Experiencing a level or constant amount of SSI each month can be a great relief, but such monthly SSI check leveling can also cause problems with SSI check amounts if it is neither reported nor understood properly.

SSI also retroactively adjusts SSI checks for an entire year based on the noted policy of applying SSI check reductions evenly to every month in a 12-month period based on yearly NESE predictions. For example, if a business is started in October and earns $3,000 NESE from October through the end of December, SSI would adjust not only those 3 start-up months but also all of the prior months of SSI receipt during that year. If this is not anticipated and accounted for, the business owner could end up owing an overpayment for the months before the business was started.

This excerpt from the SSA's policy on determining NESE illustrates elements that PBOs should remember:

Divide the entire taxable year's NESE equally among the number of months in the taxable year, even if the business:

- is seasonal;
- starts during the year;
- ceases operation before the end of the taxable year; or
- ceases operation prior to initial application for SSI.

A period of less than 12 months may be a taxable year if:

- the basis for computing and reporting income changes (e.g., fiscal to calendar year); or
- the taxpayer dies (the taxable year ends on the date of death, and net earnings are computed as of the date of death.); or
- the taxable year is closed by the Commissioner of IRS.

NOTE: An individual's taxable year is not ended when he/she goes out of business

This policy, like many other SSA policies, can be read in its entirety on line through a numbered policy and Table of Contents system. The following process allows one to obtain this SSA information and can be repeated for other policies mentioned in this chapter by substituting that policy's number in the "Search for" box.

1. Go to http://policy.ssa.gov/poms.nsf.

2. Click on the "Search" option.

3. Type the policy number in the "Search for" box (in this case, type in "SI 00820.210").

4. Select a topic of interest from the search results list.

Social Security Disability Insurance

An entirely different set of policies is used for determining self-employment income and how it affects SSDI checks. As stated previously, unlike the incrementally reduced SSI checks, SSDI checks are all or nothing. Like SSI, however, SSDI depends on income reports and the PBO's projection of estimated NESE. SSDI then requires more information than SSI that compares the NESE to gross sales, the number of hours worked per month, and, in some situations, the monthly income (versus yearly income averages for SSI). Plus, SSDI reviews and collects information on other factors such as unpaid assistance in business operations and unincurred business expenses. When dealing with self-employment income, SSDI is considerably more complicated than SSI and requires careful and thoughtful planning based on a working knowledge of the SSDI self-employment policies. Overall, SSDI reviews net earnings from self-employment but also weighs a host of other factors and (unlike SSI) does not always divide income evenly by 12 months.

Wages versus Net Earnings from Self-Employment

It is not uncommon for people with disabilities to elect to form a corporation, association, or corporate entity. For instance, a corporate entity could be an LLC that elects to be considered a corporate entity by the IRS for tax purposes and to remain an LLC for state and operating purposes. As a corporate entity, an LLC could pay the owner(s) wages depending on how the business is structured. The IRS web site "Entities: Sole Proprietor, Partnership, Limited Liability Company/Partnership (LLC/LLP), Corporation, Subchapter S Corporation" provides more information.

When the business form is chosen at start-up or altered during future expansion, it is critical to evaluate the choices—based on the general tax and liability merits—and the effects of each business form on the owner's receipt of disability-related cash and health care benefits. It is important to understand that in corporate business forms, wages can be paid to the business owner(s), and often wages are paid in corporate small businesses. Wages combined with self-employment earnings do significantly alter benefits.

SOLE PROPRIETORSHIPS AND PARTNERSHIPS

Generally, the owner(s) of sole proprietorships and partnerships receive net earnings from self-employment, often referred to as owner's draws or guaranteed payments to a partner. As noted in the previous section, a sole proprietorship or a partnership operating as an LLC can elect to be treated as a corporate entity for IRS taxes. For purposes of this section, however, it is assumed that sole proprietorships or partnerships operating as LLCs have not elected to be considered corporate entities. A section from the SSA's policies on sole proprietors and partners receiving NESE is included as an illustration. (The entire policy "When NESE are Derived" can be read at http://policy.ssa.gov/poms.nsf by searching for policy RS 01803.101.)

1. General

NESE include gains, profits and compensation credited to or set apart for the owner's or partner's use during the taxable year. The two most commonly used methods of accounting are the "cash method" and the "accrual method." The individual must use the method which most accurately reflects his income and expenses.

2. Cash Method

The cash method involves offsetting actual or "constructive" cash receipts against actual cash disbursements for deductible expenses in the same taxable year. Constructive receipt means the income becomes unqualifiedly subject to the demand of the taxpayer.

If a person's business is one in which inventories are necessary, cash basis accounting is not permitted with respect to purchases, sales, and inventories.

3. Accrual Method

Under the accrual method, net income is measured by the excess of income earned over expenses incurred. Cash, property, or services earned during the taxable year have accrued to the taxpayer and is classified as income, even though not then received.

NOTE: Do not question the method used if the taxpayer has reported consistently using the same method.

It is important to note that the SSA policy on cash versus accrual business accounting methods does not reflect the 2001 IRS policy that allows qualifying small businesses (those with less than $1,000,000 in average annual gross receipts) to potentially use the cash method. This applies to businesses even if inventory is involved. Details are available in IRS 2001 Publication No. 538 (Cash Method of Accounting for Qualifying Taxpayers), which can be obtained at the IRS web site at http://www.irs.gov or at http://www.wwwebtax.com/irs/irs_publications_list.htm.

Sole proprietorships and partnerships are the simplest, most straightforward forms of business in terms of the SSI and SSDI benefits systems. Essentially, all net income from the business is considered NESE. Partners split the income either evenly or in specified percentages based on partnership agreements. Guaranteed payments to partners are also considered NESE. Guaranteed payments to partners are a useful approach to income distribution in a partnership for benefits purposes and provide some advantages for the partners in IRS and other business matters. Possible benefits are illustrated in the following extract from the SSA's policy "Computing NE When Partners Receive Salaries" (to read the entire policy, search for policy RS 01802.375 box at http://policy.ssa.gov/poms.nsf).

A. BACKGROUND

Partners ordinarily contribute services, as well as capital, for the purpose of producing partnership profits. The partnership agreement may provide that one or more of the partners will receive payments for a salary, payments for use of capital, or interest on capital contributions, irrespective of whether the partnership has ordinary net income or loss. Such payments are called guaranteed payments.

B. OPERATING POLICY

a. The guaranteed salary of a partner is allowed as a business deduction in computing partnership income.
b. The receiving partner is not considered an employee of the partnership.
c. Guaranteed salary payments are not "wages" but NESE.

CORPORATIONS, ASSOCIATIONS, AND CORPORATE ENTITIES

Corporations, associations, and corporate entities can be put in the same category for benefits purposes. This chapter does not address the varied complexities of forming corporations other than to direct the reader to critical information in SSA policy to consider when such business forms are used.

Prior sections of this chapter noted the basics of partnership options when electing to be treated as a corporate entity for IRS purposes. Corporations can be structured in a variety of ways, and the SSA has related policies for each type

of corporation. Possible types of corporations include C corporations, S corporations, closely held corporations, associations, professional corporations, and corporate entity classifications. (Some useful links about corporations and benefits considerations are available by searching for policy RS 02101.000 at http://policy.ssa.gov/poms.nsf.) As an example, an extract of the SSA's policies regarding income in S corporations follows. (Search for policy RS 01802.015 at http://policy.ssa.gov/poms.nsf for more details on S corporations.)

A. DEFINITION

Like any other corporation, an S corporation is separate and distinct from its shareholders. See RS 02101.555. The basic difference from other corporations is it does not pay Federal corporate income tax. Income is passed directly to the shareholders for Federal income tax purposes. The corporation is carrying on any trade or business. The shareholders are not self-employed nor is their income NESE.

B. POLICY-COVERAGE

The income from an S corporation may take three forms:

- Wages, received by shareholders as employees of the corporation,
- SEI, for fees paid to a corporate director,
- Dividends, paid to shareholders.

As with any small business development, the structure or form that a business takes should be carefully considered. It is highly recommended that the PBO consult a certified public accountant (CPA) and an attorney if he or she chooses a corporate form of business. It is important to note, however, that CPAs generally do not understand SSI and/or SSDI benefits' impact and that attorneys vary widely in their experience and understanding of SSA benefits impacts. This chapter can be shared with an attorney or a CPA to provide insight and some direction in locating critical SSA policies.

After addressing the basics of self-employment related to SSI, SSDI, Medicaid, PESS, NESE, and various forms and income ranges businesses operate within, the core information for developing a small business benefits analysis is in place. The next section of this chapter addresses creating a systematic approach to gathering and organizing critical benefits, personal information, and business information; analyzing the information to create a sound, interrelated business and benefits plan; and providing a set of options from which the PBO can choose.

DEVELOPING A SMALL BUSINESS BENEFITS ANALYSIS

The first step in developing a small business benefits analysis is to collect as much detailed information as possible about the PBO's SSI, SSDI, current wage and/or self-employment income, housing, food stamps, marital status, business idea (or business plan), age, vocational services, and any anticipated future changes. The PBO and BDT should complete the Small Business Benefits Planning Initial Worksheet when conducting a small business benefits analysis (see Appendix A for a blank version of this worksheet). This worksheet is designed to gather initial benefits information necessary to start a benefits analysis to determine the impact of self-employment on benefits and also to analyze potential access to and use of Social Security work incentives. This worksheet is *not* designed to initially yield an in-depth business plan but, instead, to complement a business plan as it is developed with associated relevant benefits impacts. Additional information will be needed to complete an in-depth business plan as it relates to each small business owner's life, benefits, and business goals. The following completed Small Business Benefits Planning Initial Worksheet for Bagels to the Max illustrates the value of gathering initial benefits information.

Small Business Benefits Analysis for Max

After completing the Small Business Benefits Planning Initial Worksheet, the PBO and BDT begin the process of integrating critical benefits information into the overall business planning process by developing a small business benefits analysis from the information gathered in the worksheet. From this worksheet and Max's person-centered business planning, business feasibility analysis, business plan, and marketing/sales plans, the following information is known about Max's life, SSI, and related benefits, including his estimated business income and expense projections. A benefits analysis can now be generated with information derived from known benefits policies correlated to Max's business plan and his personal SSI benefits and living arrangements.

1. Max just turned 18. He applied for, and now receives, a monthly SSI check of $545 (in 2002). Max qualified for SSI because of his disability, his current lack of personal monthly income, and his lack of significant cash resources of more than $2,000.

2. Max lives at home with his parents. Using his monthly SSI check of $545, he pays his parents $250 per month for room and board.

3. Max lives in the state of Colorado.

4. Other than special education high school services, Max receives no social program benefits.

5. Max participates in a school program that will continue for 2 more years; he intends to graduate at age 20.

6. Max's business (Bagels to the Max) is organized as a sole proprietorship. From his business plan, Max's projected net income is $15,866 yearly or $1,322 per month. These net income figures account for all business expenses (excluding his owner's draw) but do not subtract payment of federal, state, and local taxes.

7. Using $500 from his personal savings account, Max opened a separate small business account at the local bank.

Small Business Benefits Planning Initial Worksheet

Name: __Max Barkley_____ SS#: __000-00-0000_____ DOB: __3/17/84_____

Are you married?   Yes   (No)

Are you receiving any of the following?

SSI   (Yes)   No   If yes, amount received each month __$545_____

SSDI   Yes   (No)   If yes, amount received each month _____

Are you working or operating your small business (or both) at this time?   (Yes)   No

If yes, what type of work or business? __Bagel retail sales_____   Hours worked per week __20_____

Gross monthly salary or income? __None yet_____   Supported employment?   (Yes)   No

Does it appear that you will maintain this work for the next 6 to 12 months?   (Yes)   No

I expect to start my business in the next few months and maintain it into the foreseeable future.

In what type of home do you live?

Own home? _____   Rent? __I pay rent__   Subsidy? _____   If yes to subsidy, what type of subsidy?

Live with family? __Yes___   Live with roommate(s)? _____

Other housing arrangement? If yes, please describe:

How much do you pay for rent each month? __I pay $250 per month rent to my parents and live in their home with them.__

What is your current total household monthly income?

List all sources of income that your household receives in addition to the social security benefit listed above:

__$545 total___ amount received __$545 SSI__ from __I receive SSI and because I'm older than 18, my parents' income does not count.__

_____ amount received _____ from _____

_____ amount received _____ from _____

What type of health insurance are you currently receiving? (list all types of insurance you are receiving) **I receive Medicaid and no other health insurance.**

How much do you pay per month to meet your living and medical expenses?

$250 for room and board in my parents' home, $2 per month in medication co-pays to Medicaid, $50 per month for clothing, $100 per month for discretionary use and miscellaneous household supplies and items, and $20 per month for Internet access through an Internet service provider.

Please attach a copy of your business plan and/or small business income historical information and projections for the next year.

Describe your personal living situation and benefits from any government programs (e.g., SSI, Medicaid, food stamps, Section 8 rent subsidy) and the impact of those benefits on your life. This section should include any and all government benefits information.

I receive a monthly SSI check and Medicaid health insurance. SSI and Medicaid require staying below $2,000 per month in total personal cash resources. I receive no other government benefits currently, but I am thinking of moving into my own apartment in the next few years. Depending on my income at that time, I may apply for Section 8 apartment subsidies and/or food stamps. However, I believe my new business will produce enough income that I will not apply for or need Section 8 housing or food stamps.

Describe your work history since the time you began receiving benefits (e.g., I began receiving SSDI of $1,000 per month after a car accident, have received it for 3 years, and have not worked for pay yet—but I have volunteered). This section needs to include an accurate employment history since the prospective business owner (PBO) first began receiving government benefits. This is often difficult to accomplish with someone that has worked in multiple employment and self-employment situations. If there are information gaps, it may be necessary to contact related government program offices, such as the SSA and Medicaid, to obtain the best possible information available for an accurate small business benefits analysis.

I just turned 18 a month ago and applied for SSI and Medicaid, and I am now receiving SSI of $545 per month and Medicaid. I have not worked since I began to receive SSI and Medicaid.

Describe your small business income, or projected income, and include any start-up or expansion funds needed for your business. This section often requires a fairly well-developed business idea or business plan and is often a dynamic interplay between the associated business planning efforts and the benefits analysis.

I expect to earn approximately $1,322 net from my business that will start in January 2002. Per my attached business plan I have applied for and expect to receive approximately $4,410 business start-up funds from Vocational Rehabilitation (VR). I will also need an additional $15,500–$16,000 start-up and expansion funds for my business. I'm hoping that this analysis will show me a way to acquire financial support for the additional funds for my business.

Please provide any additional information, such as a pending marriage or other income from family members that live with you or will be living with you. This section addresses needed information concerning the interactions of all income and family members in a household and how that income interacts with related government programs.

I have no current marriage plans, nor do I anticipate any such plans in the next few years. I would like to get married someday, own a home, and operate my business. I live with my parents in their home and expect to move out to my own apartment or home in the next few years. I do not receive any income from my parents or other family members.

Please note any self-directed work accommodations that you may need to run your business, such as flexible work hours or personal assistance with some business operations. Accommodations for a small business owner often directly relate to various work incentives available through government programs such as SSI's Blind Work Expense income exclusion and SSDI's self-employment unpaid help and subsidy interactions with NESE.

I will need some minor workplace accommodations, such as work-height adjustment of tables and work areas, and support in the delivery part of my business, as I do not drive due to my disability. Initially, I will be working part time due to my continued high school attendance.

List any vocational support services you are currently connected with or using (i.e., state Vocational Rehabilitation services, private rehabilitation, workers' compensation, mental health employment supports). This analysis may show gaps in services for which applications could be made. For instance, if the PBO is not working with state Vocational Rehabilitation services, it may be useful to apply for such services for business development, counseling, and funding.

I am accepted by and working with state Vocational Rehabilitation and also with my high school's "school-to-work" transition program and staff. I am also working with my local Small Business Development Center and my local Senior Corps of Retired Executives for business advice and consultation.

Self-Employment Benefits Analysis

(*Note:* Parts 1, 2, 3, and 4 of this final section may require a skilled benefits planner to complete after information is gathered from the first section of this worksheet.)

1. Impact of small business income on medical coverage

2. Impact of small business income on monthly cash benefits (SSI and/or SSDI)

3. Potential work incentives that apply to this business (e.g., PASS, IRWE, BWE, SEIE, 1619(b), Subsidy, Extended Medicare, Ticket to Work)

4. Action plan from small business benefits analysis recommendations

Steps and rationale for the specified time required to meet completion date

   a.

   b.

   c.

   d.

   e.

   f.

8. Max has applied for and expects to receive the following equipment and services from state VR services

    - Mobile bagel display and refrigeration cart (maple finish) from Unico Industries $3,000.00
    - Commercial "Electro-Drive" toaster $300.00
    - Customer self-service table (maple finish) $110.00
    - Job coaching for the summer season (25 hours at $40 per hour) $1,000.00

    Total request **$4,410.00**

9. Max's business plan has been refined and projects the following business startup and expansion needs: business insurance, business cards and advertising materials, miscellaneous operating supplies, accounting expenses, and a delivery van (to be purchased during the second year of operation with an initial 6-month deposit for van insurance). An agreement has been reached with Angelica stating that part-time employees at Angelica's Coffeehouse (the host business for Bagels to the Max) will drive the van if Max supplies it and 20% of the gross sales revenue from the delivery service. The total cost for all of these additional items and services is approximately $15,500–$16,000.

Supplemental Security Income and Medicaid Income Analysis

According to 2002 1619(b) SSI work incentives and the state of Colorado, Max can earn up to $28,765 net income from his business (net income after all business expenses but before taxes) and still be eligible for SSI and Medicaid. At these earnings, he will not continue receiving an SSI cash benefit, but he will be eligible for SSI benefits should his income drop during his lifetime. If in the future Max encounters high yearly Medicaid usage due to his disability, it may even be possible to calculate an individualized Medicaid and SSI eligibility threshold greater than $28,765. At this point, however, Max does not use Medicaid in any extensive manner. If his net personal earnings from self-employment exceed $28,765 per year, he will not be eligible for SSI or Medicaid under 1619(b) policies.

Medicaid Expanded Income Analysis

Colorado passed legislation that could extend Medicaid coverage, possibly allowing Max to earn considerably more than $28,765 in NESE. He may be able to earn up to $75,000 per year in NESE while still remaining eligible for Medicaid. Because of a law passed in December 1999, several states have implemented this Medicaid option. If Colorado adopts this option and Bagels to the Max generates high levels of personal income for Max, he could still receive Medicaid health coverage by paying up to 7.5% of his income on a sliding scale. After Max exceeds the previously noted level of $28,765, he could lose SSI eligibility but retain Medicaid eligibility through this law.

Student Earned Income Exclusion Analysis

As Max is currently a student, he is entitled to the Student Earned Income Exclusion (SEIE), an SSI work incentive. According to 2002 SEIE policies, Max's

NESE can be excluded for up to $1,320 per month or $5,340 per year. In other words, Max's SSI monthly check amount will not be reduced by the first $1,320 NESE that he earns each month up to a maximum exclusion of $5,340 per year. Without the SEIE, Max's monthly SSI check amount would be reduced $1.00 for every $2.00 NESE after the first $85 of NESE each month. The $1,320 SEIE amount is increased slightly each year, usually by approximately 3% for cost of living increases, but for purposes of this example, it is assumed that the amounts stay the same for the next few years as a worst-case benefits scenario.

In Max's situation, SSI applies his NESE of $1,322 evenly across all months. No matter when he earns the income, SSI always averages NESE evenly during the year. Therefore, starting his business in January 2002 has the following effects on his SSI checks:

January:	$1,322 NESE + full SSI of $545 = $1,867
February:	$1,322 NESE + full SSI of $545 = $1,867
March:	$1,322 NESE + full SSI of $545 = $1,867
April:	$1,322 NESE + full SSI of $545 = $1,867
May:	$1,322 NESE + no SSI
June:	$1,322 NESE + no SSI
July:	$1,322 NESE + no SSI
August:	$1,322 NESE + no SSI
September:	$1,322 NESE + no SSI
October:	$1,322 NESE + no SSI
November:	$1,322 NESE + no SSI
December:	$1,322 NESE + no SSI

$15,864 NESE + $2,180 SSI = $18,044 total projected 2002 income

Max will stop receiving his SSI check in May 2002, due to using up his entire SEIE of $5,340 by the end of April 2002. The year 2003 will repeat the same pattern, assuming Max has the same NESE and the same student status with SSI by continuing to complete his high school classes.

Plan for Achieving Self-Support Analysis

Max has the option to consider using a PASS SSA Work Incentive to pay for business expenses needed to start and grow his business (e.g., van, van insurance, advertising, business insurance). If Max incorporates a PASS into his budget, it is possible to analyze in advance (during the business planning stage) the PASS financial impacts, advantages, and funds that will be available to him, assuming that he sets aside the best-calculated amount each month in his PASS. His PASS analysis is derived from the SSI formula, which in Max's case works out as follows: [$1,322 (monthly NESE) − $85 (SSI earning exclusion)]/2 = $618.50 per month available for his PASS. If Max sets $618.50 aside for the full 24 months, he will generate $618.50 × 24 = $14,844 for his small business start-up and expansion.

Max will contribute some of his potential net income to his PASS, and SSI will also continue sending $545 (each month)—not just the first 4 months of each year. A comparison of his overall income with and without a PASS follows.

Fiscal years 2002 and 2003 (24-month period for business start-up)

Without a PASS

Total income for 2 years, including $545 SSI for only 4 months per year	$36,088
Less $15,804 in business expansion costs	$20,284

With a PASS of $618.50 per month

Total income for 2 years including $545 SSI every month each year	$44,808
Less $15,804 in business expansion costs	$29,004

From this comparison, it is clear that using a PASS increases Max's personal income by $8,720. Essentially, he will receive eight additional full SSI checks each year. This is due to Max's PASS being a start-up "match-type grant" of $8,720, which will not need to be repaid if Max agrees to cover the remaining $7,084 from his NESE. Max's PASS is included in the appendix at the end of this chapter as an example of a self-employment PASS based on the analysis in this chapter.

Resource Limits and Supplemental Security Income Treatment of Monthly Net Income for Max

Because Max receives SSI and is starting a small business, he has the opportunity to take advantage of a powerful resource expansion that would not be available to him in a wage job. Small business ownership while receiving SSI poses a potential gateway to personal wealth through a unique self-employment option to accumulate unlimited cash resources in a small business owner's business checking account. This wealth accumulation opportunity is not available for an SSI recipient working as an employee in a regular wage job, as a single, unmarried employee may only accumulate up to $2,000 in liquid cash resources and a married, wage employee receiving SSI can only accumulate up to $3,000.

The difference in self-employment versus wage employment wealth accumulation is so substantial that it is difficult to present an adequate mathematical comparison. As noted, an unmarried SSI recipient working in a wage job may not exceed $2,000 in total liquid cash resources per year. The same SSI recipient, as a small business owner, has no upper limit on cash resources in a small business account. He or she could have even $100,000,000 in cash, business-related capital, equipment, and facilities and still be eligible for SSI and Medicaid.

The critical "resource limit" difference between wage employment and self-employment is that SSI policies for self-employment exclude unlimited resources set aside in a small business account (cash in a business account does not count toward the $2,000 maximum resource limit). Business equity and

personal wealth can also be enhanced through an SSI PESS. As shown in the following SSA web site extracts on PESS policy, PESS is crucial for the opportunities that it creates:

> (A) (2) Property essential to self-support used in a trade or business is excluded from resources regardless of value or rate of return effective May 1, 1990 . . . (C) (5) Effective May 1, 1990, all liquid resources used in the operation of a trade or business are excluded as property essential to self-support.

See http://policy.ssa.gov/poms.nsf/lnx/0501130501 for more information on PESS.

Benefits Analysis Summary

Max's benefits analysis yielded the critical business and benefits planning information to be considered when Max starts his small business. First, if Max earns more than $28,765 in net business income before taxes, he could lose his Medicaid and SSI eligibility (figures based on 2002 policies). If his NESE are less than that amount, however, Max remains eligible for Medicaid and SSI as long as he keeps less than $2,000 personal cash resources. Max's small business account can hold unlimited cash resources.

In addition, Max needs to project his income to SSI and Medicaid for his first year of business activities. He must use his historical sales information to project income for the following years. If Max's actual earnings vary significantly from his projections, then he should update SSI at each quarter during his first year of business operations. This will keep Max's actual income in line with his projected income to SSI.

Max's age, school attendance, and income projections give him access to four SSA work incentives:

1. He can take advantage of SSI's 2002 SEIE of $1,320 per month (up to $5,340 per year).

2. He can develop and submit a PASS for $15,804 to pay for some business start-up and expansion costs (e.g., purchase of a van for mobile delivery).

3. He can use SSI's1619(b) work incentive and earn up to $28,765 while maintaining SSI and Medicaid eligibility.

4. He can utilize the SSI PESS work incentive. This unlimited resource exclusion for small business cash and physical business property allows Max to begin building personal wealth by increasing business cash and capital equipment equity as his business grows.

Max's graduation from high school in 2 years will be a critical transition period. At that point, he will no longer have access to SEIE. Max and his BDT need to plan for that change and anticipate its effect on his net earnings and his eligibility for SSI check receipt.

Anticipated Medicaid legislation in Colorado may soon allow Max to earn up to $75,000 NESE per year and retain Medicaid coverage by paying a sliding scale premium. However, after $28,765 is exceeded, Max may lose his SSI eligibility because of 1619(b) policy limits.

Max's business plan, income projections, and current living situation demonstrate that Max will do quite well by using SSI, Medicaid, SEIE, and a PASS for his business start-up and expansion funding. Max and his BDT must pay careful attention to his quarterly earnings and adjust the income projections given to SSI to retain his benefits eligibility and support.

SUPPLEMENTAL SECURITY INCOME AND SELF-EMPLOYMENT

This section addresses key factors related to SSI and self-employment. It covers SSI advantages and disadvantages, long-term opportunities and concerns, NESE averaging and SSI, a comparison to wage employment, and income thresholds for Medicaid.

Advantages and Disadvantages

SSI has favorable policies for operating a small business. As noted earlier in the chapter, a small business owner can have unlimited funds (under SSA's PESS policies) in a small business account and retain SSI and Medicaid eligibility. SSI has higher earnings limits for SSI eligibility and associated Medicaid eligibility, therefore allowing a small business owner receiving SSI to generate substantial net income from self-employment ($14,100–$39,228) while retaining SSI and Medicaid eligibility. Gross income from a small business for someone receiving SSI has no upper limit. Generally, a business with more than $5,000,000 would be classified as a large business (versus a small business). Nonetheless, if the owner receiving SSI and net income was in the previously noted range, there still would be no upper limit to gross sales. This is true from the simplest sole proprietorship to the most complex corporate structure.

A main disadvantage for someone receiving SSI is earning more than $14,100–$39,228. Yet, by using an individualized threshold calculation, it is possible under SSI policies to earn more than each state's threshold in some situations. Once a small business owner exceeds the state's limit, the choice to lose SSI eligibility needs to be considered or individualized threshold calculations may also apply. SSI's inherent disadvantage is its intrusive nature as a system. SSI monitors income and resources at least yearly and sometimes even monthly based on changes reported to SSI by a recipient. Small business tends to level that set of interactions to a yearly review, but additional reviews could be required based on changes reported by an SSI recipient.

Long-Term Opportunities and Concerns

Over the long term, someone receiving SSI needs to provide SSI with accurate yearly predictions of NESE. Earnings that exceed yearly predictions may cause SSI overpayments, and SSI may request repayment a year or more after the checks were sent. This is fairly easy to predict and/or correct during a business year. Because SSI only uses NESE, a profitable small business can make net earnings almost anything desired simply by spending more on the business to lower the net earnings, hiring employees, or selecting any number of choices. The best advice for the long term is to compare SSI predictions for net earnings and actual net earnings, then either adjust as needed during the year or save for the anticipated payback that SSI will require for the overpayment.

Net Earnings from Self-Employment Averaging and Supplemental Security Income

Again, SSI is a wonderful system for self-employment because of its treatment of NESE. Equal monthly averaging levels the SSI amount for NESE (versus the varying amount for wage income). Attention to SSI's yearly averaging is required, but self-employed SSI recipients fare much better than recipients with wage jobs.

Comparison to Wage Employment

Wage employment pales in comparison to self-employment opportunities and flexibility. Self-employment offers increased choices through various ways to adjust income as needed during an accounting year. Self-employment also offers opportunities for unlimited cash resources in a small business account and unlimited physical business resources, such as land, buildings, and equipment. (Note: Late adjustments to net and gross income predictions may not be possible, so it is important to track net income projections to the SSA at least every 3–6 months.)

Income Thresholds for Medicaid

Perhaps one of the most powerful opportunities for someone on SSI and Medicaid while operating a small business is the 1619(b) work incentive. This work incentive allows individuals receiving SSI and Medicaid to earn past the point that an SSI check is reduced and still be eligible for SSI and Medicaid according to varying state thresholds (see http://www.ssa.gov/work/ResourcesToolkit/Health/1619b.html for each state's threshold).

This concept is illustrated by the following example of a business owner who lived in Massachusetts during 2002. Shelly was single, received SSI, lived by herself in an apartment, and paid for her rent. According to the 2002 state (Massachusetts) threshold, she could earn up to $27,887.36 in yearly NESE and still be considered eligible for SSI and Medicaid. Yet, Shelly was also legally blind by SSA's definition of blindness, so she could earn up to $28,735.76 in NESE. As of 2002, Massachusetts was one of only five states that provided an additional state supplement to the Medicaid threshold amount for individuals whom the SSA considers legally blind (see http://www.ssa.gov/work/ResourcesToolkit/Health/1619b.html for more information).

SOCIAL SECURITY DISABILITY INSURANCE AND SELF-EMPLOYMENT

This section addresses key factors related to SSDI and self-employment. It covers SSDI advantages and disadvantages; NESE, trial work period months, and SGA; and a comparison to wage employment.

Advantages and Disadvantages

Self-employed people who receive SSDI benefit checks monthly face a complex set of policies concerning the only options available to someone receiving SSDI: Receive an entire SSDI check or lose it completely. The policies for self-employment (and some for wage employment) and SSDI are limiting and complicated. Earnings thresholds are fixed nationally and do not vary by state; they are considerably lower than those thresholds established for SSI recipients. In 2002, the threshold or SGA amount for NESE was $780 per month for individuals not considered legally blind. That equals only $9,360 per year in NESE. Individuals considered legally blind had a monthly NESE threshold of $1,300 or a yearly limit of $15,600.

Net Earnings from Self-Employment, Trial Work Period Months, and Substantial Gainful Activity

To further complicate matters, SSDI also reviews monthly work effort and monthly gross and NESE, usually on a yearly basis but sometimes on a semi-annual or monthly basis. It seems contradictory for SSDI to conduct yearly reviews or monthly reviews, but SSDI policies allow this flexibility to choose either approach. NESE for 2002 that exceeded $780 per month could have eventually caused a beneficiary to lose his or her entire SSDI monthly check. "Eventually" is used to qualify that statement because SSDI also uses an involved secondary set of policies about when a person earns more than the monthly threshold ($780 in 2002). Those policies contain 9-month gauges, called a trial work period (TWP), during which no amount of income can cause someone to lose an SSDI check. In a subsequent 36-month period, called an extended period of eligibility (EPE), earnings that exceed that amount can cause loss of an SSDI check, and earnings below the threshold can cause an SSDI check to be reinstated during the EPE time frame. Self-employment TWPs are also measured by 80 hours of work per month in a small business. If a person worked 120 hours but only had net earnings of $400, the SSA could interpret the NESE as exceeding the 2002 TWP income gauge of $560.

It is important to note that SGA has changed significantly. As of 2001, SGA dollar amounts have been indexed yearly by consumer wage index increases (approximately 2%–3% per year). However, the TWP gauge has only changed once since this policy was established. Prior to 2001, the TWP gauge was only 40 hours per month. It does not appear that the 80 hours per month will be indexed in the future, although SSA policy on this amount is not clear

as of 2003. (Note: The 80-hour TWP gauge for self-employment effort does not apply to SSDI beneficiaries who are considered legally blind.)

Comparison to Wage Employment

Wage earnings are not measured by the number of hours worked during a TWP service month. This is a bonus for wage employees because they do not have to consider the number of hours worked in a wage job, just the actual gross wages. However, the remaining policies do apply to wage employees in the same way and are as complicated.

Overall, SSDI policies affect small business operations and income in a complicated manner. Small business owners with disabilities who receive SSDI must carefully plan for the impacts of self-employment earnings and work efforts on benefits. The next sections of this chapter discuss approaches and work incentives that are directed toward benefits analysis and planning for someone receiving SSDI while operating a small business.

SOCIAL SECURITY WORK INCENTIVES AND SELF-EMPLOYMENT

Plan for Achieving Self-Support

A PASS is a powerful and useful tool for small business funding and planning. Technically, it is an SSI work incentive and tool. Often, someone receiving SSDI can also acquire a PASS by placing his or her SSDI in a PASS checking account. Then, this person may become eligible for SSI. This is especially possible for someone who qualifies for SSDI and Medicaid through state Medicaid waivers, Medicaid spend-down options, and other Medicaid receipt options. A PASS will not benefit every small business owner but is certainly applicable in many situations. Thus, conducting a PASS analysis is highly recommended for any individual receiving SSI and/or SSDI. It is beyond the scope of this chapter to offer all of the available PASS information; however, searching for policy SI 00870.000 ("Plans for Achieving Self-Support for Blind or Disabled People") at http://policy.ssa.gov/poms.nsf provides on-line access to numerous PASS resources.

Impairment Related Work Expenses

IRWE policies generally are not applicable to small business operations. This is because IRWE expenses generally would be the same as business expenses that are allowed to reduce gross sales to NESE both by the IRS and SSA. Occasionally, the use of IRWE makes sense in a small business. See the SSA's Red Book on Employment Support for more information (http://www.ssa.gov/work/ResourcesToolkit/redbook.html).

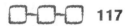

Blind Work Expenses

If an individual is legally blind according to SSA criteria and also receives SSI, he or she can use BWE. (BWE do not apply to SSDI.) Unlike IRWE, BWE apply well to self-employment. BWE policies are very liberal regarding exclusions from countable income. Income taxes are even considered a work expense that can be excluded. Again, see the SSA's Red Book on Employment Support for more information (http://www.ssa.gov/work/ResourcesToolkit/redbook.html).

Self-Employment Subsidy

Self-Employment Subsidy encompasses several powerful tools, including un-incurred business expenses and unpaid help, for self-employed individuals who receive SSDI. (It does not apply to SSI recipients.) Self-Employment Subsidy is complex, and later sections of this chapter cover it in detail. Although the Red Book on Employment Support does not provide a thorough description of Self-Employment Subsidy, additional in-depth SSA policy information can be found on line at policy number DI 10510.000 ("Evaluation and Development of Self-Employment") at http://policy.ssa.gov/poms.nsf.

BENEFIT PLANNING IN ACTION: BENEFITS STRATEGIES FOR STARTING AND OPERATING A BUSINESS

Setting up a Small Business Checking Account

Setting up a small business checking account can appear to be a fairly straight-forward and simple task. However, a PBO with a disability who receives health care, cash, employment, and living supports from the government may find this to be a critical and not-so-simple task. For example, if Maria, a PBO currently receiving SSI, sets up a small business checking account using $3,000 borrowed from her parents, she must follow these steps:

1. A loan agreement with Maria's parents must be drawn up and signed be-fore the $3,000 is given to Maria (or her business). Because SSI (as well as Medicaid, food stamps, Section 8 sliding scale rental housing, and energy assistance programs) does not count loans as income, the loan agreement needs to outline a clear method for repayment. If the money had been given to her before doing so, Maria would lose her SSI check for a month because the $3,000 counts as unearned income in the month it is received. Unearned income reduces a monthly SSI check amount $1.00 for $1.00 excluding the first $20. Therefore, $2,980 of the $3,000 would count as un-earned income in the month received and would reduce her $545 SSI monthly check to $0.00 (SSI monthly checks cannot be for less than $0.00). As an SSI check cannot be adjusted during the month that it is re-ceived, Maria would actually lose her SSI check 2 months later. So, aware that a gift of $3,000 would cost $545 in SSI, Maria and her parents have chosen a no-interest loan of $3,000 to start the small business account.

2. Maria should then visit her bank and open a small business checking account using the $3,000 loaned from her parents as the initial deposit.

3. Because $3,000 exceeds the SSI maximum allowance in personal checking, savings, and cash funds (SSI limits personal cash equity to $2,000 for a single person), Maria needs to engage in some business activities during this month to take advantage of SSI's PESS small business account exclusion. The PESS exclusion will allow Maria to have unlimited funds in her small business account, assuming that she is operating a legal small business per IRS polices and laws.

4. Maria needs to visit her local SSI office to report that her small business has been started. By the end of the month, she must send the SSI office proof of business expenses or sales to verify that she has begun conducting her business during the month the account was opened. For SSI to verify the account and account balance, Maria also needs to give the local SSI claims representative a copy of her business plan (if she has one), her business checking account number, the $3,000 deposit slip, her loan paperwork, and the bank's address and telephone number.

5. Maria needs to provide SSI with an estimate of her NESE for the entire calendar year (January 1 through December 31, regardless of the fiscal year under which the business operates). Maria gives a projection of $3,000 NESE.

6. Based on Maria's NESE predictions, SSI adjusts her SSI check using the following formula: ([yearly NESE/12] − $85)/2 = monthly SSI check reduction. SSI then calculates and adjusts her SSI check both retroactively and for the future. That is, Maria starts her small business in June, so SSI retroactively applies the formula from January to June and also projects from June to December. Based on the SSI formula, Maria's SSI check is reduced by $82.50 monthly ([$3,000/12] − 85/2 = [$250 − 85]/2 = 165/2). Starting her business in June and using the $3,000 NESE projection for the year means that Maria will receive a notice in July for 6 months of SSI overpayment (January through June). Based on SSI check reductions of $82.50 per month, the notice will show that Maria owes SSI $495 ($82.50 × 6). Each month thereafter, she will receive $82.50 less SSI.

7. Because of her state's requirements for receiving SSI and Medicaid, Maria will need to make an appointment at the local Medicaid office to show proof of her small business account. She will also have to sign a release form so that Medicaid can verify her small business account, its balance, and the loan paperwork from her parents.

8. Maria receives food stamps, so she has to show her local Food Stamps Office the same account proof, income predictions, and loan paperwork. Maria's local Food Stamps Office will reduce Maria's food stamps due to her NESE income predictions. The food stamp program uses separate calculations to determine the level of eligibility for food stamps each month. The calculations are fairly aggressive and tend to eliminate or significantly reduce food stamps at close to a $0.75 reduction in food stamps

for every $1.00 earned monthly. Therefore, even if Maria earns a small amount of income, her food stamp allocations will be eliminated.

9. Maria rents Section 8 housing and/or low-income energy assistance. As a result, she needs to show the paperwork to the U.S. Department of Housing and Urban Development (HUD). NESE projections must be given to HUD at the same time they are given to other support agencies. Based on Maria's NESE, HUD may increase her rent (or decrease her energy assistance) on a sliding scale to reflect her new income. HUD may wait until Maria's next scheduled review to adjust her rent or may wait an additional 12 months because of its tenant-based Earned Income Exclusion. The Earned Income Exclusion disregards the first 12 months of increased income for a tenant with a disability who has been unemployed or underemployed during the previous 12 months. This means that Maria's rent probably will not increase in the first year of her business operations. After the first 12 months, HUD also disregards 50% of the increased income for an additional 12 months. If Maria's business is profitable over the long term, however, HUD will eventually increase her rent based on her income.

10. Maria also must file for any other IRS reports and federal, state, and local business licenses. Depending on one's location and circumstances, it may be necessary to apply for a business license, a sales tax license, and a federal employer identification number (EIN) and to file paperwork for the form of business (e.g., an LLC), corporate filings, and/or company name registration.

As noted in Step 10, all small businesses should check if, when, and which forms are required by local, state, and federal agencies. However, this chapter is not designed to duplicate small business information, which is generally available to the public via the Internet and through local SBDCs, local chambers of commerce, and an array of publications and books for small business start-ups.

Prior to moving on to the next section, it is important to note that if Maria had been receiving just SSDI, or possibly SSDI and SSI, her SSDI claims representative may have asked Maria to predict the number of hours that she would work in her business each month for the first year of operations. SSDI would not adjust her check like SSI would; instead, Maria could lose the entire check. During the TWP of 9 months, SSDI uses both an hourly gauge and a gauge for the amount of NESE earned monthly to determine if one or more of the 9 TWP months are used. (TWP does not apply to SSI.) From January of 1990 through December of 2000, the number of hours allowed was 40 hours per month. Starting in 2001, the number of hours allowed was 80. The NESE amount varies from year to year; in 2002, it was $560 per month NESE. This amount can actually be less than $560 and still be considered a TWP month if the person is engaged in small business work for more than 80 hours per month. Once the 9 TWP months are complete, a 36-month extended period of eligibility (EPE) begins. SSDI would use more complicated measures to determine whether Maria could continue receiving her entire SSDI check. She actually could have depleted her TWP previously during a wage job or another small business venture, which complicates her future income predictions. During her EPE of 36 months, SSDI will review her SGA. SGA limits have changed over the years and now change yearly based on cost of living increases. In 2002, SGA was $780 NESE per month for SSDI beneficiaries who are not blind and $1,300 NESE per month for SSDI beneficiaries who are blind. SSDI also uses three tests to see if the SSDI check could be eliminated at lower NESE earnings levels. SSDI, self-employment reporting, and yearly and monthly NESE predictions are very complicated and are covered in depth in following sections of this chapter. See Appendix A at the end of the book for the Checklist for Setting Up a Small Business Account and Predicting Net Earnings From Self-Employment (NESE). This checklist guides SSI and/or SSDI beneficiaries in setting up, reporting, and verifying a small business account, as well as initially predicting NESE.

Predicting, Tracking, and Reporting Net Earnings from Self-Employment

Predicting, tracking, and reporting gross sales and NESE is a critical step in small business activities such as year-end tax filing and quarterly estimated tax payments to the IRS and state or local tax authorities. Disability related government program(s) use the same predicting, tracking, and yearly reporting of earnings as the IRS. However, SSDI also attempts to narrow the NESE predictions and actual NESE to individual months or periods of self-employment work activity. SSDI also requires predictions and records based on the number of hours worked in a small business each month (and/or the number of hours worked over periods of work activity, such as 3- or 6-month periods). SSDI further compounds record-keeping difficulties by requiring small businesses to keep two sets of bookkeeping records. In addition to the set for the IRS, a different set of records is needed for SSDI because SSDI allows for a series of reductions in income, which the IRS does not allow, to evaluate if the PBO is exceeding SGA.

Considering that monthly earnings exceeding SGA can cause a business owner to lose his or her entire SSDI check, understanding, evaluating, and reporting SGA is a critical factor for SSDI record keeping. For instance, a small business owner with a disability who receives a monthly SSDI check of $1,500 and has a child younger than 18 who receives $750 SSDI per month (for a family total of $2,250 SSDI monthly) could lose that monthly income if his or her NESE exceeds the monthly SGA limit of $780. A loss of that magnitude would be devastating to any family; that is why it is so important to plan carefully and keep detailed records. In addition, if the net business income is not reported on time and the SSA later discovers from the IRS that the net income exceeded $780 monthly, the family could owe SSDI the $2,250 received monthly for the 24-month period. Continuing to receive $2,250 SSDI per month for 24 months equates to owing SSDI $54,000 for SSDI checks that were received while the small business owner was earning (but not reporting to SSDI) NESE income that exceeded SGA.

PBOs receiving SSDI need to plan well beyond the traditional small business planning advice that is commonly available on the open market. Instead, they need to incorporate thorough SSDI benefits planning, tracking, and reporting into the design of their small businesses. As mentioned previously, the remaining government-sponsored disability related programs (e.g., SSI) generally divide the yearly NESE by 12 to calculate the monthly actual NESE. Occasionally, state policies for other discrete government benefit programs (e.g., food stamps) allow or disallow certain business expenses regardless of IRS-allowed business expenses. In some states, however, such discrete programs attempt to narrow income to monthly actual NESE, again adding a significant level of complexity to tracking and reporting NESE and business expenses.

The next two subsections divide the basic approaches required by disability-related government programs into two distinct categories. Category 1 has the simplest requirements, paralleling the business records that any small business owner keeps for the IRS, and is suitable for small business owners receiving SSI monthly checks. Category 2 covers the more complex SSDI-related reporting.

Category 1: Programs that Follow IRS Business Policies

SSI tends to follow IRS tax code and accounting standards for most small business forms. SSI does not attempt to track income and expenses monthly but, instead, generally uses the year-end business income tax forms and reports sent in to the IRS as verification of actual yearly business income and IRS-allowed business expenses. The SSI system interacts favorably with the cash method of small business accounting, which many small business owners prefer due to the simplicity of recording expenses when they are paid and recording income when it is received. SSI, like the IRS, looks for constructive receipt of income in a cash accounting system. Basically, *constructive receipt* means that if a customer has the money ready and available to pay a business for a product/service, the business owner must take the payment and record the income. Some small business owners attempt to stall payments that have been received to show lower income during a business year. SSI watches for such issues by using a cash accounting method, as does SSDI. In most states, Medicaid, Section 8, food stamps, and energy assistance programs use the year-end small business income tax forms and reports that are sent to the IRS. Like SSI, these associated programs work to a yearly income figure and then divide it by 12 to calculate an even monthly income figure (although most businesses have uneven monthly sales and expenses). Thus, these related systems also work best with cash accounting systems. Dividing a single yearly number by 12 clearly makes predicting, tracking, and reporting easier than trying to report NESE on a monthly basis.

Predicting Net Earnings from Self-Employment for Programs that Mirror IRS Policies

Predicting future business earnings is a mix of science, statistics, research, art, intuition, luck, and chance. There are some useful strategies that help a PBO predict income for SSI purposes. The following summary and graph of several market research and income prediction methods (conducted prior to opening a tanning salon business) is presented to illustrate a combination of such strategies used by a PBO named Tanya.

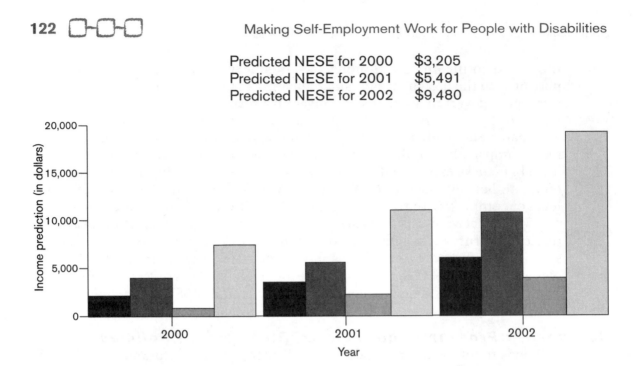

Predicted NESE for 2000 $3,205
Predicted NESE for 2001 $5,491
Predicted NESE for 2002 $9,480

Graph of market research and income prediction methods for Tanya's Tanning Salon.

3-year NESE projections for Tanya's Tanning Salon

Target market/customer profile

Initial market research was conducted on customer demographics and pro-
files. This was based on local community surveys that were distributed
through targeted vertical markets (similar businesses such as local beauty
salons and barber shops) and from a former tanning bed owner's customer
records. The tanning bed was located in a local hair salon that went out of
business. The single tanning bed business served 106 customers annually
and repeated business at an average rate of 3 times per week per customer
or 318 customer visits per month. Market projections from having two and
eventually three tanning booths available for quicker and more convenient
sessions conservatively projects 150 customers (3% of the target market
population base) within the first year. Using an average of 3 sessions per
week per customer equates to a total of 450 sessions per month. The prior
local market was limited by its location within a hair salon, which generally
targeted and provided its largest share of business for women's hair styling.
From records and recent surveys, customers' family income levels ranged
from $15,000 to $45,000 per year. The demographic breakdown of customers was shown to be 8% high school students (male and female), 5%
males 30–60 years old, and 87% females 25–65 years old. There were con-
centrations in the 30–50 age ranges for both men and women. A small percentage of prior tanning salon customers were ages 65–90 years old, sug-
gesting the opportunity for market expansion into the over-65 market.

This local market research was a significant part of the method used to develop the income predictions for Tanya's business plan. Tanya presented a simple, one-page list of research questions to local hair salon operators. She requested that these business owners ask their customers to anonymously complete the questions about anticipated use of a local tanning salon. A few weeks later, Tanya's business planner, Jeff, analyzed the completed surveys as a starting point for predicting NESE to SSI and as support for business start-up funding from SSI, VR, and WIA agencies.

The first through third years of NESE projections, developed from the previously noted methods and assumptions for the tanning salon, were used for business plan development, funding, and business start-up. Jeff then implemented an SSI income prediction strategy to reduce the predicted income estimates from $3,205 NESE in the first year by almost a third to roughly $2,400 NESE as a conservative projection of net earnings to SSI. Jeff decided to reduce Tanya's net income predictions because SSI net business income policy immediately reduces the owner's SSI check based on income prediction. He coordinated this strategy with Tanya's start-up cash and cash flow predictions. The lower NESE predictions also served as a conservative back-up plan for variations in NESE predictions and their effect on SSI monthly check amounts after the predictions were presented to SSI.

SSI applied its standard monthly check reduction formula to Tanya's $2,400 yearly NESE prediction: $2,400 NESE per year/ 12 = $200 NESE per month. This resulted in an SSI monthly check reduction of $57.50 ([$200.00 − $85.00]/2). Using 2002 SSI rates of $545 per month, Tanya received $487.50 SSI ($545 − $57.50) while earning $200 NESE monthly. As a result, her total income was $687.50 monthly ($200 NESE + $487.50 SSI). Considering that she was living on $545 SSI per month while unemployed, Tanya improved her personal finances with small business income.

Tanya actually could have earned $3,205 NESE as her business plan projected or possibly even more for the year. Had she actually earned $3,205 NESE in her fist ycar, hcr NESE projection to SSI of $2,400 would have been too low and she would have owed SSI overpayment money. Applying the same formula to $3,205 yearly NESE yields an SSI check reduction of $91 per month, versus the $57.50 reduction using the $2,400 NESE prediction. The difference in monthly check reductions ($33.50) multiplied by 12 months equals $402, which is the amount that Tanya would owe SSI. However, Tanya would have earned $805 more NESE during the year and could afford to pay the $402 overpayment from her extra $805 NESE.

Tanya also had another option if her NESE was actually $3,205 instead of the projected $2,400. During the business calendar year, she could have chosen to spend the extra $805 NESE on any number of additional IRS-allowed business expenses, such as business supplies, office equipment, advertising materials, or temporary help for peak business hours. Because SSI applies its formulas evenly every month based on the final overall NESE, Tanya had the flexibility to track her income during the year and adjust it in any number of ways to achieve her predicted NESE. If Tanya earned less NESE than predicted, she would receive an SSI "refund," or underpayment, for the additional SSI withheld each month.

Tanya had another option: Utilize a PASS work incentive. If she chose to use a PASS, based on the projection of $3,205 NESE in the first year, her SSI would not be reduced by $91 each month. She would not experience an SSI check reduction. Instead, she would receive the full SSI check amount each month under the agreement to account for $91 of start-up business expenses as PASS expenses also. This is a very useful approach for a new small business owner receiving monthly SSI checks because there is often little or no income during the first few months of business operation. Without a PASS, receiving $91 less SSI each month with no new business income could mean that Tanya might have difficulty paying her personal bills. PBOs receiving SSI seldom use PASSes for small business start-up expenses, perhaps because of misconceptions and misinformation. Yet, they are almost perfect financial solutions to business start-up and personal cash flow impacts. In Tanya's case, a PASS was not used but would have fit in her situation well and would have resulted in her receiving an additional $91 per month (or $1,092 during her first year of business operations).

The SSI PESS policy allows Tanya to have unlimited cash in her small business account. She is still subject to a $2,000 total personal cash resource limit, but, over time, can grow her business operating account to any amount.

Adding Funds

The following information addresses the mechanics of adding after-tax business income to an account. Jeff projected Tanya's NESE as $9,480 for the third year of business. Tanya started the year with $1,120 (after-tax business income) in her small business checking account and plans to add $1,580 after-tax income to her small business account by the end of the year. The goal is to increase her available cash to $2,700 for starting her fourth year of business operations. The necessary planning for personal and business cash and SSI check amounts is shown next.

Third-year income, expense, and tax summary for Tanya's Tanning Salon:

$19,570	gross sales
−$10,090	business expenses
$9,480	**NESE**
−$1,200	federal, state, and local taxes
$8,280	**after-tax personal income**

1. $9,480 third-year (before tax) NESE/12 = $790 per month third-year NESE
2. ($790 NESE − $85)/2 = $705/2 = $352.50 monthly SSI check reduction
3. $545 SSI month − $352.50 = $192.50 monthly SSI
4. $192.50 SSI × 12 = $2,310 third-year total SSI anticipated
5. $9,480 NESE − $1,200 federal and state taxes = $8,280 after-tax personal income
6. $8,280 after-tax personal income + $2,310 SSI = $10,590 personal income
7. $10,590 income − $1,580 after tax income left in business account = $9,010
8. $9,010/12 = $750.84 total per month, of which $192.50 is monthly SSI, resulting in a $558.34 personal draw from Tanya's business account each month

9. Quarterly withdrawals of $1,200 (estimated taxes; see Step 5) = $300 for federal and state estimated tax payments (does not affect Tanya's personal draw from the business, which is actually calculated after tax-income)

Had Tanya chosen to use a PASS, she would have had an additional $352.50 SSI each month in her third year. All of the other figures in her NESE predictions would have remained the same (assuming that she had at least $352.50 in business expenses each month, which the PASS could cover). With a PASS, third-year personal after-tax and SSI income would be $750.84 + $352.50 = $1,103.34. PBOs who receive monthly SSI checks prior to applying for a PASS submission have access to additional business funding. PASSes are monthly, free, business funds that assist a small business start-up. PASS policies suggest that 18 months should offer sufficient funding for business owners, but they do allow for longer individualized approvals or extensions based on each unique small business and its PASS. SSI has approved a few business-related PASSes for up to 3 years.

Summary of Supplemental Security Income Interactions with Self-Employment Funding and Earnings

SSI's system interacts favorably with the cash method of small business accounting. With basic research and planning and a reasonably accurate business plan, a PBO receiving SSI has some control over the income predictions that he or she gives to SSI (as well as to Medicaid, food stamp programs, and HUD). The PBO can choose almost any predicted NESE if the business is profitable, allowing for conservative estimates of monthly and yearly income. Using a PASS is highly recommended for a PBO receiving SSI, and it is a low-risk approach for monthly business and personal income support during a business start-up. In addition, conservatively adding after-tax personal income to a business account during each year of operations is an excellent way to build equity and take advantage of SSI's PESS exclusion. Overall, SSI provides opportunities to earn considerable NESE while maintaining SSI and Medicaid eligibility.

Category 2: Programs that Deviate from IRS Policies

In general business practice, keeping two sets of books that have different balances and expense adjustments would be considered illegal. Yet, for a small business owner receiving SSDI, it is actually a required practice. The IRS-approved set of books includes the standard records and accounting for IRS quarterly tax estimates, quarterly tax payments, and end-of-year tax returns. In the IRS-approved set of books, all of the standard allowable deductions and types of income are predicted, tracked, and reported. The IRS has no interest in the second set of books, which is required by SSDI only. The second set accounts for a series of critical factors to determine whether the business owner should continue to receive a monthly SSDI check. (The factors that necessitate a second set of books are explained in the subsection "Social Security Disability Insurance, Net Earnings from Self-Employment, and Two Sets of Books.") Anyone running a reasonably profitable small business while receiving SSDI must prepare for the possible total loss of his or her SSDI check. Even in some small businesses that are not very profitable, SSDI staff may use various complex SSDI policies to eliminate the owner's check.

A cash accounting method, which is suitable for PBOs who are SSI recipients, is not recommended for SSDI beneficiaries. SSDI interacts best with an accrual accounting method. *Accrual accounting* accounts for income when it is earned, billed, or due, which may not be when it is actually received. Expenses are accounted for when they are incurred, which also may not be when the actual expense payments are made. For a PBO receiving monthly SSDI benefits, setting up an accrual accounting method during the first month of business operations is a crucial step in business planning and operations, as errors can seriously affect personal living income. PBOs often receive little or no explanation of SSDI's complex self-employment policies. Since the 1990s, the authors have not reviewed any business plans from business owners receiving SSDI that address these critical policy issues.

Generally, only two choices exist for a PBO who receives SSDI and intends to operate a small business that generates income. The first choice is to plan to lose his or her SSDI check during the business start-up years and to design a small business that is profitable enough to replace the loss of monthly SSDI income. That loss can occur as soon as the first month of operating the business and can continue years into the future. The business operational factors that the SSA uses to evaluate SSDI check loss (or continuation) are explained and outlined in "Social Security Disability Insurance, Net Earnings from Self-Employment, and Two Sets of Books."

The second is a choice for some but not all PBOs receiving SSDI: Develop a PASS that creates SSI eligibility and generates a monthly SSI check in addition to the SSDI check. The owner then intentionally loses his or her SSDI check during the time frame in which the PASS is approved and retains SSI and Medicaid eligibility. This approach and the previous one are fairly narrow choices and are predicated on the assumption that the business is profitable in the future.

If the business is very small and only generates minimal earnings with little work effort each month, then a third choice is possible. Nonetheless, designing an intentionally low-effort, unprofitable business is not the intent of this chapter. Such an approach defeats the purpose of owning and operating a small business. If the owner is only working a few token hours in the business each month and the business continually generates very low profits, then the purpose of operating the business is questionable. In addition, over time, the SSA and/or the IRS could determine that the business is a hobby and retroactively reverse any business expenses allowed as tax deductions and SSDI-related income deductions. If the IRS determined that the business was operating as a hobby, it is possible that the owner could owe the IRS back taxes and owe the SSA overpayments.

A fourth possibility is in the realm of government support interactions with wages and dividends paid by a corporation. Wages and dividends are not forms of self-employment income and, therefore, are not NESE. An entire book would be required to address wages and corporate dividends properly; however, Appendix B at the end of this book provides web site links to access information on this topic.

This chapter is intended to help PBOs and their BDTs understand various approaches to policies that, in turn, create choices. For instance, a PBO chooses to complete a PASS form and request approval from the SSA to fund a small business start-up. On the surface, the decision to use a PASS is based on the opportunity to receive start-up funds. Choosing to use a PASS also presents a potential benefits and small business planning strategy for someone who receives SSDI and wants to become eligible for SSI and Medicaid. Once a PASS creates SSI and Medicaid due to eligibility, another option becomes available for the PBO. He or she can choose to intentionally eliminate monthly SSDI cash benefits while maintaining SSI and Medicaid eligibility.

Social Security Disability Insurance, Net Earnings from Self-Employment, and Two Sets of Books

The first set of books required for a small business operated by an SSDI beneficiary is the standard IRS-required records that any small business owner needs for income tax purposes. This set of books is as simple as small business checking account monthly transaction reports; original receipts or records of all business expenses; and records of all sales transactions, receipts, and invoices.

The second set of books is solely for SSDI purposes and is used to determine SSDI eligibility. The two specific purposes of this additional set of books are to evaluate 1) earnings and work effort during the TWP and 2) SGA efforts and earnings after the TWP. The 2002 TWP earnings levels are 80 hours of work effort, or $560 NESE, per month for people who are not blind. TWP levels for individuals who are blind only measure $560 NESE per month and do not count hours of work effort. SGA 2002 levels are $780 for SSDI beneficiaries who are not blind and $1,300 per month SSDI recipients who are blind. The first purpose (i.e., TWP month usage determinations) may or may not apply to a small business owner receiving SSDI, as some small business owners may have already used all of their 9 TWP months in a prior job or small business. Others may have used some or none of their 9 TWP months since receiving SSDI.

The second purpose (i.e., SGA determinations) applies to all business owners receiving SSDI, except possibly owners with very low NESE and very low work effort in their small businesses. Even owners who show a negative NESE (i.e., business income losses for the year) and low reported work effort are eventually reviewed by SSDI to determine SGA income, work efforts, and comparisons with other similar small businesses.

The task of checking for NESE during the TWP and SGA after TWP is made more complicated due to SSDI policy requiring an analysis of NESE. This analysis first examines monthly business income and expenses to determine exact monthly income. Those figures compare when the income was earned (regardless of when it was received) to when the associated business expenses were incurred (regardless of when the expenses were paid).

SSDI's monthly tracking of business work effort and income is much more difficult and complicated than SSI's system. For instance, in a small consulting business, the expenses are generally incurred months before the income arrives. This happens because the consultant performs the work in 1 month, invoices the work for that month, and generally is not paid for another 1–3 months. Say that a consultant works more than 80 hours total in June and has one contract for 2 days of consulting. The fees consist of $4,000 in fees plus $1,000 in travel charges for $5,000 total invoiced to her customer. The consultant also has $2,000 in business operating and travel expenses in June but because the invoice is not paid until August, the business shows a net loss of $2,000 in June. When the customer pays the $5,000 invoice in August, there are very few business expenses (totaling only $500), and the owner takes the month off for a vacation. So in August, the business net income is $5,000 − $500 operating expenses = $4,500 NESE. The business records show $4,500 NESE in August, yet no work took place that month.

In this situation, SSDI would review the business records to discover when the work was performed, when the related business expenses were incurred, and when the income was received. SSDI staff might discover that the income was earned in June and, therefore, June was 1 of the 9 countable TWP months. In June, the owner worked more than 80 hours in her business, $5,000 was earned, and $2,000 in expenses were incurred. This leaves a theoretical or accrual income that month of $3,000, which exceeds the $560 TWP gauge for NESE. It appears that SSDI would count June as a TWP month, even though the owner's cash business records show a loss of $2,000 in June. It also appears that SSDI should not count August as a TWP month because little or no work effort took place and no income was earned, even though the owner's business records showed net earnings of $4,500 in August. Nevertheless, SSDI policy is not precisely clear for such situations. Because both months meet SSDI's two either-or tests, SSDI could count one or both as TWP months. Using a cash method of accounting leaves SSDI policy ambiguous and creates the potential to count both June and August as TWP months. If the owner had used an accrual method of accounting instead, then it would be more clear that August did not count as a TWP month.

Coupling an accrual accounting method with SSDI's accrual approach to tracking monthly NESE and work effort for TWP months is helpful but can still be somewhat unclear and complicated for less simple business situations. For instance, cash sales combined with contract and invoice sales, which are paid for months after the work is completed, can make it unclear when income is actually earned. SSDI would have difficulty assigning accrual method business expenses to any single month when large business expenses for an entire year are paid in one month. Examples of such expenses include business insurance premiums, advertising paid before sales occur (i.e., advertising needed to receive the eventual sales), or one-time cash equipment purchases for equipment that is used over several years but is written off in 1 year as a business expense for tax purposes. (The latter situation exemplifies SSDI's NESE tracking dilemma not only for 1 year but for any single month during that year.) To provide local SSDI staff latitude in more complex situations, SSDI's TWP determination policy for self-employment allows periods of work effort to be averaged (e.g., several months or 6 months of work effort and NESE). It also has a "fall back position" for when business records are not clear or insufficient detail is available; this policy allows TWP determinations to average an entire year's NESE and work effort. SSDI's TWP policy does direct local SSDI staff to first seek out the highest possible level of month-by-month detail prior to using averaging approaches.

The second criteria can be problematic as well. SSDI considers 80 hours of work effort equivalent to earning more than $560 NESE for TWP month determinations (for people who are not blind). It is possible to have net income losses or earnings of less than $560 NESE in any month or in a series of months and still use up one or more of the 9 TWP months allowed. As noted in the previous example, the consulting business owner showed a cash basis net loss of $2,000 in June yet used up a TWP month because she worked more than 80 hours in the month of June. Thus, it is highly possible—even probable—that despite a first-year loss for all 12 months of business operations, SSDI will determine that the business owner worked more than 80 hours per month and, in turn, depleted the entire TWP allowance.

Once a small business owner has used up all 9 TWP months, SSDI evaluates SGA that occurs after the TWP is completed. Exceeding $780 NESE per month can cause the total loss of an SSDI check, so this is the area for which the second set of books is required. Using figures from Tanya's Tanning Salon as an example, assume that Tanya was receiving SSDI. Her third-year federal taxable income and expenses (per the required IRS records) showed her gross sales to be $19,570. Tanya's NESE for that year are $9,480. Therefore, her IRS-allowed business expenses are ($19,570 − $9,480) = $10,090. Her federal, state, and local taxes are $1,200.

Tanya's third-year income, expenses, and taxes per the first set of books (for the IRS)

$19,570	gross sales
−$10,090	business expenses
$9,480	**NESE**
−$1,200	federal, state, and local taxes
$8,280	**after-tax personal income**

Note: $9,480 NESE per year/12 months = $790 per month average NESE

Per IRS records, Tanya is earning $790 NESE monthly, which exceeds the SGA level by $10 per month. Her entire SSDI check could be in jeopardy. This is why a second set of SSDI-compliant books and SSDI-specific records for her SGA determination are needed.

In constructing this second set of books, Tanya first needs to record all unpaid help with her business operations. SSDI allows her to reduce her taxable NESE by the actual value that she would have paid for the hours worked by her unpaid help. For instance, Tanya's husband, Terry, works about 20 hours per week in a local school bus maintenance facility, but he often helps Tanya in her business when he has free time. He assists her by performing minor physical tasks, as Tanya's physical disability limits her mobility. On average, Terry assists Tanya with her business 5 hours per week. Per the local labor rate for such work, he would be paid $7.50 per hour. Tanya needs to record the number of hours that Terry assists and then multiply that time by the local labor rate of $7.50 per hour. At 5 hours per week, for 4.3 weeks per month, the value of his unpaid help is $7.50 × 4.3 × 5 = $161.25 per month.

Tanya's second set of books begins to take shape. She can now show SSDI a business expense on her second set of books. (Note: The IRS does not allow unpaid help to be counted as a business deduction.) This first-line item is subtracted from her IRS NESE.

Tanya's second set of business income and expense books (for SSDI)

   $790.00 Tanya's Tanning Salon monthly NESE from IRS books
 −$161.25 Terry's monthly unpaid help
   $628.75 **NESE countable for Tanya's SGA determination**

Tanya also records the free monthly accounting support received from a local community rehabilitation provider, which she can count as unpaid help. That support is recorded as 2 hours per month at the local bookkeeping practice rate of $25 per hour, totaling $50 per month in unpaid help. This second-line item is subtracted from the SSDI set of books.

$790.00 Tanya's Tanning Salon monthly NESE from IRS books

 −$161.25 Terry's monthly unpaid help
  −$50.00 monthly bookkeeping unpaid help
  $578.75 **NESE countable for Tanya's SGA determination**

Tanya also records telephone calls made and received regarding her local SBDC advisor, her chamber of commerce advisor, a local attorney who is a family friend, and another small business owner. All of these people provide free business advice that would otherwise need to be purchased. Records of her telephone calls average 1 hour per month for all calls (an average of four calls per month at 15 minutes each equals 1 hour per month). The average local hourly rate of such business consulting and legal advice is $75. The third line item is subtracted from the SSDI set of books.

$790.00 Tanya's Tanning Salon monthly NESE from IRS books

 −$161.25 Terry's monthly unpaid help
  −$50.00 monthly bookkeeping unpaid help
  −$75.00 business and legal unpaid help
  $503.75 **NESE countable for Tanya's SGA determination**

Carefully recording unpaid help throughout the year allows Tanya to lower her SSDI countable NESE for her SGA determination to $503.75, which is below the monthly SGA level of $780. Tanya also records unincurred business expenses, SSDI SGA income exclusion, in her second set of books. Tanya does not pay for unincurred business expenses, so she has no receipts and cannot claim them in her first set of books (taxable income to the IRS). Because of her business- and disability-related needs (that changed/worsened toward the end of her second year in business due to her disability) for an adapted office space, desk, and chair, Tanya reopened her case for postemployment services with VR during her third year of business operations. She could not claim these items as business expenses, as VR paid for them. The adapted office equipment cost

$1,200, thereby costing $100 per month for 12 months. This fourth line item is subtracted from the SSDI set of books.

$790.00 Tanya's Tanning Salon monthly NESE from IRS books

- −$161.25   Terry's monthly unpaid help
- −$50.00   monthly bookkeeping unpaid help
- −$75.00   business and legal unpaid help
- −$100.00   VR-purchased office furniture as unincurred business expenses
- **$403.75**   **NESE countable for Tanya's SGA determination**

Because of her disability, Tanya also requires monthly medications. The IRS does not allow these to be counted as business expenses, but SSDI considers them IRWE. Tanya keeps all her receipts for her second set of books. Her medications cost her $60 per month. The fifth line item is subtracted from the SSDI set of books:

$790.00 Tanya's Tanning Salon monthly NESE from IRS books

- −$161.25   Terry's monthly unpaid help
- −$50.00   monthly bookkeeping unpaid help
- −$75.00   business and legal unpaid help
- −$100.00   VR-purchased office furniture as unincurred business expenses
- −$60.00   monthly medications as IRWE
- **$343.75**   **NESE countable for Tanya's SGA determination**

By keeping this second set of books, Tanya can prove to SSDI that her NESE, although $790 monthly per IRS requirements, is only $343.75 monthly when adjusted per SSDI-allowed deductions (i.e., unpaid help, unincurred business expenses, and IRWE). Because $343.75 is below the monthly SGA level of $780, Tanya has an improved chance of retaining her SSDI check.

Tanya's review by SSDI is not over yet. SSDI has determined that she is performing significant services in her business because she is the sole owner, but she is not producing substantial income due to her unpaid help, unincurred business expenses, and IRWE. Therefore, SSDI reviews local similar small businesses and the local economy to compare her business operations to the other businesses and local business NESE. The nearest small business that is similar to Tanya's Tanning Salon is in another town 50 miles away. That business generates approximately three times the NESE of Tanya's business. The comparable business has considerably higher operating costs. Tanya's overall efficiency is less than that of the comparable small business owner. Tanya's income is not regarded as adequate because her NESE is only $9,480 per year. The income regarded as an adequate standard of living in Tanya's community, based on the comparison's business, is actually quite low but still rated at $12,000 per year.

Considering hours, skills, energy output, efficiency, duties, and responsibilities, SSDI was not able to show that Tanya was performing at a level comparable to that of individuals without disabilities. SSDI's lack of conclusive evidence resulted in a finding that the work performed was not SGA. For SSDI to conduct such comparisons between people with and without disabilities, the

---

Important points to remember for small business owners who receive SSDI

SSDI interacts best with an accrual accounting method. This differs dramatically from SSI, which interacts best with a cash accounting system.

All of the following factors need to be carefully reviewed before giving SSDI predicted NESE:

- Past TWP month usage
- Future predictions of NESE that will exceed SGA
- Anticipated hours worked
- Any unpaid help, unincurred business expenses, or IRWE

SSDI requires two set of books. The first set only includes the standard IRS income and expense records, preferably using the accrual method of accounting. The second set tracks and documents unpaid help, unincurred business expenses, and IRWE for SSDI determinations of SGA.

A PASS should be considered to fund a small business start-up and to establish the owner's eligibility for SSI and Medicaid. Once a PASS is approved, the business owner's SSDI check should intentionally be eliminated *during the PASS* (not after the PASS is completed). When this strategy is followed, the owner retains SSI and Medicaid eligibility indefinitely and has access to all of SSI's and Medicaid's small business advantages.

Even with a moderately profitable small business, monthly SGA levels make it is very difficult to continue receiving SSDI. If a PASS cannot be used, which at times it cannot, then the PBO needs to plan to either lose his or her SSDI check as the business becomes profitable or to intentionally not earn over SGA. It is very difficult to operate a profitable small business, not earn over SGA, and not lose an SSDI check.

SSDI reviews of SGA are complex and critical. When NESE exceed SGA or SSDI staff confirm comparable work effort to another similar business, the owner loses his or her SSDI check. This loss, if unplanned, can be devastating financially, often resulting in large overpayments and, in turn, debts to the SSA.

---

type of self-employment compared must be the same. In addition, the individuals without disabilities must maintain a standard of living regarded as adequate for a particular community. SSA policy also concludes that well-established businesses are generally the most reasonable choice for comparison.

Tanya's small business is well developed but still in a tenuous position. It has the capacity to grow beyond $9,480 NESE per year. However, it is clear from the review of her third year of operations that if Tanya earns near $12,000 NESE per year, she is in jeopardy of losing her entire SSDI check. The complexity of SSDI and self-employment cannot be stressed enough. In actual practice, many small business owners receiving SSDI do not keep records of unpaid help, unincurred business expenses, and IRWE. Generally, business owners who receive SSDI do not know that such record keeping is required. Also, SSDI-conducted comparisons to other businesses are interpretive and give SSDI latitude in interpreting reports from other businesses in any number of ways.

PUTTING IT ALL TOGETHER

The combination of SSA policies, IRS policies, and self-employment seems complicated. Nevertheless, even the most complex system can be understood to operate in fairly simple and helpful patterns. When addressing SSA and self-employment considerations, the following thinking tools may be helpful for PBOs and BDTs. First, document the PBO's SSI and/or SSDI benefits. Also, document other benefits (e.g., Section 8 housing, supported living, food stamps, Medicare, Medicaid, employment supports), as well as pertinent personal information (e.g., marital status, total household income). Remember that someone receiving SSI and considering self-employment has increased earning potential through SSI and Medicaid. Even someone who has both SSI and SSDI has all the opportunities afforded to someone on SSI considering a small business.

Plan carefully for the interaction between the small business income and SSDI's "all-or-nothing check" receipt. This is crucial for individuals who only receive SSDI. A useful approach might be to develop a PASS, if possible, which would enable the PBO to set aside the SSDI check and to qualify for SSI. Using a PASS is the only way for a PBO with a large SSDI check to qualify for SSI benefits. In such a situation, a PASS must be carefully planned to "lose" the SSDI check while the PASS is still active and then to maintain SSI and Medicaid eligibility after the PASS is completed. If a PASS is not possible for someone receiving SSDI, then carefully consider self-employment subsidies such as unpaid help, unincurred business expenses, IRWE, and comparable work effort to another business. If a busines owner receiving SSDI exceeds SGA ($780 per month NESE in 2002), then the owner could lose his or her entire SSDI check. Self-employment subsidies could prevent the unexpected or unplanned loss of an SSDI check due to earnings over SGA.

CONCLUSION

Small business owners with disabilities have unique financial opportunities and critical financial concerns that are neither opportunities nor concerns for small business owners without disabilities. Typical assistance for small business financial planning does apply to PBOs with disabilities; however, only using typical business financial planning is a serious error for many business owners with disabilities. This specifically applies to owners with substantial disabilities who receive SSI and/or SSDI. Yet, with strategic financial and benefits planning tailored to each owner's specific business, to IRS policies, and to the self-employment policies and services of government-funded support systems, opportunities for success increase exponentially for small business owners with disabilities.

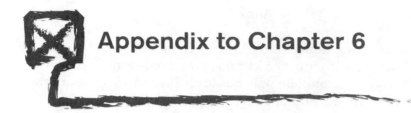

Appendix to Chapter 6

Max's Sample PASS

PLAN FOR ACHIEVING SELF-SUPPORT	Date Received
In order to minimize recontacts or processing delays, please complete all questions and provide thorough explanations where requested. If you need additional space to answer any questions, use the Remarks section or a separate sheet of paper	

Name ___Max Barkley___ SSN ___000-00-0000___

PART 1 – YOUR WORK GOAL

A.   What is your work goal? *(Show the specific job you expect to have at the end of the plan. If you do not yet have a specific work goal and will be working with a vocational professional to find a suitable job match, show "VR Evaluation." If you show "VR Evaluation," be sure to complete Part II, question F on page 4.* ___To own and operate Bagels to the Max, my own bagel sales and delivery small business (see attached business plan)___

If your goal involves supported employment, show the number of hours of job coaching you will receive when you begin working ___25 hours___ per week/(month) *(circle one).*

Show the number of hours of job coaching you expect to receive after the plan is completed. ___1 hour___ per week/(month) *(circle one).*

B.   Describe the duties you expect to perform in this job. Be as specific as possible *(standing, walking, sitting, lifting stooping, bending, contact with the public, writing reports/documents, etc.)* ___I will operate my own bagel sales and delivery business through a variety of business tasks, including standing, walking, sitting, lifting, stooping, making contact with the public, and packaging and preparing a variety of fresh bagels. My attached business plan details my activities in the business.___

C.   How did you decide on this work goal and what makes this job attractive to you? ___I chose this work goal through a person-centered vocational planning process, using a vocational profile with my high-school "school-to-work" transition planning team, my Vocational Rehabilitation (VR) counselor, the local SCORE small business advisor, and my family. Given my life experiences, interests, and local, natural community business relationships I chose this goal as a reflection of my skills and opportunities in my local economic___

D.   If your work goal does not involve self-employment, how much do you expect to earn each month ___environment.___ (gross) after your plan is completed? $___N/A___/month

E. If your work goal involves self-employment, explain why working for yourself will make you more self-supporting than working for someone else.

My business plan clearly shows the economic opportunities and financial justifications for choosing self-employment over wage employment in the rural community where I live. My projected net earnings from self-employment are 2-10 times higher than an average minimum wage job. In my hometown, people of all ages with developmental disabilities are still statistically more likely to earn minimum wage (or less).

NOTE: If you plan to start your own business, attach a detailed business plan. At a minimum, the business plan must include the type of business; products or services to be offered by your business; a description of the market for the business; the advertising plan; technical assistance needed; tools, supplies, and equipment needed; and a profit-and-loss projection for the duration of the PASS and at least one year beyond its completion. Also include a description of how you intend to make this business succeed.

F. Did someone help you prepare this plan?   ☑YES ☐ NO   If "No," skip to G.
If "YES," show the name, address and telephone number of that individual or organization.
Mr. Jones, School-to-Work Transition teacher. Rural High School
_____
_____

May we contact them if we need additional information about your plan? ☑YES ☐NO

Do you want us to send them a copy of our decision on your plan?   ☑YES ☐NO

Are they charging you a fee for this service?   ☐YES ☑NO
If "YES," how much are they charging? _____

G. Have you ever submitted a Plan for Achieving Self Support (PASS) to Social Security? ☐YES ☑NO
If "NO," skip to Part II.
If "YES," complete the following:

Was a PASS ever approved for you?   ☐YES ☐NO If "NO," skip to Part II.
If "YES," complete the following:

When was your most recent plan approved (month/year)? _____
What was your work goal in that plan? _____

Did you complete that PASS?   ☐YES ☐NO
If "NO," why weren't you able to complete it? _____
_____
_____

If "YES," why weren't you able to become self-supporting? _____
_____

Why do you believe that this new plan you are requesting will help you go to work? _____
_____

PART II – MEDICAL/VOCATIONAL BACKGROUND

A. What are your disabling illnesses, injuries, or conditions? _Cerebral palsy with associated musculature and neurological developmental effects_

B. Describe any limitations you have because of your disability (e.g., limited amount of standing or lifting, stooping, bending, or walking; difficulty concentrating; unable to work with other people, difficulty handling stress, etc.) Be specific. _My disability limits my lifting capacity and affects my speech, physical coordination, fine motor skills, handwriting, and a variety of associated daily living and working activities._

In light of the limitations you described, how will you carry out the duties of your work goal?
My work goal as described in this PASS document and in my attached business plan does not involve heavy lifting, nor does it require fine motor skill coordination for most tasks. Some people find my speech difficult to understand at first, but after only a few minutes of conversation, I am understood well by the general public. By owning my own business, I will be able to continually customize any needed job accommodations because I will be the business owner and in control of the work tasks and accommodations that I may need.

C. List the jobs you have had **most often** in the past few years. Also list any jobs, including volunteer work, which are similar to your work goal or which provided you with skills that may help you perform the work goal. List the dates you worked in these jobs. Identify periods of self-employment. If you were in the Army, list your Military Occupational Specialty (MOS) code; for the Air Force, list your Air Force Specialty (AFSC) code; and for the Navy, Marine Corps, and Coast Guard, list your RATE.

Job Title	Type of Business	Dates Worked	
		From	To
1. Assistant Manager at my high school's office. Healthy Breakfast bagel enterprise in the school	High School office + cafeteria	The school years 2001+2002 (9 months each year)	
2. Lawn Care provider (mowing lawns for my family + neighbors)	Hobby business	1999	– 2002
3. Volunteer for my church's bagel and pancake breakfasts	Volunteer/church fund-raising events	1998	– 2002

D.   Circle the highest grade of school completed.

      0   1   2   3   4   5   6   7   8   9   10   (11)   12   GED   or   High School Equivalency

      College: 1   2   3   4   or more

1.   Were you awarded a college or postgraduate degree?   ☐YES   ☒NO   If "NO," skip to 2.
      When did you graduate? _____
      What type of degree did you receive? (B.A., B.S., M.B.A., etc.) _____
      In what field of study? _____

2.   Did you attend special education classes?   ☒YES ☐ NO If "NO," skip to E.
      If "YES," complete the following:

      Name of school _Rural High School_____
      Address: _88800 Rural Road_____
      Dates attended: From _1992_____   To _2002 still in school___
      Type of program _Inclusive education support in general education classrooms_

E.   Have you completed any type of special job training, trade or vocational school?   ☐YES   ☒NO
      If "NO," skip to F.
      If "YES," complete the following:

      Type of training _____
      Date completed _____
      Did you receive a certificate or license?   ☐ YES   ☐ NO If "NO," skip to F.
      If "YES," what kind of certificate or license did you receive?

      _____
      _____

F.   Have you ever had or expect to have a vocational evaluation or an Individualized Written Rehabilitation
      Plan (IWRP) or an Individualized Employment Plan (IEP)?   ☐ YES ☒NO _But I have completed a_
      If "NO," skip to Part III (page 5).   _Vocational Profile with my_
                                                                                              school-to-work planning team.

      If "YES," attach a copy of the evaluation and skip to Part II (page 5). If you cannot attach a copy,
      complete the following: _I have attached a copy of my Vocational Profile to this PASS._

      When were you evaluated or when do you expect to be evaluated or when was the IWRP or IEP done or
      when do you expect it to be done? _2000 - 2002_____

      Show the name, address, and phone number of the person or organization who evaluated you or will
      evaluate you or who prepared the IWRP or IEP or will prepare the IWRP or IEP.
      Mr. Jones, High School — School-to-Work Transition teacher
      Rural High School   _Phone: 555-555-5550_

PART III – YOUR PLAN

I want my Plan to begin __January 2002__ (month/year)
and my Plan to end __December 2003__ (month/year)

List the steps, in sequence, that you will take to reach this work goal. Be as specific as possible. If you will be attending school, show the courses you will study each quarter/semester. Include the final steps to find a job once you have obtained the tools, education, services, etc., that you need.

Step	Beginning Date	Completion Date
1. PASS submitted and approved by the Social Security Administration	Dec. 2001	Jan. 2002
2. PASS checking account opened	Jan. 2002	Jan. 2002
3. Small business operations started in June of 2001. The first 6 months business involved business set up, with VR support and the development of trial product sales (to prove feasibility of business). The supports purchased by VR during first 6 months are noted below: • Mobile bagel display and refrigeration cart: $3,000.00 • Commercial "Electro-Drive" toaster: $300.00 • Customer service table (maple finish): $110.00 • Job coaching for the summer season (25 hours at $40/hour): $1,000.00 TOTAL $4,410.00	June 2000	Dec. 2001
4. PASS business startup funded supports for 2002–2003: • Business insurance, business cards and advertising materials, miscellaneous operating supplies, accounting expenses, and a delivery van (to be phased-in during the second year of operations with an initial 6-month deposit for van insurance) • An agreement has been reached with the owner of Angelica's Coffeehouse (my host business) that her part-time employees will drive the van if I supply it and 20% of the gross sales revenue from the delivery service. The total cost for all the items and services required equals $15,500 – $16,000.	Jan. 2002	Dec. 2003
5. A detailed plan with the business progression and activities during startup is attached.	Jan. 2002	Dec. 2003

6. The PASS will eliminate SSI cash benefits,   Dec. 2003   Dec. 2003
   SSI eligibility will be maintained through
   Section 1619(b) Medicaid policies.

Form SSA-545-BK (2/99)   Page 5

PART IV – EXPENSES

A.   If you propose to purchase, lease, or rent a vehicle, please provide the following additional information:

1.   Explain why less expensive forms of transportation *(e.g., public transportation, cabs)* will not allow you to reach your work goal.

    The van described in This application and in my business plan is a necessary component of my small business startup and development. There is no cheaper alternative, such as public transportation, for a small business bagel delivery service.

2.   Do you currently have a valid driver's license?   ☐ YES   ☒ NO
      If "YES," skip to 3.
      If "NO," complete the following:

      Does Part III include the steps you will follow to get a driver's license?
      ☐ YES   ☒ NO
      If "YES," skip to 3.
      If "NO," complete the following:

      Who will drive the vehicle? Part-time employees of Angelica's Coffeehouse (my host business)
      How will it be used to help you with your work goal? When I supply the van and receive 80% of the gross sales from the delivery service, Angelica's Coffeehouse (the host business) will receive 20% of the gross sales revenue from the delivery service. The delivery van is a critical component of my small business development and expansion.

3.   If you are proposing to **purchase** a vehicle, explain why renting or leasing are not sufficient.

    As noted previously, the van described in this PASS application and in my business plan is a necessary component of my small business startup and development. There is no cheaper alternative such as public transportation or leasing or renting, for a small business bagel delivery service. I plan on buying a good used van (as a business expense), and used vehicles cannot be leased.

4.   Explain why you chose the particular vehicle. (**Note:** the purchase of the vehicle should be listed as one of the steps in Part III.)

    My van purchase is noted in Step 4 of Part III. I plan on purchasing a Ford Windstar (1-year-old, low mileage). This van was chosen because of its low entrance height and my ability to negotiate that height per my walking and mobility coordination. Also, the used van fits within my PASS and small business plan budget sales projections, and it provides a low-cost, yet reliable business start-up purchase.

B.   If you propose to purchase computer equipment or other expensive equipment, please explain why a less expensive alternative (e.g., rental of a computer or purchase of a less expensive model) will not allow you to reach your goal. Explain why you need the capabilities of the particular computer/equipment you identified. Also, if you attend (or will attend) a school with a computer lab for student use, explain why use of that facility is not sufficient to meet your needs.

N/A I am not proposing to purchase expensive equipment — VR has purchased my necessary business start-up equipment.

C.   Other than the items identified in A or B above, list the items or services you are buying or renting or will need to buy or rent in order to reach your work goal. Be as specific as possible. If schooling is an item, list tuition, fees, books, etc. as separate items. List the cost for the entire length of time you will be in school. Where applicable, include brand and model number of the item. **(Do not include expenses you were paying prior to the beginning of your plan; only <u>additional</u> expenses incurred because of your plan can be approved.)**

   NOTE: Be sure that Part III shows when you will purchase these items or services or training.

1.   Item/service training: *1-year-old (2001) Ford Winstar Van* Cost: $ *$11,000*

   Vendor provider: *Rural Ford Dealership*

   How will this help you reach your work goal? *The delivery van is a necessary component of my small business startup and success. It is not something that VR can purchase for my business. Yet, without it, my business would be seriously undercapitalized —a common cause for small business failures.*

   How did you determine the cost? *Comparison quotes from multiple car dealerships.*

   Why wouldn't something less expensive meet your needs? *I have priced less expensive vans and the mileage on used vans and repairs would outweigh the initial savings. Potentially large and unexpected repair bills would jeopardize my business startup cash flow projections.*

2.   Item/service training: *Business liability + vehicle insurance* Cost: $ *3,100*

   Vendor provider: *Rural Insurance Agency*

   How will this help you reach your work goal? *Insurance is required for my vehicle and for my business. Operating a vehicle without insurance is illegal, and lack of insurance for my business is not sound business practice.*

   How did you determine the cost? *Comparison quotes from local insurance agents*

   Why wouldn't something less expensive meet your needs? *I have not been able to locate any lower priced insurance. This is the lowest price.*

3. Item/service training: Advertising + business cards Cost: $ 600

   Vendor provider: Rural Marketing and Printing Services

   How will this help you reach your work goal? Please see the marketing section of my small business plan. Marketing and advertising is a critical support for my business start-up.

   How did you determine the cost? Comparison quotes from local printing and marketing firms.

   Why wouldn't something less expensive meet your needs? This is the least expensive marketing approach for my small business start-up. Please review the justification in my business plan.

4. Item/service training: Small business start-up accounting expenses Cost: $ 440

   Vendor provider: Rural C.P.A., Inc

   How will this help you reach your work goal? Required accounting support to start my business

   How did you determine the cost? Comparison quotes from local accounting firms

   Why wouldn't something less expensive meet your needs? This is the least expensive accounting support that I have been able to find in my local community.

5. Item/service training: Miscellaneous start-up office supplies Cost: $ 440

   Vendor provider: Office Max and Staples stores

   How will this help you reach your work goal? Required office supplies for my business

   How did you determine the cost? Averaged costs from research of similar small businesses

   Why wouldn't something less expensive meet your needs? There is no less expensive alternative.

D.   If you indicated in Part II (page 4) that you have a college degree or specialized training, and your plan includes additional education or training, explain why the education/training you already received is not sufficient to allow you to be self-supporting.

_N/A_

E.   What are your current expenses each month *(rent, food, utilities, phone, property taxes, homeowner's insurance automobile repair and maintenance, public transportation costs, clothes, laundry/dry cleaning, charity contributions, etc.)*?

$ ___545___ /month

If the amount of income you will have available for living expenses after making payments or saving money for your plan expenses is **less than** your current living expenses, explain how you will pay for your living expenses.

The amount of income that I will have available for living expenses after making payments or saving money in this PASS will be the same or more than my current account. My plan is based on current receipt of SSI only. Therefore, it will only be affected if my business provides the projected net earnings outlined in my business plan to set aside a portion of my net income for use in this PASS.

I will monitor my business records daily, weekly, monthly, and quarterly for both SSI and IRS tax purposes and will therefore know whether the income projections are sufficient to support this PASS.

Should my income projections fluctuate significantly above or below my business plan projections, I will subsequently request a revision to my PASS to either reduce the amount set aside and my PASS expenses or to increase these PASS funds to reach my goal sooner than projected. In either case, my SSI will remain at its current amount, which is sufficient to meet my current and projected living expenses.

PART V – FUNDING FOR WORK GOAL

A. Do you plan to use any items you already own (e.g., equipment or property) to reach your work goal?

    ☑ YES   ☐ NO
If "NO," skip to B.
If "YES," complete the following:

Item _mobile display & refrigeration cart, commercial toaster, commercial service table,_
Value _$3,000 + $300 + $110 + $1,000 = $4,410.00_   _job coaching_
How will this help you reach your work goal? _These items services and pieces_
of equipment, outlined in my small business plan, are critical to the
Item _____ success of my business._
Value _____
How will this help you reach your work goal? _____
_____

B. Have you saved any money to pay for the expenses listed on pages 6-8 in Part IV? (*Include cash on hand or money in a bank account.*)   ☑ YES ☐ NO If "NO," skip to C.
If "YES," how much have you saved? _$500_ _____

C. Do you receive or expect to receive income other than SSI payments?   ☑ YES ☐ NO
If "NO," skip to F.
If "YES," provide details as follows:

Type of Income	Amount	Frequency (*Weekly, Monthly, Yearly*)
Net earnings from Self-Employment (NESE)	$1,322 NESE	Monthly

D. How much of this income will you use each month to pay for the expenses listed in Part IV?
$660 per month from my NESE × 24 months = $15,840 total
for this PASS
_____
_____

E. Do you plan to save any or all of this money for a future purchase which is necessary to complete your goal?

☑ YES ☐ NO If "NO," skip to F.

If "YES," how will you keep the money separate from other money you have? *(If you will keep the savings in a separate bank account, give the name and address of the bank and the account number.)*

I will open a separate bank account for my PASS once the PASS is approved.

F. Will any other person or organization (e.g., Vocational Rehabilitation, school grants, Job Partnership Training Assistance (JPTA) pay for or reimburse you for any part of the expenses listed in Part IV or provide any other items or services you will need?

☑ YES ☐ NO If "NO," skip to Part VI.

If "YES," provide details as follows:

Who Will Pay	Item/ service	Amount	When will the item/ service be purchased?
VR	Items listed in Part V-F	$4,410	Already purchased (July 2001)

PART VI- REMARKS

For further details on or clarifications of my business research and business start-up plans, please see the following: my attached business plan, SCORE analysis, SBA business plan analysis, vocational profile, VR-IPE, and business trial sales income and expense records from June 2001 - December 2001.

PART VII – AGREEMENT

If my plan is approved, I agree to:

☐ Comply with all of the terms and conditions of the plan as approved by the Social Security Administration (SSA);

☐ Report any changes in my plan **to SSA** immediately:

Form SSA-545-BK (2/99) Page 11

❑   Keep records and receipts of all expenditures I make under the plan until asked to provide them to SSA:

❑   Use the income or resources set aside under the plan **only** to buy the items or services shown in the plan as approved by SSA.

I realize that if I do not comply with the terms of the plan or if I use the income or resources set aside under my plan for any other purpose, SSA will count the income or resources that were excluded and I may have to repay the additional SSI I received.

I also realize that SSA may not approve any expenditures for which I do not submit receipts or other proof of payment.

I know that anyone who makes or causes to be made a false statement or representation of material fact in an application for use in determining a right to payment under the Social Security Act commits a crime punishable under Federal Law and/or State Law. I affirm that all the information I have given on this form is true.

Signature _Max Barkley_____ Date_July 29, 2002___

Address _Post Office Box 345_____

_Lynnwood, CO   80101_____

Telephone:

Home_555-555-5555_____

Work_same as above_____

PRIVACY ACT STATEMENT

The Social Security Administration is allowed to collect the information on this form under section 1631(e) of the Social Security Act. We need this information to determine if we can approve your plan for achieving self-support. Giving us this information is voluntary. However, without it, we may not be able to approve your plan. Social Security will not use the information for any other purpose.

We would give out the facts on this form without your consent only in certain situations. For example, we give out this information if a Federal law requires us to or if your congressional Representative or Senator needs the information to answer questions you ask them.

PAPERWORK REDUCTION ACT NOTICE AND TIME IT TAKES STATEMENT:

The **Paperwork Reduction Act of 1995** requires us to notify you that this information collection is in accordance with the clearance requirements of section 3507 of the Paperwork Reduction Act of 1995. We may not conduct or sponsor, and you are not required to respond to, a collection of information unless it displays a valid OMB control number. We estimate that it will take you about 120 minutes to complete this form. This includes the time it will take to read the instructions, gather the necessary facts and fill out the form.

OUR RESPONSIBILITIES TO YOU

We received your plan for achieving self-support (PASS) on _____.
Your plan will be processed by Social Security employees who are trained to work with PASS.

The PASS expert handling your case will work directly with you. He or she will look over the plan as soon as possible to see if there is a good chance that you can meet your work goal. The PASS expert will also make sure that the things you want to pay for are needed to achieve your work goal and are reasonably priced. If changes are needed, the PASS expert will discuss them with you.

You may contact the PASS expert toll-free at 1-_____.

YOUR REPORTING AND RECORDKEEPING RESPONSIBILITIES

If we approve your plan, you must tell Social Security about any changes to your plan. You must tell us if:

☐ Your medical condition improves.

☐ You are unable to follow your plan.

☐ You decide not to pursue your goal or decide to pursue a different goal.

☐ You decide that you do not need to pay for any of the expenses you listed in your plan.

☐ Someone else pays for any of your plan expenses.

☐ You use the income or resources we exclude for a purpose other than the expenses specified in your plan.

☐ There are any other changes to your plan.

You must tell us about any of these things within 10 days following the month in which it happens. If you do not report any of these things, we may stop your plan.

You should also tell us if your decide that you need to pay for other expenses not listed in your plan in order to reach your goal. We may be able to change your plan or the amount of income we exclude so you can pay for the additional expenses.

YOU MUST KEEP RECEIPTS OR CANCELLED CHECKS TO SHOW WHAT EXPENSES YOU PAID FOR AS PART OF THE PLAN. You need to keep these receipts or cancelled checks until we contact you to find out if you are still following your plan. When we contact you, we will ask to see the receipts or cancelled checks. If you are not following the plan, you man have to pay back some or all of the SSI you received.

Form SSA-545-BK (2/99)   Page 14

Chapter 7

Small Business Finance and Small Business Owners with Disabilities

IMPORTANT TERMS IN THIS CHAPTER

Assets: What a business owns or is legally due, such as equipment and property, including all cash the business has currently.

Balance sheet: A key financial document in a business plan. It lists the current assets and liabilities of the business. The result of all assets minus all liabilities of the business should always equal zero.

Cost of goods sold (COGS): The direct costs associated with buying or producing a product or service, such as inventory, raw materials, or employee labor. COGS is summarized as a dollar value and as a percentage of total sales revenue.

Gross profit margin (GPM): The total sales revenue of the business minus the COGS. GPM is summarized as a dollar value and as a percentage of total sales revenue.

Industry averages: The costs and percentage comparison factors for businesses of similar type and size in the industry within which a business operates.

Liabilities: Business debts or what a business legally owes, such as the balance due on a small business loan or the equity in a business due to the owner.

Net profit margin (NPM): The net earnings of a small business after all business expenses are deducted from total sales revenue but before income taxes are paid. NPM is summarized as a dollar value and as a percentage of total sales revenue.

Owner's draw: NESE due to the owner, generated from any nonincorporated business (i.e., sole proprietorship, partnership, or limited liability company) after all business expenses are deducted from total sales revenue but before income taxes are paid. Typically, owner's draws are taken out of a business operating account monthly. Yet, even if draws are not removed from the operating account, they are the owner's taxable earnings.

Owner's equity: A liability of the business to the owner, such as an owner's initial personal cash used to start a business.

Profit and loss statement/projections (P&L): The detailed monthly and yearly income projections for a business derived from the sales and expense assumptions and goals of the business outlined in the earlier research, business idea/niche, pricing, sales, and marketing sections of the business plan.

Stable small firms: Small businesses that do not strive to achieve quick returns on investments and substantial profits but, instead, focus on providing a solid income for the owner(s).

Business start-up funding, financial planning, and accurate income and expense records are critical tools for every small business. Traditional methods for small business record keeping, planning, and finance abound in small business books, courses, and software. Business owners have almost unlimited access to relevant information on the Internet from the SBA (http://www.sba.gov) and the IRS (http://www.irs.gov/businesses/small). CPAs, bookkeepers, financial advisors, and financial planners offer business and personal financial support. Therefore, abundant talent and information exist for small business owners in all financial areas except the interaction of small business income and financial planning with the myriad of government support programs used by business owners with disabilities. The demand for financial planning support that addresses financial considerations for small business owners with disabilities appears so low that few related books, courses, software, or planning services are available.

As outlined in Chapter 6, almost without exception, small business owners with significant disabilities rely on one or more government-sponsored cash, health care, housing, vocational, or daily living assistance programs. To be eligible for such long-term services and supports, many people with disabilities have little or no financial or personal resources, living a life of poverty in order to receive necessary supports. Millions of people receive SSI and Medicaid, which require (by 2002 specifications) personal cash resources to be less than $2,000 for a single person and $3,000 for a married couple. This chapters builds on Chapter 6 in an effort to illustrate tools for business start-up funding, financial planning, and record keeping that incorporate both standard business finance practices and disability service program finance interactions.

FINANCING A BUSINESS START-UP

It is difficult to acquire conventional small business loans and investors for business start-ups. In addition, loans often carry heavy interest rates and result in high levels of anxiety-causing debt. Banks prefer not to make small business loans unless substantial collateral is available. Obtaining loans often requires the business plan to be well developed and to show high growth potential. As noted in Chapter 1, wealthy individual and/or "angel" investors are the exception, but self-employed people with disabilities almost always have access to alternate sources of free capital from which to build their business.

Powerful social, economic, and business start-up support for small business owners with disabilities is available from three well-established U.S. programs: state VR, the SSA, and WIA agencies. VR, the SSA, and WIA agencies can fund a small business start-up for someone with a disability by providing free, individual, grant-type funds and services. Each program also can potentially pay a small business consultant to assist in developing a business plan for a prospective business owner with a disability. Because the start-up funds from VR, the SSA, and WIA agencies are grants (not loans), they are available for small enterprises that appear economically viable but do not predict dramatic growth. It is important to note that these funds do not have to be repaid and can be used to leverage small business loans and microloans if additional start-up dollars are required.

Continuing with the example of Bagels to the Max, it is clear that Max has access to business start-up funds from VR and the SSA. Max's example illustrates a typical combined funding approach available to prospective business owners with disabilities. Max receives $4,410 from VR, plus an additional $9,000 from the SSA through a PASS work incentive, for a total of $13,410 in free/grant business start-up funding. Max also receives support from his high school special education department in the form of support personnel. Beyond his direct start-up funds and high school support services, Max obtains free support services from his local SBDC, the local chapter of SCORE, VR, and the SSA in the form of advice, counseling, and on-the-job training (supported employment). The value of these additional services equals, at a conservative estimate, an extra $5,000. The net result becomes a grant-type start-up package of funds and services in excess of $18,000 for Max and his new business.

Stable Small Firms

A feasible business plan is required to receive business start-up funds from VR, the SSA, and WIA agencies. The plan must clearly show the potential for the proposed small business to become a stable small firm. Regarding the goal of becoming a stable small firm and obtaining start-up funding, there is distinction between small businesses started by people with disabilities and businesses started by owners without disabilities. To obtain funds, PBOs without disabilities are generally required to demonstrate a substantial financial projection with greater profitability than PBOs with disabilities are required to demonstrate when seeking funds from VR, the SSA, or WIA agencies. In other words, a small business owner with a disability does not need to show high growth and income potential to acquire start-up funding. The business plan only needs to show that the company has the potential to become a stable small firm. For instance, for the SSA to approve a small business plan from someone receiving SSI and using a PASS for funding, the business income projection simply has to demonstrate a significant increase in income.

A prospective business owner with a disability on SSI could potentially develop a business plan that is funded by a PASS with projections as low as $400 NESE per month, as $400 per month ($4,800 per year net earnings) is a significant increase in income for someone who, prior to starting a business, did not earn income and lived on a monthly SSI check. In 2002, an SSDI PASS application for a PBO receiving monthly SSDI checks needed to show a projected net earnings capacity in a business plan of at least $780 per month ($9,360 per year net earnings) to secure business start-up funding from SSA. The difference between SSI and SSDI is that SSI may only require a prediction of $400 NESE per month while SSDI definitely requires a prediction of at least $780 NESE per month for PASS funding. SSI and SSDI PASS start-up funding approval thresholds have relatively low minimum net earning projection requirements to secure business start-up funds from the SSA.

VR and WIA requirements vary from state to state but are generally flexible enough to allow for low net earnings from self-employment in a business plan. In some states, projected net earnings can even be less than $400 per month to secure start-up funding from VR and WIA. In these states, the projected net earnings are allowed to be almost any amount customized for the PBO's situation and disability as well.

Not having to project high earnings and high growth outcomes opens the door to starting a small business with adequate funding while reducing potential investment risks, fears, and anxieties. Although it is certainly desirable to develop a business plan that projects high net earnings, the looser requirements of SSA, VR, and WIA provide funding opportunities for PBOs with disabilities to gain access to financing without facing the rigors of justifying high income projections.

Additional Business Start-Up Resources

In addition to VR, the SSA, and WIA agencies, a variety of other financial resources are generally available for financing a small business start-up. The PBO may have some personal savings, cash, or trust funds and possibly even a home that can be mortgaged. In some states, disability-specific councils (e.g., State Developmental Disability Planning Councils) provide grant-type small business start-up funds. Loans and microloans from the SBA, banks, credit unions, and a variety of private and commercial loan companies are possible sources for start-up funds. Often, family members contribute start-up funds through personal loans, investments, or direct funding support. The Temporary Assistance for Needy Families (TANF) program, administered through the U.S. Office of Family Assistance, can support small business start-ups through Individual Development Accounts (IDAs). IDAs offer match-type funding; a variety of programs and banks match the funds saved in IDAs in ratios from 1:1 to 1:9. Some states have national disability and grant-funded employment programs, such as those funded by the Rehabilitation Services Administration (RSA), which can potentially support small business start-ups. The Business Start-Up Financial Resources worksheet, located in Appendix A at the end of this book, is a useful tool for listing and analyzing potential start-up financial resources.

SMALL BUSINESS FINANCIAL PLANNING AND RECORD KEEPING

The three core disability programs—the SSA, VR, and WIA—are potential sources for financing a business start-up. Each source of free start-up funding affects cash-flow projections and actual cash flow differently while an individual operates a small business. Using the Chapter 3 sample business of Earl's High Performance Lawn Care, the following three examples show how VR, WIA agency funding, and a PASS (from the SSA) interact with the cash flow, net earnings, and Earl's equity. In these examples, net profit margin (NPM) equals the owner's taxable income/draw.

Example 1: Monthly cash flow with no VR, WIA, or PASS (SSA) financing

  $500 gross sales
−$100 COGS
−$300 operating costs
=$100 NPM
+$200 starting cash
=$300 subtotal
−$100 owner's draw
=$200 ending cash

Example 2 shows the cash flow and NPM impact of VR/WIA paying for the $300 monthly operating costs needed for the business operations. Notice in Example 2 that VR/WIA artificially inflates the profits by $300 from $100 net earnings to $400 net earnings by paying for (or wiping out) the operating costs needed to run the business. Because VR and WIA pay for the expenses directly as a free grant and do not give the business owner the receipts for the expenses, the owner cannot claim the expenses as tax deductions. To the IRS, the business looks like it has no operating costs that month, and net earnings are increased substantially.

Example 2: Monthly cash flow with $300 in operating costs paid by VR/WIA

  $500 gross sales
−$100 COGS
  −$0 operating costs ($300 in operating costs paid by VR/WIA funds)
=$400 NPM
+$200 starting cash
=$600 subtotal
−$400 owner's draw
=$200 ending cash

Example 3 outlines the addition of $300 monthly though a PASS provided by the SSA. The NPM remains the same as in the first example ($100). Examples 2 and 3 list VR/WIA agency funds or a PASS for the $300 monthly operating costs but show very different effects on the NPM. A PASS allows Earl to keep the receipts. Because a PASS creates an increase in SSI benefits, it is considered the owner's personal money (as an owner's equity contribution to the business account) going into the business each month via the SSA. Of the three sources, VR, WIA, and PASS, only PASS increases Earl's owner's equity and ending cash by $300. VR/WIA agency financial support increases the net profit margin by $300 from $100 to $400, in contrast to a PASS, which does not increase the net profit but does increase the owner's equity and ending cash from $200 to $500, yet all three (VR, WIA and PASS) pay for the fixed costs to operate the business.

Example 3: Monthly cash flow with a PASS paying for $300 of the operating costs

  $500 gross sales
−$100 COGS
−$300 operating costs
=$100 NPM
+$200 starting cash
+$300 PASS funding
=$600 subtotal
−$100 owner's draw
=$500 ending cash

As demonstrated in the previous three examples, free business start-up funding from VR, WIA, and SSA affects profits, cash flow, and owner's equity in very different ways depending on the source of the funds. Prior to incorporating the varying effects of VR, WIA, and SSA start-up funds (if VR, WIA or PASS apply, which often is the case for a PBO with a disability), it is important to initially understand the general principles and applications of small business finance and record keeping.

This chapter depicts fairly simple NESE from businesses operating as sole proprietorships, partnerships, or single taxation LLCs (LLCs that do not elect to be treated as corporations for IRS tax purposes), all of which *cannot and do not pay wages to owners.* Instead, the owners receive self-employment income as "owners' draws" that equal the NESE of the business. The yearly NESE from sole proprietorships, partnerships, and LLCs is the owners' yearly taxable self-employment income. NESE is often referred to as net profit in a P&L statement. NESE is the net profit after all IRS-allowed business expenses and before taxes of the business; therefore, NESE is the owners' taxable self-employment earnings before paying IRS taxes. This is a critical point for the rest of this chapter and bears repeating although it has been referenced in several other chapters of the book.

If a sole proprietorship, partnership, or LLC earns $24,000 in gross sales and has receipts for $12,000 in business expenses allowed by the IRS, then the NPM, owner's draw, or NESE is ($24,000 gross sales − $12,000 business expenses) = $12,000 NESE. The IRS, the SSA, Medicaid, the food stamps program, and HUD count the NESE of $12,000 as the owner's self-employment income for the year. The owner still has to pay income, Social Security, and self-employment taxes from the $12,000 NESE. The $12,000 NESE is the owner's draw or owner's self-employment income before taxes are paid.

Often in the planning and operational stages of a business, the owner sets a fixed amount as the owner's draw to be taken out of the business account on a monthly basis. Using the previous example, if the owner had conservatively taken out $800 per month as an owner's draw, by the end of the year the owner would have taken out $800 × 12 = $9,600. However, the business owner in the previous example actually earned $12,000 NESE, and that owner is required to pay income, Social Security, and self-employment taxes on NESE of $12,000 even though the owner only withdrew $9,600 from the business as an owner's draw during the year. If the owner chooses to leave the remaining $2,400 ($12,000 − $9,600) in the business and not take the $2,400 out as an owner's draw, then taxes are still due on the $2,400. The remaining amount after all taxes are paid becomes an increase in the owner's cash equity in the business.

Essentially, in this scenario, the owner is considered to be paid the full $12,000 NESE as if one lump sum of $2,400 was paid at the end of the year if only $9,600 was paid during the year to the owner. Then, the owner pays taxes on the $12,000 and, at that point, can choose to put (or leave) the remaining after-tax income back into the business operating account. Any amount that is after-tax income left in the business operating account becomes an increase to the owner's cash equity in the business.

For instance, if the owner received $9,600 during the year in monthly owner's draws and paid 15% in taxes on the $12,000 NESE (15% × $12,000 = $1,800), then the owner's after-tax income would be $10,200 ($12,000 NESE − $1,800 tax = $10,200 after tax owner's income). If the owner chooses to keep the $9,600 in owner's draws as personal income and leave the remaining $600 of the $10,200 after-tax income in the business operating account, this is similar to the owner's setting aside $600 after-tax income in a savings account. The $600 left in the business operating account becomes an increase in the owner's cash equity in the business account as if it were a $600 increase in equity set aside in a personal savings account.

A very favorable and critical factor that affects SSI, Medicaid, HUD, and food stamps benefits in this scenario is that the $600 left in the business operating account is after-tax personal income left in the business account. The IRS and all of the noted benefits systems have now accounted for the $600 as income once in the owner's life when taxes were paid on the $12,000 NESE. The $600 left in the business operating account can never be treated as income to the owner again. If the owner chooses someday to remove the $600 from the business account and place it in his or her personal account, then the SSI, Medicaid, HUD, and food stamps systems cannot count it as income again. The $600 moved into the owner's personal account is not "unearned income," nor is it the owner's "earned income" when it is moved from his or her business account into his or her personal account. It is simply $600 moved from an excluded (by SSI, Medicaid, HUD, and food stamps) sort of savings account (his or her business account) into a nonexcluded savings or checking personal account. The $600 can then be used for any purpose allowed by such benefits systems (e.g., purchasing a home, buying a personal vehicle, paying personal debts) without being treated as income to the owner again by any of the programs from which the owner receives benefits.

Increasing owner's equity in a small business account is a flexible and useful approach to accumulate large amounts of business account owner's equity funds, which can quickly and easily be converted to personal funds and are not counted by SSI, Medicaid, HUD, and food stamps. Yearly owner's equity increases in a business account can lead to unlimited savings toward a home purchase that otherwise could not be saved in a personal savings account restricted to less than $2,000 in wage employment situations by SSI, Medicaid, HUD, and food stamps. For instance, if the owner earned and paid taxes on NESE of $15,000 each year for 10 years and left $3,000 after-tax income in his or her business account each year as owner's equity increases, the owner would accumulate $30,000 in owner's equity in the business account. Because the $30,000 is not counted as a resource in the business account due to PESS policies, it will not count toward the owner's $2,000 cash resource restriction for SSI and Medicaid receipt. If the owner then moves the $30,000 from the business account into his or her personal account and in the same month purchases a home with the $30,000 as a down payment, then SSI, Medicaid, HUD, and food stamps will ignore the $30,000, as the programs already treated it once as income in the owner's life. Also, because the owner spends the $30,000 before the end of the month, his or her personal account will then again be back below $2,000 in cash resources, and the individual will continue to be eligible for SSI, Medicaid, HUD, and food stamps. Without owning and operating a small business (e.g., instead working in a wage job for another employer), individuals receiving benefits cannot save $30,000 in their personal accounts for a home down payment, as they will be restricted to less than $2,000 in total cash resources in their personal accounts to continue to receive the noted benefits.

The following two critical business financial concepts provide the core logic for understanding the basic organization of the required financial data for a business plan:

1. NESE equals the owner's before-tax self-employment earnings

2. The owner's cash equity in the business account equals after-tax earnings in a business account

Business financial planning and information is required for two distinct applications for any business. The first application occurs during the development of a business plan to start a business. The second application addresses the ongoing operations, record keeping, taxes, and long-term success of a business.

The list of financial data required for a business plan can initially seem overwhelming to a PBO and BDT. It is important to understand that many successful business owners are not highly skilled in accounting and business finance principles. The goal for such business owners is not to become experts in business finance but, instead, to achieve a useful understanding of their business's specific financial tools well enough to benefit from them. An account-

Financial data required for a business plan
_____

1. Loan applications (including SSA, VR, and WIA as potential free funding)

2. Start-up budget, capital equipment, and start-up expenses list

3. Balance sheet

4. Break-even analysis

5. Income projections (P&L statements/projections)

   3-year summary

   Detail by month for the first year

   Detail by quarters for the second and third years (or detail by month for the second and third years if an SSA PASS is anticipated for start-up funding)

   Assumptions used as a basis for the financial projections

6. Cash-flow projections

   3-year summary

   Detail by month for the first year

   Detail by quarters for the second and third years (or detail by month for the second and third years if an SSA PASS is anticipated for start-up funding)

   Assumptions used as a basis for the financial projections
_____

ant or financial advisor can and often should be utilized to assist with achieving the goal of a PBO and BDT developing and then understanding the financial tools needed well enough to benefit from those tools. The following sections of this chapter provide a very basic guide for developing initial financial planning and operating information for PBOs using the simplest forms of self-employment. This material is not meant to be the exact or best approach for any specific business.

Loan Applications

Business start-up loan applications—including SSA, VR, and WIA funding applications—need to be included in the financial section of a business plan, when applicable. The need for a loan or application for SSA, VR, and WIA funding is driven by the business plan and the remaining financial sections of the business plan. Although this section is listed first in the business plan's financial section, it generally requires most—if not all—of the plan's other financial sections to be completed prior to understanding whether a loan application or SSA, VR, or WIA funds are needed for the business start-up. This material seems to be listed first in the financial data required for a business plan due to the premise that many business plans are written mainly for gaining access to start-up funds. Certainly, if applications have been made for business loans or VR, SSA, or WIA funds, then including such applications and funding requests in this section is necessary. Some owners fully fund business start-ups from personal savings or other personal resources and, therefore, no applications are required. In the case of a business start-up that is fully funded by the owner with no other application for start-up funding, it is still useful to account for the amount and source of the owner's personal funding to clearly represent in this financial section of the business plan the owner's personal investment in starting the business.

Start-Up Budget, Capital Equipment, and Start-Up Expenses List

This financial section, like the prior section, tends to develop as a function of the business plan assumptions, research, and equipment needed to begin to operate the business; sales projections; and the remaining financial sections. For instance, in the P&L and cash-flow sections of the financial data, the cash-flow projections may show the need for $10,000 in cash-flow shortfalls due to start-up expenses (or almost any amount derived from the cash-flow analysis) that cannot be paid by projected earnings from the business for perhaps the first 6 months (or shorter/longer period during the start-up of the business). As the business start-up expenses are identified in the business plan, P&L, and cash-flow projections, this section of the financial data begins to take shape.

Each piece of capital equipment needed to start the business should be listed in this section with an associated cost and rationale for the proposed use and need. Also, the expected source of start-up funds for each item should be identified at this point in the financial section.

Balance Sheet

A balance sheet is a key financial document in a business plan. It lists current assets (what the business owns or is legally due, such as equipment and property, including all cash the business has) and liabilities (business debts or what the business legally owes, such as the loan balance due on a small business loan) of the business. Balance sheets fluctuate constantly due to the fluid and changing nature of business income and expenses. Corporate forms of businesses develop balance sheets monthly. Monthly balance sheet preparation is not required for simpler forms of businesses (e.g., sole proprietorships, partnerships, LLCs) yet is a sound accounting practice and very useful for the ongoing financial planning and monitoring of any business. A new business start-up and business plan should show the initial month's balance sheet when the business opens.

Before proceeding to a review of a standard balance sheet used by typical small businesses, it is important to note that there are several major exceptions to a standard balance sheet, cash flow, depreciation of capital items, and taxable income that apply to business owners with disabilities who apply for and receive VR/WIA funding to start their businesses. VR/WIA policies in this area of start-up support in each state vary considerably around the United States, so the following information is also based on the conditions applied in each state and sometimes even by each local VR/WIA counselor within each state. Several key questions need to be asked of each VR/WIA counselor for each business start-up and are discussed as they apply in each of the following sections. Generally, business start-up support from VR/WIA falls into three possible categories:

1. Large expenditures for capital assets, such as capital equipment, that VR/WIA purchases for the business start-up. Examples are large equipment or start-up inventory purchases.

2. VR/WIA prepaid expenses, such as goods, benefits, or services VR/WIA buys or rents in advance. Examples are office supplies, insurance protection, and floor space.

3. Smaller, recurring, nonprepaid operating expenses, such as VR/WIA payment for goods, benefits, or services each month as they occur (not in advance) during the first 1–12 months of business start-up operations. This may occur for a longer period of time if VR/WIA continues to pay for recurring business expenses beyond the first 12 months of business operations, which is unlikely yet possible in some situations. Examples are ongoing business rent and monthly operating expenses.

Large Expenditures for Capital Assets

When paid for by VR/WIA funds, large expenditures for capital assets may involve local or state VR/WIA restrictions on the "ownership of the capital asset," in which VR/WIA retains ownership of the asset for some agreed-on period of time or upon completion of negotiated performance goals met by the business owner. Here are the key questions that need to be asked of and answered by local VR/WIA counselors at this point:

When a local VR/WIA counselor purchases large assets for a business, does VR/WIA retain ownership of the asset/equipment? If VR/WIA retains ownership, then when and/or under what circumstances does ownership transfer to the owner from VR/WIA?

For instance, VR/WIA in some states retains ownership of a capital asset purchased for a business through a negotiated depreciable life of the asset. Often VR/WIA calls this agreement, which is generally put in writing, a "loan" of the equipment from the agency to the business owner for a specific period of time (with no "loan payments" due to VR). In such a case, if VR/WIA purchased an $18,000 mobile hot dog sales cart for a business start-up in January 2003, depreciated that asset on paper for 60 months at $300 depreciation per month, and "loaned the cart at no cost" to the business owner until it was fully depreciated, then the following balance sheet entries would be required for the first 2 months (and every month thereafter for 60 months, reducing the value of the asset by $300 per month each month for VR/WIA purposes).

It is important to note that as long as VR/WIA retains ownership of an asset, the owner's equity in the business is neither increased nor decreased by the asset that VR/WIA owns. Also, it is critical to understand that the asset is not actually being depreciated from a tax standpoint, as VR/WIA owns the asset and it cannot be depreciated by the business until VR relinquishes ownership of the asset to the business owner. When VR/WIA transfers ownership to the business owner, even if VR/WIA believes the asset to be fully depreciated (from their perspective or agreement negotiated with the business owner), the asset becomes the owner's property. It may have a fair market value at the time of transfer, which could be depreciated from that point forward using standard IRS depreciation schedules.

Balance Sheet

Company: <u>Mobile Hot Dog Sales</u>

As of: <u>January 31, 2003</u>

ASSETS

Mobile hot dog sales cart: **$17,700**

($18,000 less a $300 adjustment similar to $300 of depreciation each month, based on a 60-month schedule [60 x $300 = $18,000], which cannot be used for tax reduction purposes while VR/WIA retains ownership of the asset)

LIABILITIES

VR/WIA: **$17,700**

(Not actual depreciation but a value assigned that needs to equal the previously given VR/WIA adjustment to assets in the balance sheet)

Balance (assets minus liabilities):   **$0**

Balance Sheet

Company: <u>Mobile Hot Dog Sales</u>

As of: <u>February 28, 2003</u>

ASSETS

Mobile hot dog sales cart: **$17,400**

($18,000 less a $600 adjustment similar to $300 of depreciation for 2 months, based on a 60-month schedule, which cannot be used for tax reduction purposes while VR/WIA retains ownership of the asset)

LIABILITIES

VR/WIA: **$17,400**

(Not actual depreciation but a value assigned that needs to equal the previously given VR/WIA adjustment to assets in the balance sheet)

Balance (assets minus liabilities):   **$0**

For instance, using the previous example, after 60 months, the value of the mobile hot dog sales cart asset will be "$0.00" according to VR/WIA's agreement with the business owner, and VR/WIA will transfer ownership to the owner. The owner in this situation has not been able to deduct depreciation for tax purposes for the entire 60 months due to VR/WIA owning the asset for 60 months. On the 61st month, when VR/WIA transfers ownership to the business, a fair market value can be assigned to the mobile cart and the business can begin to deduct IRS-allowed depreciation from the business taxable income based on the fair market value of the asset at the time it becomes the owner's property. If the fair market value of the cart is $6,000 at month 61, then the owner can set up a 60-month depreciation schedule for "used equipment" and begin to deduct $100 in depreciation each month from that point forward. A new balance sheet will be required to accommodate the ownership of the asset starting at $6,000 in month 61 and the actual $100 depreciation per month of the asset for the following 60 months (versus the prior 60 months, during which the asset was not actually being depreciated for IRS tax purposes and was only being reduced in value on paper for VR/WIA purposes).

In some situations, VR/WIA negotiates with the business owner to release ownership of the asset to the business owner upon completion of certain business performance goals. For example, if VR/WIA agrees to relinquish ownership of the mobile hot dog sales cart when the owner achieves earnings more than $800 for 10 months (and the owner does earn more than $800 per month in the first 10 months of business operations), then the balance sheet and fixed assets in the business will change significantly in the eleventh month. To illustrate this very significant change in transfer of ownership option that VR/WIA may agree to with the business owner, the same mobile hot dog sales cart example, altered to show changes in the tenth and eleventh months of business operations, is used. The balance sheet would appear as follows in October and November of 2003 (when VR/WIA transfers ownership of the asset to the business owner on the eleventh month).

Balance Sheet

Company: <u>Mobile Hot Dog Sales</u>

As of: <u>October 31, 2003</u>

ASSETS

Mobile hot dog sales cart: $15,000
($18,000 less $3,000 based on $300 less
VR/WIA value/month for 10 months)

LIABILITIES

VR/WIA: $15,000
(VR/WIA still retains ownership in October)

Balance (assets minus liabilities):　　　**$0**

Balance Sheet

Company: <u>Mobile Hot Dog Sales</u>

As of: <u>November 30, 2003</u>

ASSETS

Mobile hot dog sales cart: $14,750
($15,000 fair market value at time of transfer of ownership to the small business from VR/WIA less an actual IRS-allowed $250 depreciation per month for the new actual IRS-approved period of 60 months depreciation)

Depreciation reserve account: $250
(When VR/WIA transfers ownership at the fair market value of $15,000, the operating cash in a business account of a profitable business will increase to compensate for the $250 of depreciation; the assets value is reduced by $250 to $14,750 that month, which reduces the net taxable earnings of the business by $250 and increases the cash assets in the business by $250. A common practice is to track the monthly accumulated depreciation in a depreciation reserve account.)

Total assets: $15,000

LIABILITIES

Owner's equity: $15,000
(VR/WIA transfers ownership to the business owner and the cart's fair market value of $15,000 becomes part of the net worth/owner's equity in the business. The $15,000 owner's equity remains a constant $15,000 for this asset from this point forward, unless the owner withdraws some or all of the owner's equity in the business.)

Total liabilities: $15,000

Balance (assets minus liabilities): $0

It is critical to note that in November of 2003 (and beyond), the prior business liability to VR/WIA from January through October of 2003 significantly changes to an "owner's claim on assets"—that is, a liability of the business to the owner when VR/WIA relinquishes its ownership claim on the mobile hot dog cart in November. Whenever VR/WIA relinquishes its claim on or transfers ownership of assets to a business owner, not only does the monthly balance sheet change significantly, but also the owner's equity, cash flow, and business profits and losses change dramatically from that point forward. This is because the owner now has a personal claim on the asset and the asset's depreciation can be used as a tax deduction after VR transfers ownership of the asset to the business. The new IRS-allowed depreciation begins at the time of transfer, based on the fair market value of the asset. In this example, the fair market value of the asset at time of transfer was considered to be $15,000. The asset is then treated as used equipment (versus new equipment) for depreciation purposes and is depreciated over a standard 60-month depreciation schedule at $250 per month for 60 months (60 × $250 = $15,000) starting in No-

vember of 2003 (versus the prior $300 per month value reduction of the asset during the first 10 months when VR/WIA owned the asset).

Smaller VR/WIA Prepaid Expenses

The second category, smaller VR/WIA prepaid expenses (e.g., goods, benefits, or services a business buys or rents in advance), needs to be tracked on a balance sheet but cannot be used as business expenses for tax purposes. These expenses cannot be used as business expenses because VR/WIA pays for them directly and the owner has no receipts for the business expenses to write off as tax deductions. Generally, VR/WIA does not retain ownership of these prepaid items or services and, therefore, the value of the prepaid expenses becomes an asset to the business and also a liability to the business in the form of owner's equity, where both values are reduced as the prepaid items or services are used each month. An example might be VR/WIA agreeing to support the business start-up by prepaying $3,000 for the first 6 months of office space rent at $500 per month during the first month the business opens. The balance sheet tracks the prepaid rent by VR/WIA in this example as follows.

Balance Sheet

Company: <u>Mobile Hot Dog Sales</u>

As of: <u>January 31, 2003</u>

ASSETS

Prepaid rent: $2,500

($3,000 prepaid rent by VR/WIA, less $500 for January rent)

LIABILITIES

Owner's equity/prepaid rent: $2,500

($3,000 prepaid rent by VR/WIA, less $500 for January rent)

Balance (assets minus liabilities): $0

Smaller, Recurring, Nonprepaid Operating Expenses

The third category—smaller, recurring, nonprepaid operating expenses (e.g., VR/WIA payment for goods, benefits, or services each month as they occur but not prepaying the expenses months in advance), generally does not need to be tracked on a balance sheet. The effects of VR/WIA paying for recurring operating expenses will alter the owner's net earnings, which is transferred to the balance sheet from the P&L statement, but the actual VR payments in this case are not directly entered or tracked on the balance sheet. When VR/WIA pays for a monthly recurring expense, it cannot be used as a business expense for tax purposes and, therefore, has the effect of increasing the owner's income. VR/WIA payments for recurring operating expenses artificially increase the net earnings of the business in the month the expenses are paid for by eliminating the expenses from the normal operating costs for the business during that month.

Balance Sheet

Company: Mobile Hot Dog Sales_____

As of: February 28, 2003_____

ASSETS

Prepaid rent:	$2,000
($3,000 prepaid rent by VR/WIA, less $500 for January and $500 for February rent)	

LIABILITIES

Owner's equity/prepaid rent:	$2,000
($3,000 prepaid rent by VR/WIA, less $500 for January and $500 for February rent)	

Balance (assets minus liabilities):	**$0**

There are many public sources for information on balance sheets for business plans. The SBA's web site offers a balance sheet format with instructions (go to http://www.sbaonline.sba.gov/starting/indexbusplans.html).

Break-Even Analysis

A break-even analysis is used in business planning, tracking, and decision making for a wide variety of applications. It is typically required for at least two purposes during the development of a business plan and a business start-up:

1. To determine the amount of gross sales required to pay for all business expenses during each predicted year of business operations

2. To determine the amount of gross sales required to pay for all business expenses during an average month in each predicted year of business operations

The information required for a break-even analysis is derived from the monthly and yearly P&L detailed income and expense projections for the business in a business plan. After the business is operating, a break-even analysis is based on actual income and expense information each month (and each year) and is a very useful tool to use at least once every 6 months or as often as once each month.

From the business plan P&L projections or actual information when a business is operating, particular sets of information and a certain process is required to develop a break-even analysis. The first set of information needed for a break-even analysis is the gross profit margin (GPM) of a business expressed as a percentage. The GPM percentage is derived from the gross sales of the business less the COGS. The COGS consist of any expense directly related to one unit of sales. As a simple example using Earl's High Performance Lawn Care, the average (per unit of sales) lawn "gross sales" price is $10 per lawn. In this example, the COGS are the costs associated with mowing each lawn (but do not include the owner's labor in this sole proprietorship) and are estimated to be $1.00 per lawn. This figure comes from the average cost of gas and oil for the lawn mower for each lawn mowed. The GPM, expressed as a decimal percentage, is then calculated as follows:

Earl's COGS per unit sold (i.e., per lawn mowed) = $1.00 (for gas and oil per each lawn mowed)

Earl's gross sales per lawn (i.e., what Earl charges to mow one lawn) = $10.00

The following formula always uses 1 as a constant because it is calculating an inverse percentage. Percentages less than 100% are initially expressed as their decimal equivalent, which is always less than 1. This approach may sound difficult, but it is actually fairly simple to calculate the GPM percentage by using the formula and steps:

1. GPM% = [1 − (COGS/gross sales)] × 100
2. GPM% = [1 − ($1.00 COGS/$10.00 gross sales)] × 100
3. GPM% = [1 − ($1.00/$10.00)] × 100
4. GPM% = [1 − 0.1] × 100
5. GPM% = 0.9 × 100

    GPM% = 90%

The second set of information needed for a break-even analysis is an estimate (or actual information, if available) of the total fixed operating costs of the business. Fixed operating costs of the business are the business operating expenses that do not vary with each sale, such as a business telephone/fax, transportation, business insurance, monthly office space rent and utilities, advertising, administrative salaries, interest on business loans, and office supplies. Fixed operating costs are those costs that are needed regardless of the number of sales per month or year. In Earl's business, the average monthly fixed costs are estimated to be $200 transportation, $60 telephone/fax, $100 advertising, $50 office supplies, and $40 business liability insurance for a total of $450 per month or $5,400 per year ($450/month × 12 months) in fixed costs.

Using $5,400 per year (or $450 per month in fixed costs) and a GPM of 90% (0.9), the break-even point for the year and for each month can be calculated. The break-even point is a result of dividing the fixed costs by the GPM decimal percentage. Thus, the yearly break-even point in this case is the fixed costs/ year of $5,400 divided by the GPM of 0.9 = $5,400/0.9 = $6,000. For Earl to break even and pay for all of his business expenses, he needs to sell at least $6,000 per year in lawn mowing services. His monthly average gross sales to break even needs to be at least $450/0.9 = $500 average sales per month.

After completing a break-even analysis, it is possible to evaluate a few key pricing and operational cost variables to see if the business can break even and also generate an income for Earl that will work for his business and income goals. Earl estimates that each lawn will take 30 minutes to mow, plus an additional 10 minutes to get to and from each lawn, with contracts set up in local areas for small yards in close proximity. He projects that he will mow an average of 10 lawns per day at $10 per lawn = $100 per day, times an average of 20 days per month = 200 lawns per month at $10 per lawn = $2,000 per month gross sales. Earl's GPM is 90% or 0.9 × $2,000 = $1,800 per month, less his fixed costs (operating expenses) of $450/month results in Earl earning ($1,800 − $450) = $1,350 per month for 200 lawns per month. His yearly owner's draw before taxes is $1,350 × 12 = $16,200. Earl mows 200 lawns per month at 40 minutes per lawn = 8000 minutes/60 minutes = 134 hours of direct lawn mowing work per month. Earl's income before taxes and hourly rate is a factor of the $1,350 monthly owner's draw (his earnings from the business operations), divided by 134 hours = $10.08 per hour when he is mowing lawns.

Assuming Earl is also engaged in business sales and operations management activities for an additional 26 hours per month, his hourly rate is actually $1,350 divided by 160 hours per month = $8.43 per hour. In a sole proprietorship (also applies to a partnership or LLC), Earl cannot be paid wages as the owner of his business and is actually paid an owner's draw each month. It is useful to compare his owner's draw income to what it would be as an hourly wage to get an idea if Earl is earning the amount of income that he would like to earn and, if not, what needs to be reevaluated or altered to increase his income.

Assuming that Earl is not satisfied with his break-even analysis, he has three options to lower his break-even point and thereby earn increased profits:

1. Earl can work on lowering his direct costs (COGS), which in this example is the $1.00 for gasoline and oil per lawn and the time it takes to mow each lawn. He could evaluate perhaps purchasing a larger and more efficient lawn mower that cuts more lawns faster, reduces the time to mow each lawn by 5 minutes, and reduces the gas and oil requirements per lawn from $1.00 to $0.75 per lawn. If Earl lowered his direct cost to $0.75 per lawn, his GPM would increase to 0.925 (or 92.5%) from 0.9 (90%) and his break-even point would be reduced from $500 per month to $486 per month.

2. Evaluating Earl's fixed costs and potentially lowering them is another option that would increase his profit and lower his break-even point. If Earl reduced his telephone and transportation costs by $50 per month total, his fixed costs would be lowered to $400 per month, and his break-even point would change from $500 per month to $444 per month. If Earl were to combine the changes in his reduced direct costs (given in the first option) with the changes proposed to his fixed costs, his break-even point would be reduced from $500 per month to $432 per month.

3. The third option to lower Earl's break-even point would be for Earl to increase his prices. Even a small 5% change in pricing will increase his profits and lower his break-even point. If Earl charges 5% more per lawn at $10.50 per lawn, his break-even point is lowered from the original $500 per month to $452 per month.

If Earl incorporates all three options, his break-even point is lowered to $430 per month or $5,160 per year (compared with $500 per month and $6,000 per year). Applying the new lowered break-even analysis figures to Earl's projected number of lawns per year plus one extra lawn mowed per day (240 more sales per year due to the time savings of his new faster equipment) results in yearly gross sales of $27,720 at a GPM of 0.928 (92.8%) or $25,724 GPM, with operating expenses (fixed costs) of $4,800 for an owner's draw (net profit) of $20,924 (versus his original projection of $16,200 net profit/owner's draw). Earl's comparative hourly rate for 128 direct hours (6 hours less than the original 134 direct hours due to his increased efficiency) of lawn mowing plus 26 hours of business management activities now totals 154 hours of work per month (versus 160) and increases to $11.31 per hour versus $8.43 per hour. His monthly owner's draw before taxes increases from $1,350 per month to $1,743 per month.

The results of his efforts to lower his break-even point equate to an increase of $393 per month in additional profits through implementing the changes outlined previously from his break-even point analysis. Assuming he needs to purchase the new, more efficient lawn mower to accomplish the increased efficiency part of his changes and the lawn mower costs $1,572 (from a fairly simple view of such a purchase not including potential depreciation options), his investment in his new lawn mower is paid for in the first 4 months of business operations, yielding a 4-month return on his investment (ROI) into more efficient capital equipment.

In the business plan development stage of Earl's business, using the given analysis of the three potential options for lowering Earl's break-even point (assuming they are applied based on solid facts and prove to be reasonably predictable) could justify in his business plan the need and the expected quick 4-month ROI for a more efficient lawn mower in the start-up month of his business. Such an analysis would also potentially affect a slight 5% sales price increase and a reduction in operating (fixed) costs.

In the operational stages of Earl's business, as he experiences actual sales and actual business expenses, a break-even analysis using the same approach could certainly be used to develop practical financial decision information after the first few months of business operations. Using a break-even analysis to assist with ongoing interactive business management decisions is a common business practice. Break-even analyses often produce timely and relevant information that can be used to stabilize business operations in unprofitable times, invest in improvements and new equipment, and support changes that reduce the break-even point of a business and increase profits.

There is a balance that needs to be created in any business between financial decision support tools and nonfinancial decision support tools. For instance, cutting advertising expenses and Internet support personnel expenses as a result of break-even analysis financial data could appear to be useful in the short run from a simple short-term cost-cutting perspective during cyclical low earnings months of operations. In the long run, however, it could cause employees and customers to lose confidence and eventually produce substantial losses in employee turnover and service or product sales. Although a break-even analysis is a fairly simple and very practical financial tool needed in most businesses, it is only one financial analysis tool from a variety of broader financial and non-financial management tools in any business. Understanding and using a break-even analysis is important in business plan development and in most ongoing business operations over time, yet it certainly needs to be tempered with all other possible financial and nonfinancial management decision tools and processes.

Income Projections (Profit and Loss Statements/Projections)

Business plans submitted to obtain loans or VR/WIA funding support generally require a 3-year summary of all P&L projections in detail by month for the first year and then are detailed by quarters (every 3 months) in the second and third years. VR/WIA may in some situations require shorter, less formal projections, such as only 6–12 months of projections based on state policy differences and individual VR/WIA counselor's discretion. State and local VR/WIA policies vary widely on criteria and often have multiple criteria based on the amount of funding requested.

If a business plan is being submitted to SSA for potential PASS funding, SSA by policy uniformly in each state requires at least 1 year's P&L projections past the end of the PASS timeline for funding. PASSes for small business start-up support funding tend to last at least 18 months per SSA/PASS policy yet can be approved for shorter or longer periods of time; sometimes, PASSes are retroactively approved. Because 18 months is the average length of small business PASSes, adding a year onto 18 months for P&L projections results in 30 months of P&L projections detailed by month as a minimum required by SSA. The result typically is that P&L projections for PASS funding requests are detailed, month-by-month projections for 36 months.

P&L projections in a business plan's financial section generally are the detailed financial results derived from the sales and expense assumptions and goals of the business outlined in the earlier research, business idea/niche, pricing, and sales and marketing sections of the business plan. For instance, at this point in the business plan development process, it is prudent to assume that the lawn care business based its assumption of 10 to 11 customers' lawns projected to be mowed each day on reasonable sales and expense projection data. These data likely came from local surveys, local and national lawn mowing business research and statistics, a few trial sales, a few repeat customers already under contract, and some potential customers who have confirmed their intent to contract once the business is officially open for business. Essentially, a substantial amount of the business plan preparation and research effort has been completed, and it is now time to clearly organize and synthesize the business sales and expense information gathered to date into a set of financial projections. It is critical at this stage to have supporting rationale for business income and expense projections. Simply stating a capacity to mow 11 lawns per day is generally not enough rationale. However, as noted previously (from all of the prior work in the business plan process), sound back-up rationale for projections from multiple sources and methods gives income and expense projections a critically needed level of credibility for the business owner to develop sound financial projections confidently.

During the process of developing P&L projections, it is important for the PBO and BDT to develop a P&L narrative that explains the research and assumptions used for estimating future sales and expenses. The P&L projections can and generally should also be compared with industry standards for similar businesses when the P&L projections are developed and refined. When comparing the projections to industry standards, any significant variances from industry standards could help a PBO and BDT to discover over- or underestimated sales and expense projections. If there are significant variations that are not considered to be over- or underestimated, then it is useful to develop a narrative to explain the differences compared to industry averages.

Often, PBOs with disabilities apply for and receive significant free start-up funds from VR, WIA, and/or the SSA. Free start-up funding, which is not a factor in industry standards, tends to significantly alter expense and income entries in a P&L statement in the areas of depreciation, COGS, operating costs, GPM, net profit, and owner's draws. The result is that comparisons of the P&L projections for the PBO's business to industry standards may be (and often are) significantly skewed or vary widely from the industry standards during the start-up period of the business while the PBO is receiving free start-up financial support. In some areas, such as asset depreciation, the effects of VR/WIA retaining ownership of a major capital asset purchase for its depreciable life in some situations could alter the average net earnings for up to 5 years or more. If VR/WIA retains ownership of an asset, then the asset cannot be depreciated while VR/WIA owns it. As an example, an $18,000 asset required to operate a specific business that is depreciated at a rate of $300 per month for 5 years would, in an average industry standard business profile, reduce taxable net income by $3,600 per year. If VR/WIA retains ownership of that asset, then the asset cannot be depreciated and the owner's draw and net profits are increased by $3,600 each year for 5 years. In a business that is projected to earn $14,400 per year, the net profit is significantly altered compared with industry standards if $3,600 of the business earnings are inflated taxable net income due to not deducting the $3,600 depreciation of the capital asset that VR/WIA owns each year for the first 5 years.

There are a variety of methods and options for gaining access to industry standard comparison information. Trade associations may provide industry standard information to their members and guests and can be obtained from the Internet. See the Industry Standard Information section of Appendix B (at the end of the book) for some useful web sites that include such information (most charge a fee) that could save research time. SBA's web site also suggests traditional research at local libraries: "The reference librarian in your nearest public library can refer you to documents that contain the percentage figures, for example, Robert Morris Associates' Annual Statement Studies" (from http://www.sbaonline.sba.gov/starting/indexbusplans.html).

At first glance, the recommendations to find industry standards for similar businesses for a PBO and BDT may seem overwhelming, unnecessary for a small business, and time consuming. There is at least one short cut that can provide a quick general industry standard comparison for starters: the more general yet limited free industry standard data and tools on the free BizStats.com web site (http://www.BizStats.com). To illustrate the relative ease of obtaining some comparison data, after using BizStats.com for 5–10 minutes, Earl could locate and print some quick general comparison data tailored to his gross sales projections. On the site's home page, there is a bold "Benchmark Your Business in 5 Seconds!" note with an entry form area where Earl can enter the expected yearly gross sales from his business sales projections. Using the rough projections in the last break-even analysis section of this chapter, Earl would enter $27,200 as his estimated gross sales projections. He would then scroll through a small list and select a broad category for services related businesses. Assuming that Earl then selects the category of service-related businesses and refines that to the closest match of services (real estate), the web site results would then provide the following business comparison statistics tailored to his yearly gross sales projection of $27,200.

The P&L for Earl's lawn care business, as roughly estimated so far in the initial example break-even analysis, has resulted in a 7.2% COGS, which was derived previously in this chapter from an estimate of $0.75 for gas and oil for each sale of $10.50 for mowing a small residential lawn in his target/niche mar-

Services: Real estate	Average profitability	Expense percentage
Total revenue (sales)	$27,720	100.0%
Total expenses as percentage of revenue	$13,201	47.6%
Net income to owner as percentage of revenue	$14,519	52.4%
Detail of expenses (as percentage of revenue)		
Cost of goods sold (COGS)	$1,715	6.2%
Salaries and wages	$375	1.4%
Advertising	$948	3.4%
Auto and truck expenses	$1,855	6.7%
Depreciation	$660	2.4%
Employee benefits	$34	0.1%
Home office business expenses	$160	0.6%
Insurance	$164	0.6%
Interest expense	$221	0.8%
Legal and professional services	$245	0.9%
Meals and entertainment	$293	1.1%
Office expense	$633	2.3%
Retirement plans	$29	0.1%
Rent–equipment	$216	0.8%
Rent–office and business property	$339	1.2%
Repairs	$156	0.6%
Supplies	$359	1.3%
Taxes–business and payroll	$159	0.6%
Travel	$229	0.8%
Utilities	$567	2.0%
Other expenses	$3,842	13.9%
Total expenses as percentage of revenue	$13,201	47.6%

Source: BizStats.com (http://www.BizStats.com).

ket. Earl's 7.2% COGS estimate seems to compare reasonably well with the industry standard of 6.2% noted in the table of BizStats.com industry standard data. COGS can vary widely from almost 0% to 90% in different industries. Earl's estimate is quite close at less than a 1% variance from the average (7.2% versus 6.2%). Earl can feel somewhat confident that his COGS may be in the correct range compared with a general related industry average. In reviewing the comparison of net earnings, Earl notices that his initial estimate of net earnings of $20,924 varies significantly from the industry standard of $14,519 net income to the owner. Such a wide variance is a red flag that there may be something incorrect in Earl's estimates or in the general industry average that he selected on the web site for business comparison, or there may be a skewed variance that may be due to his projected use of free start-up funds from VR/WIA or SSA. Another red flag that Earl notices is the industry standard, which has 20 operating expense line items to operate a business similar to Earl's, yet Earl currently projects only 5 operating expense line items. With such a significant variance, Earl decides to review his operating expense projections to evaluate whether there may be more expenses required to operate his business than his original estimated expenses for telephone calls, insurance, transportation, advertising, and office supplies.

This quick research and rough comparison analysis, which is based on a broad industry category from only a few possible choices, might be inaccurate, and a more accurate comparison could be desired. If so, Earl will need to research a possible free industry standards report at his local library or on trade association web sites, or he will need to purchase an industry standard report that is as close as possible to a lawn mowing industry standard. There is a Standard Industry Classification (SIC) number for lawn mowing (782) and North American Industry Classification System (NAICS) number for lawn mowing (561730), so Earl can obtain a much more refined industry standard set of data for more accurate comparison with his business P&L. His business may not compare precisely, even with exact SIC and NAICS code matches, because industry standard averages for income levels as low as his business plan is projecting are generally not clearly represented in large data profiles/reports. Earl and his BDT may be able to effectively use the general related services industry data from BizStats .com but probably will not need to (although may choose to) gather additional comparison standards at this point due to the small size of Earl's business. If Earl's business plan/design grows into a larger business operation, there will be a logical point at which gathering much more specific industry standard comparison data will probably be an essential element of his business plan.

Developing and modifying a P&L projection on a monthly basis for 1–3 years can be accomplished easily with spreadsheet software, commercial business plan writing software such as Biz Plan Pro, and manual paper methods. Free P&L spreadsheet public access files are available on the web in a number of places. These preformatted, free spreadsheets work well with the customized information supplied in this chapter regarding SSA, VR, and WIA impacts. The three web sites included under "Spreadsheet Public Access Files" in Appendix B at the end of the book also include free templates for all other related financial business planning tools (e.g., break-even analysis, cash flow, balance sheet).

The 12-month P&L spreadsheet on page 173 illustrates Earl's lawn care business income and expense projections for the first year of operations. Earl revised his earlier projections to accommodate for a series of expenses he had not considered until he reached this stage of his planning process. In the far right column of the table, the general industry standard percentages he researched on BizStats.com are recorded in all of the areas he was able to locate standards data. The standard percentages are compared with his actual projection percentages two columns over from the right. Overall, Earl's gross and net profits are very close to the industry standards.

Earl's P&L statement is now completed for the first year of operations. Because Earl plans on using a PASS to support his business start-up for the first 12 months of his business, he will also need to complete at least one more year of detailed month-by-month P&L projections per SSA PASS policy. He will also need to complete a quarterly P&L set of projections for his third year of operations.

To demonstrate both general business P&L practices and adjusted practices for VR, WIA, and SSA effects on P&L, there are a number of expenses included in Earl's projections illustrating how various general business operating income and expenses are accounted for monthly/yearly, as well as examples of how VR/WIA and SSA/PASS expenses are accounted for monthly/yearly. Earl's P&L example also works well for individuals who do not receive VR/WIA or SSA funding support, yet the example would need to be adjusted to remove the variances caused by the VR/WIA and PASS adjustments illustrated in the P&L projections. The following list illustrates the major steps taken to create Earl's projections.

1. Earl carefully listed both the expected gross sales and contract sales that he expects to receive from customers who contract with his company for ongoing lawn mowing services and for individual customers who prefer not to be bound by a contract yet purchase his services each month.

2. Next, Earl projected his COGS each month from his estimate of $0.75 per lawn to arrive at his COGS estimates.

3. He then calculated his gross profit each month by subtracting his COGS from his revenue (sales) projections.

4. Earl expects both VR and SSA/PASS financial support for his business start-up and estimates that support to be $12,960 from VR and $6,900 from SSA/PASS. A common error at this point is to list PASS and VR funds as income to the business. Notice in Earl's P&L projections that VR and PASS funds are not listed as income. The reason is that neither source of start-up funds is derived from sales of the business and should never be listed on a P&L statement as income. PASS and VR/WIA funds are accounted for on cash-flow projections but not on P&L projections.

5. Earl then lists all of his expected fixed (or operating) expenses *except* expenses paid for or expected to be paid for by VR. Any expense expected to be paid for by VR is removed from the P&L fixed expenses with a notation on the left describing the equipment and purchase price that has been removed from the projections. In Earl's P&L projections, three expenses are

12-month profit and loss (P&L) for Earl's High Performance Lawn Care in 2003 (in dollar amounts)

	Jan.	Feb.	Mar.	Apr.	May	June	July	Aug.	Sept.	Oct.	Nov.	Dec.	Actual percentage	Total	Standard percentage
Revenue (Sales)															
Lawn mowing yearly contract sales	1,260	1,260	1,260	1,680	1,680	1,680	1,680	1,680	1,680	1,680	1,680	1,680		$18,900	
Lawn mowing individual sales	210	210	420	630	840	1,050	1,260	1,260	1,050	840	630	420		$8,820	
Total revenue	1,470	1,470	1,680	2,310	2,520	2,730	2,940	2,940	2,730	2,520	2,310	2,100	100	$27,720	100
Cost of goods sold (COGS)															
Oil and gasoline at $0.75/ yard mowed	105	105	120	165	180	195	210	210	195	180	165	150	7.2	$1,980	6.2
Gross profit	1,365	1,365	1,560	2,145	2,340	2,535	2,730	2,730	2,535	2,340	2,145	1,950	92.8	$25,740	93.8
Expenses															
Contract labor (Virtual Assistant)	100	100	100	100	100	100	100	100	100	100	100	100	4.4	$1,200	1.4
Advertising ($480 VR first month)	0	90	90	90	90	90	90	90	90	90	90	90	3.6	$990	3.4
Auto and truck expenses	200	200	200	200	200	200	200	200	200	200	200	200	8.7	$2,400	6.7
Depreciation (PASS—purchased truck; 60 months x $105)							105	105	105	105	105	105	2.5	**$630**	2.4
Employee benefits													0	$0	0.1
Home office business expenses													0	$0	0.6
Insurance ($480 VR first month)	0												0	$0	0.6
Interest expense													0	$0	0.8
Legal and professional services	125	25	25	50	25	50	100	100	125	100	100	200	3.7	$1,025	0.9
Meals and entertainment	50	50	50	50	50	50	50	50	50	50	50	50	2.2	$600	1.1
Office expenses	60	60	60	60	60	60	60	60	60	60	60	60	2.6	$720	2.3
Retirement plans													0	$0	0.1
Rent—equipment			100			100			100			100	1.4	$400	0.8
Rent—PASS paid $400	100	100	100	100	100	100	100	100	100	100	100	100	4.4	$1,200	1.2
Equipment (VR first month $12,000)	0													**$0**	
Repairs—PASS paid $200	50	50	50	50	50	50	50	50	50	50	50	50	2.2	$600	0.6
Supplies	40	40	40	40	40	40	40	40	40	40	40	40	1.7	$480	1.3
Taxes—business and payroll													0	$0	0.6
Travel													0	$0	0.8
Utilities													0	$0	2.0
Other expenses	55	55	55	55	55	55	65	65	65	65	65	65	2.6	$720	13.9
Total operating expenses	780	770	870	795	770	895	960	960	1,085	960	960	1,160	39.5	$10,965	41.4
Net profit (before taxes)	585	595	690	1,350	1,570	1,640	1,770	1,770	1,450	1,380	1,185	790	53.3	$14,775	52.4

removed from his P&L projections: $12,000 for the purchase price of the major business equipment (lawn mowers, trailer, and trimmers) in January 2003; $480 for business insurance expense for 1 year, prepaid in January 2003; and $480 for advertising expenses in January 2003 for a telephone book business listing. Because Earl has the option of claiming all $12,000 in equipment expenses as business operating expenses due to the IRS allowance for up to $25,000, he notes that this expense was paid for by VR in his operating expense columns.

6. Next, Earl identifies any operating expenses expected to be paid by the SSA through his PASS. These expenses are left as operating expenses in the P&L sheets (versus VR-paid expenses that are removed from the P&L operating expense categories). Capital item expenses paid for by a PASS that are planned to be depreciated over time are not listed in P&L sheets. Only the depreciation is listed on P&L projections. Earl is using his 12-year-old personal car with a trailer until the PASS generates enough to make a down payment in June to purchase the needed pickup truck and then pay off the 6-month note on the balance owed to a local bank by the end of 2003. Earl expects to purchase the $6,300 pickup truck in June 2003 (using a 6-month note from his bank) for his business as a capital item purchase, so he lists neither the down payment nor the monthly payments for the truck as operating expenses. He does, however, identify the $105 monthly depreciation expenses in his P&L projections as being paid for by PASS funds. Unlike VR-paid expenses, expenses paid for by PASS funds are left in the P&L projections and are simply noted or shown in bold print, indicating that PASS funds are expected to pay for the related expenses.

7. Earl totals all of his monthly/yearly expenses and then subtracts those totals from his gross profit to determine his net profits. In this example, Earl's business earns a profit of $14,775 in its first year of operation. If VR does not fund Earl's request for $12,960 and PASS does not fund his request for $6,900, then Earl will not be able to start his business because he will not have the needed equipment. Assuming that Earl just receives $552 SSI to live on in the beginning of 2003 (and SSI requires his personal cash assets to be below $2,000 in saving or checking accounts), he would have no resources or equity to leverage a bank loan and will not be able to acquire the funds needed to start his business. His projected $14,775 without $12,960 from VR and $6,900 from SSA would equate to a business loss for his first year and, logistically, without the needed equipment, he could not even start the business.

8. Earl begins to prepare his request to VR to pay for the equipment, start-up insurance, and advertising that VR can fund within their policies. Earl prepares a PASS request for the SSA to fund his pickup truck, as SSA polices allow for the purchase of a vehicle with PASS funds, including loan interest and operating costs. However, Earl is not finished yet; he still needs to prepare a cash-flow analysis projection to evaluate whether he has the needed cash each month to operate his business. Cash flow is often considered the most critical survival concern of any business. Cash-flow projections address the actual monthly cash available and address multiple other business expenses not covered in P&L projections.

9. Before proceeding to cash-flow projections, a final P&L projections note needs to be stated concerning depreciation. Large capital equipment and vehicle purchases can be depreciated over time, usually across 5–7 years, with 5 years as a general guideline. Depending on the expense and IRS laws, it is possible in small business to deduct up to $25,000 in capital purchases in 1 year. Yet, it often may be more prudent in the long run to not write off such an expense in 1 year but, instead, to depreciate the cost of that item over perhaps 60 months. Depreciation is an important component of P&L projections and needs to be accounted for in P&L. However, depreciation is not accounted for in cash-flow projections because it is not an actual expense. Some variations of these policies exist when accountants use net profit from the P&L projections to create a short cut for cash-flow projections. When such short cuts are used, depreciation needs to be added back in to cash-flow projections, as it was used to reduce net earnings in the P&L projections. This chapter does not use such short cuts and, therefore, depreciation will not appear anywhere on the cash-flow projections that follow in the next section. In either case, depreciation is not an actual cash exchange. The cash result of using depreciation is to lower taxable income (which results in less cash paid to the owner as net earnings) while increasing operating cash by monthly building a reserve of actual cash available (not paid to the owner as net earnings). This provides funds to replace the needed equipment or vehicle in some future time frame, such as in a typical 5-year depreciation approach. Depreciation is a very useful and important strategy for someone receiving SSI monthly cash benefits because that person cannot save or have more than $2,000 in a personal cash each month but can have unlimited funds in a business account. If depreciation is not used and a capital purchase is written off completely in 1 year for an item purchased only once by PASS or VR/WIA (versus slowly over time), then the net effect is that the owner will have no other personal means to save for the replacement of the capital item. Depreciation of any depreciable asset is recommended for any-one receiving one-time VR/WIA or SSA start-up funding support, and it is highly recommended for anyone receiving SSI cash benefits. P&L projections account for depreciation, as demonstrated in Earl's P&L. The actual purchase of the related capital item is not found in P&L projections, however, and is accounted for in cash-flow projections. In the next section on cash-flow, the purchase of the pickup truck, depreciated in the P&L projections, is shown in the cash-flow projections as a capital purchase and coordinates the two sets of projections.

Cash-Flow Projections

Cash-flow projections, similar to P&L projections, can be developed by using free, preformatted spreadsheet software; by purchasing commercial business plan development software; or manually on paper. The web sites listed under "Spreadsheet Public Access Files" in Appendix B contain free spreadsheet software for cash-flow projections and links to sites where popular commercial business plan writing software can be purchased on line. Cash-flow projection spreadsheets start with the sales and expense information used in the P&L projections, then expand that information considerably.

To demonstrate both general business cash-flow projection practices and adjusted practices for VR, WIA, and SSA effects on cash flow, a number of expenses are included in Earl's projections, illustrating how various general business operating income and expenses are accounted for monthly/yearly, plus examples of how VR/WIA and SSA/PASS expenses are accounted for monthly/ yearly. Earl's cash flow example also works well for individuals who do not receive VR/WIA or SSA funding support, yet the example would need to be adjusted to remove all of the variances caused by the VR/WIA and PASS adjustments illustrated in the cash-flow projections. The major points illustrated by Earl's projections are as follows:

1. Cash-flow projections add an additional column for tracking "Pre-start-up" cash equity infusions (in this case, Earl's personal savings, which he uses to start the business) and any purchases or expenditures prior to the first month of starting the business. The process of cash-flow projections and analysis of the projections tends to change based on information derived from developing different cash-flow impacts from monthly sales and expenses. Earl had approximately $1,600 in personal savings and was not sure if he needed to use some, none, or all of his savings to start his business, even with VR/ WIA and SSA/PASS financial support. His first cash-flow projections showed a negative cash ending balance in the second month of operations (his business was broke by the second month and not able to pay its bills) without some other cash, so Earl tried adding $500 to his projections from his personal savings. That took care of his second month, but in his third month he was broke again. He tried several different starting cash amounts and found that a $1,500 cash infusion from his personal savings to start the business worked well and that he had the needed cash in his savings account. Earl also could have increased his request to VR for start-up funding support in the first few months to solve his initial cash-flow problems, but he decided instead to use his personal savings.

2. Earl still had a concern that even with the $1,500 start-up cash he personally uses for his business, in his sixth month of operations he was dangerously close to not having enough cash. His ending cash in the sixth month was only $1,144 and did not allow much room for error. Part of the problem was created by his calculated and fairly fixed owner's draw each month. Earl already understood from his P&L projections that he expected the business to produce $14,775 net earnings and felt comfortable with his P&L projections and believed them to be accurate, conservative projections. Because Earl receives SSI and SSI averages all net profits or net earnings for the year evenly over every month, Earl needs to receive his full owner's draw ($1,231 per month × 12 months = approximately $14,775) each month for three reasons. First, he needs to fund his PASS of $575 per month, which is based on recovering his SSI check reduction of the full SSI check amount of $552. Due to his earnings, he needs to be able to set aside $575 from his net earnings evenly every month in his PASS equity infusion. Second, if he were to not use a PASS, then his SSI of $552 would be reduced to $0 each month and he would still be very close to not being able

to cover his monthly living expenses. Third, based on his P&L earnings projections, Earl also needs to set aside roughly 20% of his owner's draw/ earnings each month to pay his estimated quarterly self-employment and income taxes personally (20% × $1,231 = $246 taxes). The net income result for Earl is that every month, he is evenly paid his calculated $1,231 owner's draw as his business income, plus he receives $552 SSI (due to his projected PASS) for a total income of ($1,231 + $552) = $1,783. Earl's monthly personal and tax expenses are $246 for self-employment and income taxes; $575 monthly PASS expenses; and $780 minimum room and board expenses, which increased from $552 prior to his business based on his expected HUD Section 8 rent increase (due to his projected income) and his food stamp reductions. Earl's total projected personal expenses are ($246 + $575 + $780) = $1,601. The result of his personal income less expenses is ($1,783 income − $1,601 expenses) = $182 remaining discretionary income. Earl cannot afford to not pay himself his projected net earnings averaged evenly over every month. If he does not pay himself through his owner's draw (the income he projects to SSA, HUD, food stamps), he will not have enough income to use his PASS, pay taxes, pay rent, or buy food. However, Earl still has the business cash-flow dilemma of being dangerously close to not having enough cash in June 2003, so he decides that out of his remaining after-tax income of $182 per month, he will add back into his business $100 per month as an owner's equity contribution to the business. By adding back in $100 per month from his after-tax personal funds by June, he now projects that $1,744 will be left in his business account at the end of the month instead of only $1,144.

3. Following down the first month (January) after his owner's equity monthly $100 cash infusion, VR's payments in Earl's first month for his business insurance, advertising, and capital equipment are entered. It is important to note that VR does not actually give him the funds, and this is a significant deviation from standard cash-flow practices. To account for this deviation from standard practice (in the center "Cash paid out" section, where operating expenses are listed), VR is again noted on the left-hand side expense descriptions as paying for the three expenses. However, the expenses cannot be claimed as business expenses, as VR keeps the receipts. Instead, an entry of $0 expense is input for an expense in January, whereas without VR funding support, the same expenses would have been paid from gross sales earnings in any other business. In the lower section of the January cash flow column, the same amounts are noted once more as a "Cash flow out expense" to cash flow (not to earnings) to account for adding the exact same VR contribution amount in the beginning (upper) "Cash on hand" section in January. It may seem like a lot of work to add VR funds in to the cash flow and then take them right back out, yet it has proven effective to do the extra few entries and work required to clearly show the effect of VR support to banks, VR, the SSA, and the IRS.

4. The next January entry in the upper "Cash on hand" section is the PASS amount of $575 per month. PASS is not income to any business and is actually a cash equity infusion into the business that is assigned by the PASS document and the SSA to occur monthly to accumulate, then pay for ex-

12-month cash flow for Earl's High Performance Lawn Care in 2003 (in dollar amounts)

	Pre–start-up	Jan.	Feb.	Mar.	Apr.	May	June	July	Aug.	Sept.	Oct.	Nov.	Dec.	Total
Cash on hand (beginning of the month)	0	1,500	1,529	1,568	1,702	2,496	3,510	1,744	2,488	3,232	3,656	4,009	4,167	
Owner's cash equity infusion	**1,500**	**100**	**100**	**100**	**100**	**100**	**100**	**100**	**100**	**100**	**100**	**100**	**100**	**$2,700**
VR–insurance	**480**													**$480**
VR–advertising	**480**													**$480**
VR–business and equipment purchase	**12,000**													**$12,000**
PASS/SSA cash infusion	**575**	**575**	**575**	**575**	**575**	**575**	**575**	**575**	**575**	**575**	**575**	**575**	**575**	**$6,900**
Cash sales receipts	1,470	1,000	1,200	1,500	1,620	1,730	1,840	1,840	1,730	1,620	1,500	1,400		$18,450
Collections from credit accounts		470	480	810	900	1,000	1,100	1,100	1,000	900	810	700		$9,270
Total cash available (before cash paid out)	16,605	3,674	3,923	4,687	5,691	6,915	5,359	6,103	6,637	6,851	6,994	6,942		
Cash paid out														
Oil and gasoline at $0.75/ yard mowed	105	105	120	165	180	195	210	210	195	180	165	150		$1,980
Contract (Virtual Assistant)	100	100	100	100	100	100	100	100	100	100	100	100		$1,200
Advertising–VR paid $480	**0**	**90**	**90**	**90**	**90**	**90**	**90**	**90**	**90**	**90**	**90**	**90**		**$990**
Auto and truck expenses	200	200	200	200	200	200	200	200	200	200	200	200		$2,400
Employee benefits														$0
Home office business expenses														$0
Insurance–VR paid $480	**0**													**$0**
Interest expense														
Legal and professional services	125	25	25	50	25	50	100	100	125	100	100	200		$1,025

Table (landscape orientation). Columns: Start, months 1–12, and Total.

Item	Start	1	2	3	4	5	6	7	8	9	10	11	12	Total
Meals and entertainment		50	50	50	50	50	50	50	50	50	50	50	50	$600
Office expenses		60	60	60	60	60	60	60	60	60	60	60	60	$720
Retirement plans														$0
Rent—equipment		100			100			100			100			$400
Rent—PASS paid $400		**100**	**100**	**100**	**100**	**100**	**100**	**100**	**100**	**100**	**100**	**100**	**100**	**$1,200**
Repairs—PASS paid $200		**50**	**50**	**50**	**50**	**50**	**50**	**50**	**50**	**50**	**50**	**50**	**50**	**$600**
Supplies		40	40	40	40	40	40	40	40	40	40	40	40	$480
Taxes—business and payroll														$0
Travel														$0
Utilities														$0
Other Expenses		55	55	55	55	55	55	65	65	65	65	65	65	$720
Subtotal		835	875	990	960	950	1,090	1,065	1,065	1,175	1,035	1,020	1,205	$12,315
VR—"loaned equipment" (not depreciable until VR transfers ownership on 12/31/2003)		12,000												$12,000
VR—first month insurance		480												$480
VR—first month advertising		480												$480
PASS—capital equipment purchase (pickup truck)							2,850							$2,850
$3,450 loan payments—paid by PASS								575	575	575	575	575	575	$3,450
Owner's draw		**1,231**	**1,231**	**1,231**	**1,231**	**1,231**	**1,231**	**1,231**	**1,231**	**1,231**	**1,232**	**1,232**	**1,232**	**$14,775**
Total cash paid out	0	15,076	2,106	2,221	2,191	2,181	5,171	2,871	2,871	2,981	2,842	2,827	3,012	$46,350
Cash position—end of month	1,500	1,529	1,568	1,702	2,496	1,744	2,488	3,232	3,656	4,009	4,167	3,930		

penses or to pay monthly for expenses for only SSA-approved and agreed-on specific business start-up expenses. It is important to understand that PASS funds affect cash flow dramatically but are not listed on P&L projections, just on cash-flow projections and impacts. A bonus feature of PASS funds is that while they are accumulating to pay for a large item, such as the truck in Earl's business, the same funds also help stabilize cash flow in the early months of the business operations, which are often low income producing months as the business gets started. If a PASS is planned well and worked into cash flow and the design of the business, it also adds significant cash equity to a profitable business over time. PASS is often a critical financial component for someone who receives SSI or both SSI and SSDI and is starting any profitable business. Due to the interactions of SSI and net income averaging noted previously, if Earl's PASS is not used, his business will be short $6,900 in funding from the PASS. Because his ending cash at the end of the year when using a PASS is $3,390, if $6,900 is subtracted out, Earl will end up going out of business due to a ($6,900 − $3,390) = a $3,510 lack of cash. (He would be short $3,510 and run out of money in the first few month of business operations.) As noted in the previous section, if Earl does not pay himself all of his net earnings, that does not solve his cash-flow problems. In fact, it makes them worse, and he would not be able pay his rent. PASS funds balanced with VR/WIA funding create very favorable conditions for operating a cash solvent business for someone receiving SSI.

5. The center "Cash paid out" section of the cash-flow projections parallels any standard business cash flow and accounting for expenses from the P&L projections, except for a few entries related to VR-paid expenses. VR-affected lines have been bolded to show their impacts in the cash-flow projections.

6. In Earl's example, VR has chosen to release the equipment purchased by VR to him at the end of the last month of the first year of operations. VR had Earl sign an agreement that he was "conditionally borrowing and using" the equipment for the first year. Therefore, the equipment cannot be depreciated until the second year Earl is in business, at which point the fair market value at the time that VR transfers ownership to Earl will be established. Earl can depreciate the equipment from that point forward as "used equipment." Used equipment is important because it cannot be written off in a single year under the $25,000-maximum gauge that the IRS allows for "new equipment purchases." Earl will need to set up depreciation schedules that are allowable by the IRS in 2004 when VR transfers the ownership to him. As noted previously, depreciation is not entered on cash-flow projection sheets, but depreciation entered in a P&L and net income analysis does affect cash flow by causing more cash to be available for the business each month and over the years (due to reducing taxable earnings and thereby reducing owners' draws). Depreciation increases operating cash for the purchase of replacement equipment in the future. Often on balance sheets and cash-flow sheets, a "depreciation reserve account" is set up to show the extra cash as an expense in cash flow. This also allows a business owner to track the excess cash (created by depreciation effects) in balance sheets to ensure that funds are available for future equipment purchases.

SAMPLE FINANCIAL DOCUMENTS

This section provides sample financial documents to summarize the concepts discussed in this chapter. The samples are based on the example business of Earl's High Performance Lawn Care.

Date: January 1, 2003   Business: Earl's High Performance Lawn Care

Source of funds	Amount requested	Use of funds
Vocational Rehabilitation (Grant/not a loan)	$12,960	Capital equipment: $12,000 Advertising: $480 Business insurance: $480
Social Security–PASS (Grant/not a loan)	$6,900	Used pickup truck: $6,900 (including interest on short-term note)
6-Month bank note (Short-term $3,400 loan)	*	*Used pickup truck: 6-month loan for $3,400 paid by monthly PASS funds noted above; already in $6,900 total PASS
Personal cash equity	$2,700	Start-up $1,500 Total monthly equity infusion $1,200
Total	$22,610	$22,610

Loan applications (including SSA, VR, and WIA as potential free funding).

Date: January 1, 2003   Business: Earl's High Performance Lawn Care

Item	Cost	Use of item/expense
Capital equipment	$12,000	Required mowing, trimming, and miscellaneous tools, including a two-wheel trailer
Advertising	$480	First month: prepaid 12-month telephone book listing
Business insurance	$480	Business liability insurance: 12 months prepaid
Used pickup truck	$6,900	Business vehicle required to transport equipment
Operating cash	$2,700	Initial operating expenses, contract labor, mileage, legal, office expenses, office and equipment rent, repairs, supplies, and miscellaneous expenses
Total	$22,610	

Start-up budget, capital equipment, and start-up expenses list.

Balance Sheet

Company: <u>Earl's High Performance Lawn Care</u>

As of: <u>January 31, 2003 (end of first month)</u>

ASSETS

Current Assets

Cash:	$1,529
VR-prepaid expenses ($960–$80 for 1 of 12 months):	$880
Total current assets:	$2,409

Fixed (Long-Term) Assets

VR equipment (less one month $200 VR value reduction):	$11,800
Adjustment due to VR ownership of asset until 12/31/03:	–$11,800
Total fixed assets:	$0

Total assets:	**$2,409**

LIABILITIES

Current Liabilities

(VR-owned equipment less 1 month value reduction):	$11,800
Adjustment due to VR ownership until 12/31/03:	–$11,800
VR-prepaid expenses (less 1 of 12 months):	$880
Total current liabilities:	$880

Long-Term Liabilities

None	$0
Total liabilities:	**$880**

NET WORTH

Owner's initial $1,500 equity:	$1,500
Owner's personal monthly paid in equity:	$100
Owner's PASS monthly paid in equity:	$575
*Retained earnings:	–$646
Total net worth:	**$1,529**
TOTAL LIABILITIES AND NET WORTH:	**$2,409**

*Note: Retained earnings = –$646 in January due to a low first month net profit of $585, less an owner's monthly draw of $1,231, which reduces owner's equity by $646

Balance sheet for the end of the first month of operations, January 2003.

Balance Sheet

Company: <u>Earl's High Performance Lawn Care</u>

As of: <u>December 31, 2003 (end of twelfth month)</u>

ASSETS

Current Assets

Cash:	$3,930
Total current assets:	$3,930

Fixed (Long-Term) Assets

Equipment: VR transferred ownership to owner on 12/31/03 at fair market value of $9,600 (as used equipment):	$9,600
Equipment: $6,300 truck (net after $630 depreciation):	$5,670
Total fixed assets:	$15,270
Total assets:	**$19,200**

LIABILITIES

Current Liabilities	$0
Long-Term Liabilities	$0

NET WORTH

Equipment transferred 12/31/03 from VR liability to owner's equity:	$9,600
Owner's initial $1,500 equity:	$1,500
Owner's personal $100 monthly paid in equity:	$1,200
Owner's PASS $575 monthly paid in equity:	$6,900
Retained earnings	$0
Total net worth:	**$19,200**
TOTAL LIABILITIES AND NET WORTH:	**$19,200**

Balance sheet for the end of the first year projections, December 2003.

Break-Even Analysis

Company: <u>Earl's High Performance Lawn Care</u>

As of: <u>January 1, 2003</u>

Note: The following cost of goods sold (COGS) percentage and fixed expenses information is from Earl's High Performance Lawn Care's 12-month profit and loss (P&L) and cash flow projections.	
V% Expressed as a percentage of yearly variable expenses (COGS)	7.2%
<u>V</u> Expressed as a decimal conversion (COGS/100) or (V%/100)	<u>0.072</u>
F Total Yearly Fixed (Operating) Expenses	$10,965
Note: Break even = F/(1 − V)	
Yearly revenue (sales) required to break even (with no owner's draw)	$11,816
Monthly revenue (sales) required to break even (with no owner's draw)	$985
Yearly revenue required to break even with additional fixed expenses of $14,775/year as the projected yearly profits/owner's draw	$27,720
Monthly revenue required to break even with additional fixed expenses of $1,231/month as the projected monthly profits/owner's draw	$2,311

Break-even analysis.

For a sample 12-month P&L spreadsheet, see page 173. For a sample 12-month cash flow spreadsheet, see pages 178–179.

CONCLUSION

At this point, the two core components of a business plan are completed: 1) the narrative and 2) the five business financial documents (loan applications, start-up expenses, break-even analysis, P&L projections, and cash-flow projections). If business loans or investors are involved in the business start-up, then banks and investors typically require a personal financial statement from each owner or major stockholder summarizing personal assets and liabilities outside of the business. Owners with disabilities who also receive SSI, SSDI, Medicaid, Medicare, housing assistance, or other related benefits will also need a completed benefits analysis as outlined in Chapter 6.

This stage of the business planning process often feels like the end, yet is actually the beginning of the financial work involved in operating a small business. A well-developed and sufficiently funded business start-up moves quickly from the planning stages into the daily financial activities of running a business. Several of the financial documents generated in the business planning stage now become critical long-term financial planning, tracking, and monitoring tools. First, the cash-flow projections need to be tracked and compared with the actual cash flow of the business at least monthly. Some business owners track cash flow weekly and even daily and adjust for changes in actual versus projected cash flow as quickly as possible. P&Ls are important to investors and business owners, and actual P&Ls certainly need to be compared with projected P&Ls. Yet employees, creditors, and suppliers want to be paid in cash, and most have little or no awareness or interest in the P&L aspect of businesses.

Constant attention is required to maintain accurate records of expense receipts; payments to suppliers/creditors; invoices sent to customers; and income paid in cash, by check, or by credit card. As noted previously in this chapter, a variety of commercially available software is available for tracking small business finances. Also, the free web site spreadsheets (preformatted for small businesses) noted in this chapter are quite useful as a starting point and even as an ongoing tracking set of tools. Using Earl's business as an example, if his cash flow and P&Ls were created on the free spreadsheets, it would be a fairly simple financial task to copy those files and create an "actual" spreadsheet to compare with the "projected spreadsheet" created from the business plan. Thus, with almost no financial investment in software, a reasonable system can be set up on a computer not only to account for income and expenses, but also to compare actual versus projected values and use that information for business decisions as needed.

Generally, even when using the best software, some manual filing and accounting systems need to be set up in most businesses. At least one checking account that is only used for the business is highly advised, even in the smallest and simplest business. Some small businesses do get started using the owner's personal checking account when business income and expense are commingled with all other daily personal finance activities. This certainly seems simple and less costly in the short run but often can be a problem in the long run. Spending hours going through personal checkbook entries to discover which entry (income or expense) was related to a small business can be frustrating and is clearly not a standard business practice. For a business owner receiving SSI, SSDI, Medicaid, or any other social system support, mixing business income and expenses in a personal checking account can cause serious financial and health care coverage issues. Anyone receiving SSI and/or Medicaid while operating a business needs to open and use a separate checking account for his or her business. Those two benefit systems interact in financially painful ways with business income and expenses commingled with personal checking and savings accounts. Chapter 6 addresses setting up and using a checking account for a business from a SSI/Medicaid benefits perspective, and the reader should review this information again if applicable.

Next, there is the issue of saving for and paying income and self-employment taxes to the IRS. More often than not, the IRS is the number one reason to set up and use some sort of reliable accounting system for a business. A typical error of a new small business owner is to not track profits and net business income, then pay too little or no taxes to the IRS. Self-employment income (versus wage income when working for someone else as an employee) requires quarterly tax payments to the IRS based on as accurate as possible estimates of net profits (owner's income) yearly, which are paid in four quarterly payments to the IRS. The funds for paying taxes are deductions from the owner's draw and owner's income even if not taken out of the business. In this chapter's example, Earl needs to set aside an accurate estimated tax percentage of his monthly $1,231 owner's draw (calculated roughly in the example as being 20% for taxes, or $246 for taxes) to pay his taxes every 3 months (3 × $246 = $738). However, if Earl spends his entire owner's draw each month personally, he will owe the IRS $738 each quarter but not have the funds to pay the IRS. If he does not pay his taxes, then he will owe the IRS 4 × $738 = $2,952 after 1 year. The IRS will not only want his taxes paid but also will probably charge him penalties and interest for late payments. It could take the IRS a while to catch up with Earl; if it takes the IRS a few years, he could easily owe the IRS $10,000–$50,000 or almost any amount, as the penalties and interest accumulate on the tax debt that he owes the IRS.

SSI and SSDI pose the same type of risks and repayment problems if income is not tracked and accounted for appropriately. If Earl does not account for and report his income and expenses timely and accurately, SSI or SSDI cash benefits could be lost completely. Also, Medicaid health care could be lost, and Earl could owe large sums of funds to those systems just as he could owe the IRS if he does not pay his taxes. Financial benefits planning for a business owner receiving social systems benefits is a critical tool that can avoid problems and assist in creating unlimited individual equity wealth in a profitable small business.

FINAL THOUGHTS

Unlimited wealth? There's an idea! It seems like it might be helpful to get used to the word *profit,* too, because it shows up all over the place in small business activities. Is unlimited wealth possible? Is it all around each of us? It appears to be right there and then it is gone again. We know it is there, somewhere. It seems logical that unlimited wealth is also all around PBOs with disabilities, as we-are-they and they-are-we (and we all kind of know that intuitively). Plus, not to hurry you along too much, just in case you've not noticed yet, the entire trip we call life is pretty short. Wealth and business creation are interconnected. The genesis of each can only be found in a single PBO's mind. Every new business first started in someone's thoughts. No doubt about it—the future is waiting, and we hope that you think it is time to stop wasting so many lives and business ideas in the thoughts of close to half the world's minds. What was your last business idea? What's your current idea? Perhaps tomorrow there will be another idea, then another, and perhaps so many people (with or without disabilities) somewhere near you right now have so many business ideas at this very instant that unlimited wealth does exist all around. So, what are you thinking? We are thinking we would like to thank you for your interest in self-employment and *Making Self-Employment Work for People with Disabilities!* We certainly wish you all the best in all that you do!

Thank you!
Cary and Dave

Afterword

In the not too distant past, individuals with significant disabilities lived in state institutions and nursing homes and only attended special schools. There was a time when people with significant developmental disabilities were considered unemployable in the competitive labor force. Fortunately, since the 1960s, there has been gradual and steady progress away from such segregation toward policies and practices that foster inclusion in society. Advocacy, research into practice, and legislation have facilitated these policies and practices. The advocates recognized that these abuses were wrong, and individuals such as Blatt and Kaplan (1966), Boggs (1959), Taylor (1988, 2001), and Wolfensberger (1972), led efforts to change these practices. The research that gradually led to better practices in the field was led in education by Brown and colleagues (e.g., Brown & York, 1974); in employment by Bellamy, Horner, and Inman (1979), Gold (1973), and Wehman (1981); and in community living and participation by Bradley, Ashbaugh, and Blaney (1994) and Bruininks and Lakin (1985). The statutes include the Education for All Handicapped Children Act of 1975 (PL 94-142), the Americans with Disabilities Act (ADA) of 1990 (PL 101-336); the Rehabilitation Act of 1973 (PL 93-112) and its amendments in 1986, 1992, and 1998 (PL 99-506, PL 102-569, PL 105-220); and the Ticket to Work and Work Incentive Improvement Act (TWWIIA) of 1999 (PL 106-170).

Advocacy, research into practice, and legislation became the critical foundation for people with significant developmental disabilities to be recognized as viable citizens with real human potential who should be educated with their peers in neighborhood schools (Wehmeyer & Patton, 2000). This foundation was the bedrock for creating the concept of supports—that is, accept people where they are and build the necessary network of supports around them. From this, the practices of supported employment (Wehman, 1981) and supported living (e.g., Bauer & Smith, 1993) grew, and, eventually, the entire definition of *mental retardation* changed (American Association on Mental Retardation [AAMR], 1992, 2002). As of 2003, the definition reflects the necessity of supports in determining the level of mental retardation that one exhibits. The definition takes into account that people with appropriate amounts of support will not exhibit "mentally retarded" behaviors (AAMR, 2002). This evolution has direct bearing on how self-employment has become an increasingly viable option.

The growth of competitive employment, as well as other inclusive employment options as outcomes for people with significant disabilities since the 1990s, has been fostered by the ADA, which promotes full community inclusion for people with disabilities. Because of the ADA, the Supreme Court upheld *Olmstead v. L.C.* (1999), a landmark community inclusion decision. However, the impact of this growth in competitive employment outcomes is still relatively small when compared with the total number of people with disabilities who work in segregated or sheltered employment settings. For example, *The State of the States in Developmental Disabilities: 2000 Study Summary* (Braddock, Hemp, Parish, & Rizzolo, 2000) reported that in fiscal year 1998, state mental retardation/developmental disabilities (MR/DD) agencies served approximately 372,000 individuals in day programs or sheltered employment. In comparison, these agencies served roughly 97,500 people in supported/competitive employment. Thus, an approximate 4:1 ratio of noncompetitive to competitive work outcomes exists for people served by MR/DD agencies.

For individuals served through the Medicaid Home and Community-Based (HCB) Waiver, West et al. (2002) indicated that in fiscal year 1999, only 15% of the more than 130,000 people receiving day habilitation services through the HCB Waiver were in supported employment. The rest were in a variety of day habilitation service categories that were not competitive work oriented and, frequently, not inclusive. These reports demonstrate that for many people with significant disabilities, being served in segregated settings continues to be the dominant experience. Many of these people receive SSI or SSDI as well or have been hard to serve previously (Institute on Community Inclusion, 2002). Unfortunately, hundreds of thousands of people with disabilities remain in segregated centers. Many more are on waiting lists for employment despite the fact that people with significant cognitive, physical, and behavioral challenges have demonstrated their competence in the workplace (Abery, 1994).

With this in mind, it is noteworthy that Cary Griffin and David Hammis have developed a refreshingly new approach to helping people with significant disabilities become employed. In *Making Self-Employment Work for People with Disabilities*, Griffin and Hammis have taken the concept of support for integrated and competitive employment to a higher level: one that is more innovative and provides greater control and empowerment over one's life. Arguably, owning one's business *is* the American dream in terms of being able to control one's work conditions and see the direct result of the time invested into the amount of pay, economic self-sufficiency, and benefits attained. There is a much greater outcome associated with self-employment, however: the self-esteem that results from knowing that you designed, created, and implemented a new entity that responds to a community need. This is the type of productive contribution that the Supreme Court justices sought in *Olmstead v. L.C.* (1999) and will yield higher levels of awareness by other community members toward people with disabilities. Owning a business or being a stakeholder in a business helps to significantly demystify the concept of disability. When an individual plays a guitar and sings so well that these musical services are in frequent demand in the community, for example, that person's multiple sclerosis, paraplegia, or Asperger syndrome becomes irrelevant. These are only clinical labels that have been applied by professionals but are surpassed through competence in the world of work. All work is good, all work has value—but work by people who own their own businesses, employ others, pay taxes, and can show an increasing stake of business ownership is truly a personal and societal contribution.

With that said, many questions linger about self-employment for people with disabilities. Griffin and Hammis do an outstanding job of dispelling stereotypes and, more important, providing the nuts and bolts for creating businesses: careful analysis of community needs, careful benefits planning, careful personnel recruitment and training, and use of important resources such as small business and other economic development programs that are available to all people—with or without disabilities.

Although this book has many strengths, perhaps the greatest is the underlying and continually present theme of universality. The authors never consider that people with disabilities cannot start and run their own businesses successfully. The book's rich case studies present a positive scenario. There is no sense that it is impossible, no caveats of failure; instead, there are only constructive and well-planned strategies for success. We strongly recommend this book for providers who aspire to help people with disabilities move to a higher level of success in the community, as well as for individuals with disabilities themselves. It is an outstanding piece of work.

Paul Wehman, Ph.D.
Professor of Physical Medicine and Rehabilitation
Director of the Rehabilitation Research
and Training Center on Workplace Supports
Virginia Commonwealth University, Richmond

John Kregel, Ed.D.
Professor of Special Education
Associate Director and Research Director
of the Rehabilitation Research and
Training Center on Supported Employment
Virginia Commonwealth University, Richmond

REFERENCES

Abery, B.H. (1994). A conceptual framework for enhancing self-determination. In M.F. Hayden & B.H. Abery (Eds.), *Challenges for a service system in transition: Ensuring quality community experiences for persons with developmental disabilities* (pp. 345–380). Baltimore: Paul H. Brookes Publishing Co.

American Association on Mental Retardation. (1992). *News and Notes, 5*(1), 1–8.

American Association on Mental Retardation. (2002). *Mental retardation: Definition, classification and systems of supports* (10th ed.). Washington, DC: Author.

Americans with Disabilities Act (ADA) of 1990, PL 101-336, 42 U.S.C. §§ 12101 *et seq.*

Bauer, L., & Smith, G.A. (1993). *Community living for the developmentally disabled: State legislative report, 18* (12), 1–6.

Bellamy, T., Horner, R., & Inman, D. (1979). *Vocational training of severely retarded adults.* Austin, TX: PRO-ED.

Blatt, B., & Kaplan, F. (1966). *Christmas in purgatory: A photographic essay on mental retardation.* Boston: Allyn & Bacon.

Boggs, E.M. (1959). *Decade of decision.* New York: National Association for Retarded Children.

Braddock, D., Hemp, R., Parish, S., & Rizzolo, M. (2000). *The state of the states in developmental disabilities: 2000 study summary.* Chicago: University of Illinois, Department of Disability and Human Development.

Bradley, V.J., Ashbaugh, J.W., & Blaney, B.C. (Eds.). (1994). *Creating individual supports for people with developmental disabilities: A mandate for change at many levels.* Baltimore: Paul H. Brookes Publishing Co.

Brown, L., & York, R. (1974). Developing programs for severely handicapped students: Teacher training and classroom instruction. *Focus on Exceptional Children, 6*(2), 1–15.

Bruininks, R.H., & Lakin, K.C. (Eds.). (1985). *Living and learning in the least restrictive environment.* Baltimore: Paul H. Brookes Publishing Co.

Education for All Handicapped Children Act of 1975, PL 94-142, 20 U.S.C. §§ 1400 *et seq.*

Gold, M. (1973). Vocational Habilitation for the Mentally Retarded. In N. Ellis (Ed.), *International review of research in mental retardation: Vol. 6.* New York: Academic Press.

Individuals with Disabilities Education Act (IDEA) Amendments of 1997, PL 105-17, 20 U.S.C. §§ 1400 *et seq.*

Institute on Community Inclusion. (2002). *Report prepared by Dana Gilmore on Rehabilitation 911 Database related to MR/DD clients on SSI/SSDI.* Unpublished manuscript, University of Massachusetts, Boston.

Olmstead v. L.C., 119 S. Ct. 2176 (1999).

Rehabilitation Act Amendments of 1986, PL 99-506, 29 U.S.C. §§ 701 *et seq.*

Rehabilitation Act Amendments of 1992, PL 102-569, 29 U.S.C. §§ 701 *et seq.*

Rehabilitation Act Amendments of 1998, PL 105-220, 29 U.S.C §§ 701 *et seq.*

Rehabilitation Act of 1973, PL 93-112, 29 U.S.C. §§ 701 *et seq.*

Taylor, S.J. (1988). Caught in the continuum: A critical analysis of the principle of the least restrictive environment. *Journal of The Association for Persons with Severe Handicaps, 13*(1), 45–53.

Taylor, S.J. (2001). The continuum and current controversies in the USA. *Journal of Intellectual & Developmental Disability, 26*(1), 15–33.

Ticket to Work and Work Incentive Improvement Act (TWWIIA) of 1999, PL 106-170, 42 U.S.C. §§ 1305 *et seq.*

Wehman, P. (1981). *Competitive employment: New horizons for severely disabled individuals.* Baltimore: Paul H. Brookes Publishing Co.

Wehmeyer, M., & Patton, J. (2000). *Mental retardation in the 21st century.* Austin, TX: PRO-ED.

West, M., Hill, J., Revell, G., Smith, G., Kregel, J., & Campbell, L. (2002). Medicaid HCB waivers and supported employment: Pre- and post-Balanced Budget Act of 1997. *Mental Retardation, 40*(2), 142–147.

Wolfensberger, W. (1972). *Principles of normalization.* Toronto: National Institute for Mental Retardation.

References

Access to Credit. (1998). *Small enterprise, big dreams* [Videotape]. Frederick, MD: Access to Credit Media Project.

Americans with Disabilities Act (ADA) of 1990, PL 101-336, 42 U.S.C. §§ 12101 *et seq.*

Arnold, N. (Ed.). (1996). *Self-employment in vocational rehabilitation: Building on lessons from rural America.* Missoula: Rural Institute, The University of Montana.

Bivins, B. (1994). *Operating a really small business: An owner's guide.* Menlo Park, CA: Crisp Publications.

Blohowiak, D. (1995). *How's all the work going to get done?: Now that your company has downsized, restructured and reengineered.* Franklin Lakes, NJ: Career Press.

Brodsky, N. (February, 2002). Street smarts: Opportunity knocks [Electronic version]. *Inc.* Retrieved February 2002 from http://www.inc.com

Brown, L., Branston, M., Hamre-Nietupski, S., Pumpian, I., Certo, N., & Gruenwald, L. (1979). A strategy for developing chronological age appropriate content for severely handicapped adolescents and young adults. *Journal of Special Education, 13,* 81–90.

Brown, L., Udvari-Solner, A., Frattura-Kampschroer, L., Davis, L., Ahlgren, C., Van Deventer, P., & Jorgensen, J. (1987). The Madison strategy for evaluating the vocational milieu of a worker with severe intellectual disabilities. In L. Brown, A. Udvari-Solner, L. Frattura-Kampschroer, L. Davis, & J. Jorgensen (Eds.), *Educational programs for students with severe intellectual disabilities* (Vol. XVII, pp. 1–372). Madison, WI: Madison Metropolitan School District.

Butterworth, J., Gilmore, D., Kiernan, W., & Schalock, R. (1999). *State trends in employment services for people with developmental disabilities.* Boston: Institute for Community Inclusion.

Callahan, M.J., & Garner, J.B. (1997). *Keys to the workplace: Skills and supports for people with disabilities.* Baltimore: Paul H. Brookes Publishing Co.

Callahan, M.J., & Nisbet, J. (1997). *The vocational profile: An alternative to traditional evaluation.* Gautier, MS: Marc Gold & Associates.

Doyel, A.W. (2000). *No more job interviews: Self-employment strategies for people with disabilities.* St. Augustine, FL: Training Resource Network.

Education for All Handicapped Children Act of 1975, PL 94-142, 20 U.S.C. §§ 1400 *et seq.*

Etzioni, A. (Ed.). (1998). *The essential communitarian reader.* Lanham, MD: Rowman & Littlefield Publishers.

Forest, M., & Pearpoint, J. (1992). Family, friends, and circles. In J. Nisbet (Ed.), *Natural supports in school, at work, and in the community for people with severe disabilities* (pp. 65–86). Baltimore: Paul H. Brookes Publishing Co.

Forrester, A. (1996). Beyond job placement: The self-employment boom. In N. Arnold (Ed.). *Self-employment in vocational rehabilitation: Building on lessons from rural America* (pp. 1–5). Missoula: Rural Institute, The University of Montana.

Freiberg, K., & Freiberg, J. (1996). *Nuts! Southwest Airlines' crazy recipe for business and personal success.* Austin, TX: Bard Press.

Friedman, S. (1996). *Forming your own limited liability company.* Chicago: Upstart Publishing Company.

Gerson, R.F. (1994). *Marketing strategies for small businesses.* Menlo Park, CA: Crisp Publications.

Gretz, S. (1992). Citizen participation: Connecting people to associational life. In D.B. Schwartz (Ed.), *Crossing the river: Creating a conceptual revolution in community and disability* (pp. 11–30). Cambridge, MA: Brookline Books.

Griffin, C.C. (1999a). *Working better, working smarter: Building responsive rehabilitation programs.* St. Augustine, FL: Training Resource Network.

Griffin, C.C. (1999b). Rural routes: Promising supported employment practices in America's frontier. In G. Revell, K.J. Inge, D. Mank, & P. Wehman (Eds.), *The impact of supported employment for people with significant disabilities: Preliminary findings from the National Supported Employment Consortium* (pp. 161–178). Richmond, VA: Rehab Research and Training Center on Workplace Supports.

Griffin, C.C., Flaherty, M., Hammis, D., Katz, M., Maxson, N., & Shelley, R. (2001). *People who own themselves: Emerging trends in rural rehabilitation.* Missoula: Rural Institute, The University of Montana.

Griffin, C.C., & Hammis, D. (1996). *StreetWise guide to person-centered career planning.* Denver, CO: Center for Technical Assistance and Training.

Griffin, C.C., & Hammis, D. (2001a). Choose, launch, grow: Self employment for individuals with psychiatric disabilities. *The Field Report, 14*(1), 1–5.

Griffin, C.C., & Hammis, D. (2001b). What comes after what comes next: Self employment as the logical descendant of supported employment. In P. Wehman (Ed.), *Supported Employment in Business* (pp. 251–267). St. Augustine, FL: Training Resource Network.

Griffin, C., & Hammis, D. (2002). Jimbo's Jumbos: A primer on small business planning. *Journal of Vocational Rehabilitation, 17*(2), 87–96.

Griffin, C.C., Hammis, D., Katz, M., Sperry, C., Flaherty, M., Shelley, R., Snizek, B., & Maxson, N. (2001). *Making the road by taking it: Team and individual exercises for self employment training.* Missoula: Rural Institute, The University of Montana.

Hagner, D., & DiLeo, D. (1993). *Working together: Workplace culture, supported employment, and persons with disabilities.* Cambridge, MA: Brookline Books.

Hammis, D., & Griffin, C.C. (2002). *Social Security considerations for entrepreneurs with significant disabilities.* Florence, MT: Griffin-Hammis Associates, LLC.

Individuals with Disabilities Education Act (IDEA) of 1990, PL 101-476, 20 U.S.C. §§ 1400 *et seq.*

Kawasaki, G. (1995). *How to drive your competition crazy.* New York: Hyperion.

Ketchum, B.W. (Ed.). (1998). *How to really start your own business.* Boston: Inc. Business Resources.

Kroth, J. (2001). Terry's story. In C. Griffin, M. Flaherty, D. Hammis, M. Katz, N. Maxson, & R. Shelley (Eds.), *People who own themselves* (pp. 53–56). Missoula: Rural Institute, The University of Montana.

Mariotti, S. (2000). *The young entrepreneur's guide to starting and running a business.* New York: Times Books.

McGaughey, M., Kiernan, W., McNally, L., Gilmore, D., & Keith, G. (1994). *Beyond the workshop: National perspectives on integrated employment.* Boston: Institute for Community Inclusion.

McKnight, J. (1995). *The careless society: Community and its counterfeits.* New York: Basic Books.

Miyares, U. (2002). Twenty reasons why it's the "best of times" to launch your small business. In C. Griffin, M. Flaherty, D. Hammis, M. Katz, N. Maxson, & R. Shelley (Eds.), *People who own themselves* (pp. 57–61). Missoula: Rural Institute, The University of Montana.

Mount, B. (1987). *Personal futures planning: Finding directions for change.* Unpublished doctoral dissertation, University of Georgia, Athens.

Mount, B. (1994). Benefits and limitations of personal futures planning. In V.J. Bradley, J.W. Ashbaugh, & B.C. Blancy (Eds.), *Creating individual supports for people with developmental disabilities: A mandate for change at many levels* (pp. 97–108). Baltimore: Paul H. Brookes Publishing Co.

Newman, L. (2001). Montana/Wyoming Careers through Partnerships. In C. Griffin, M. Flaherty, D. Hammis, M. Katz, N. Maxson, & R. Shelley (Eds.), *People who own themselves* (pp. 57–61). Missoula: Rural Institute, The University of Montana.

O'Brien, J., & Mount, B. (1991). Telling new stories: The search for capacity among people with severe handicaps. In L.H. Meyer, C.A. Peck, & L. Brown (Eds.), *Critical issues in the lives of people with severe disabilities* (pp. 89–92). Baltimore: Paul H. Brookes Publishing Co.

Olmstead v. L.C., 119 S. Ct. 2176 (1999).

Rehabilitation Act of 1973, PL 93-112, 29 U.S.C. §§ 701 *et seq.*

Shelley, R., Snizek, B., Westfall, M., Newman, L., Griffin, C., & Fogerty, L. (2002). *No lone wolves: Partnering for self-employment success.* Missoula: Rural Institute, The University of Montana.

Sirolli, E. (1999). *Ripples from the Zambezi.* Gabriola Island, British Columbia, Canada: New Society Publishers.

Small Business Administration. (1996a). *Small business growth by major industry, 1988–1995.* Washington, DC: Office of Advocacy.

Small Business Administration. (1996b). *The 3rd millennium: Small business and entrepreneurship in the 21st century.* Washington, DC: Office of Advocacy.

Straughn, G., & Chickadel, C. (1994). *The new American business system.* El Sobrante, CA: Meridian Learning Systems.

Sumner, S. (1999). *Business plan basics: NxLevel guide for micro-entrepreneurs.* Denver, CO: NxLevel Education Foundation.

Taylor, J., & Wacker, W. (1997). *The 500-year delta: What happens after what comes next.* New York: HarperBusiness.

Ticket to Work and Work Incentives Improvement Act (TWWIIA) of 1999, PL 106-170, 42 U.S.C. §§ 1305 *et seq.*

Underhill, P. (2000). *Why we buy: The science of shopping.* New York: Touchstone Books.

U.S. Census Bureau. (2001). *Statistical abstract of the United States: 2001.* On-line edition. Retrieved July 2002 from http://www.census.gov/statab/www

U.S. Department of Commerce. (2000). *Report on small business success.* Retrieved November 2002 from http://www.commerce.gov.

Wehman, P. (2001). *Life beyond the classroom: Transition strategies for young people with disabilities* (3rd ed.). Baltimore: Paul H. Brookes Publishing Co.

Wehman, P., & Kregel, J. (1998). *More than a job: Securing satisfying careers for people with disabilities.* Baltimore: Paul H. Brookes Publishing Co.

Workforce Investment Act (WIA) of 1998, PL 105-220, 29 U.S.C. §§ 2801 *et seq.*

Zyman, S. (1999). *The end of marketing as we know it.* New York: HarperBusiness.

Appendix A

Blank Forms

Background Map
Balance Sheet
Business Concept Refinement Chart
Business Owner Profile Worksheet
Business Promotion Matrix
Business Start-Up Financial Resources
Checklist for Setting Up a Small Business Account and Predicting
   Net Earnings from Self-Employment (NESE)
Dreams Map
Features and Benefits Analysis
Financial Map
Five Senses Exercise
Market Positioning Worksheet
Places Map
Preferences Map
Relationships Map
Skills and Needed Supports
Small Business Benefits Planning Initial Worksheet
Telephone Survey Worksheet
Template for Business Plan

Background Map

Use this map to list the prospective business owner's critical life experiences, the people involved in these experiences, and other relevant information. Family members and the individual are the most critical participants in developing this map of significant personal history.

Where/when I was born

**Significant events in
my life up to this point**

Where I'm headed now

From Griffin, C.C., & Hammis, D. (1996). *StreetWise guide to person-centered career planning* (p. 8). Denver, CO: Center for Technical Assistance and Training; adapted by permission.

Balance Sheet

Company: _____

As of: _____

ASSETS

Current Assets

Cash: _____

Petty cash: _____

Accounts receivable: _____

Inventory : _____

Short-term investment: _____

Prepaid expenses: _____

Long-term investment : _____

Fixed (Long-Term) Assets

Land: _____

Buildings: _____

Improvements: _____

Equipment: _____

Furniture: _____

Automobile/vehicles: _____

Other Assets

1. _____ : _____

2. _____ : _____

3. _____ : _____

4. _____ : _____

Total assets: _____

LIABILITIES

Current Liabilities

Accounts payable: _____

Notes payable: _____

Interest payable: _____

Taxes payable _____

Federal income tax: _____

State income tax: _____

Self-employment tax: _____

Sales tax (SBE): _____

Property tax: _____

Payroll accrual: _____

Long-Term Liabilities

Notes payable: _____

Total liabilities: _____

NET WORTH

Owner equity: _____

Proprietorship or Partnership

(_____ 's) equity: _____

(_____ 's) equity: _____

OR

Corporation

Capital stock: _____

Surplus paid in: _____

Retained earnings: _____

Total net worth: _____

TOTAL LIABILITIES AND TOTAL NET WORTH: _____

Business Concept Refinement Chart

1. My business idea is:		
2. Possible names for my company are:	Name A:	Name B:
3. I like this business idea because:	Reason A:	Reason B:
4. This business makes sense for me to own because:	Reason A:	Reason B:
5. My business will provide the following services/products:	Service A: Service B: Service C:	Product A: Product B: Product C:
6. This business is unique because:	Reason A:	Reason B:
7. Customers will buy my product/service because:	Reason A:	Reason B:
8. I *know* who my customers are because they have already purchased the following from me:	Services sold:	Products sold:
9. I *think* I know who my customers are because they will purchase the following from me:	Services people want:	Products people want:
10. I don't know who my customers are; here's how we'll find out:	Method #1:	Method #2:

Making Self-Employment Work for People with Disabilities by Cary Griffin and David Hammis
© 2003 Paul H. Brookes Publishing Co., Inc. All rights reserved.

Business Owner Profile Worksheet

Past work/business experience:

Talents:

Personal qualities:

Desires (career goals):

Positive personal traits:

Education and training:

Professional and personal interests:

Communication style:

Testimonial statements and letters of recommendation:

From Griffin, C.C., & Hammis, D. (1996). *StreetWise guide to person-centered career planning* (p. 7). Denver, CO: Center for Technical Assistance and Training; adapted by permission.

Business Promotion Matrix

Promotion type	Description	Timing	Cost/benefit
Business cards			
Brochure			
Fliers for public bulletin boards			
Newspaper coupons			
Yellow pages advertisement			
Personal sales calls			
Direct mail			
Telemarketing			
Web page			
Internet auction			
Storefront window signs			
Good customer discount club			
Radio advertisements			

Business Promotion Matrix

Promotion type	Description	Timing	Cost/benefit
Radio interviews			
Press releases			
Civic group membership			
Television advertisements			
Infomercial			
Public access television			
Human interest story			
E-mail advertising and coupons			
Novelties			
Logo			
Presentations at house of worship			
Other:			

Business Start-Up Financial Resources

I. Core programs, available in every state, with free, grant-type resources:

$ _____ Vocational Rehabilitation (VR)

$ _____ Workforce Investment Act (WIA) agencies

$ _____ Social Security Administration (SSA), particularly Plan for Achieving Self-Support (PASS)

II. Personal financial resources:

$ _____ Personal savings and/or trust funds

$ _____ Personal family resources and support

$ _____ Personal home/property equity

III. Other programs and resources:

$ _____ State Disability Planning Councils/employment service providers

$ _____ Individual Development Account (IDA)

$ _____ Bank, credit union, Small Business Administration (SBA), and other small business loans

$ _____ Rehabilitation Services Administration (RSA) projects and grants

$ _____ Private investors/equity financing/receivables financing

$ _____ Business partners/basis contributions

$ _____ Other

Total business start-up financial resources available = $ _____

Making Self-Employment Work for People with Disabilities by Cary Griffin and David Hammis
© 2003 Paul H. Brookes Publishing Co., Inc. All rights reserved.

Checklist for Setting Up a Small Business Account and Predicting Net Earnings from Self-Employment (NESE)

	Business account	Yearly NESE	Business plan	Proof of business expenses or sales	Monthly hours
Supplemental Security Income (SSI)					N/A
Social Security Disability Insurance (SSDI)					
Food stamps					N/A
Medicaid					
U.S. Department of Housing and Urban Development (HUD) rent					N/A
Energy assistance			N/A	N/A	N/A
Other (e.g., Veteran's Administration [VA] benefits)					
Other (e.g., long-term disability benefits)					
Other (e.g., Vocational Rehabilitation [VR] and/or Workforce Investment Act [WIA] benefits)					

Note: This checklist represents the minimum information required by each local program to set up a small business account, with the funds in the business account totally excluded as a resource. NESE predictions are also included. NESE predictions may cause some systems to either reduce benefits or increase charges, such as reductions in SSI or increases in HUD rent. In the case of SSDI receipt, monthly hours worked in a small business and NESE income predictions can cause the entire loss of an SSDI check. It is strongly advised that a benefits analysis be conducted prior to reporting predicted monthly hours worked in a small business and/or NESE predictions to any of the above local offices, specifically if SSDI is involved.

Making Self-Employment Work for People with Disabilities by Cary Griffin and David Hammis

Dreams Map

This map is used to capture a variety of desires that the potential business owner (PBO) hopes to realize in his or her lifetime. Caution should be taken because during this "dreaming" phase, as team members can sometimes impose artificial or presumed limits on dreams. Often, the phrase "that's unrealistic" is used. This derails the process of creating a desirable future. The future is not to be judged in terms of realistic or unrealistic; the future is something to be shaped and created.

On a flipchart in full view of the business design team (BDT), the PBO and the facilitator list various dreams or hopes. The BDT brainstorms a few possible ways for the dream to be realized and brainstorms who in the room or in the community might be able to assist in accomplishing or pursuing the desired outcome. Being inventive, nonjudgmental, and enthusiastic helps to energize a positive, lively, and hopeful discussion. This activity offers encouragement and creates new ideas and avenues of exploration.

The dream	A few steps that might help the dream become reality	Who can help

From Griffin, C.C., & Hammis, D. (1996). *StreetWise guide to person-centered career planning* (p. 10). Denver, CO: Center for Technical Assistance and Training; adapted by permission.

Features and Benefits Analysis

Features	Benefit(s) to customers

Features that might be added later to improve business	Potential benefit(s) to customers

Financial Map

People or agencies from which resources are currently available	Resources that I can use right now	Resources that can be developed for later use
Developmental disability day program funding		
Job/business development from Vocational Rehabilitation (VR)		
Job/business coaching		
Small business mentoring		
Plan for Achieving Self-Support (PASS)		
Family support (if available)		
The total support now available to me is $_____. With some development efforts (i.e., assistance with pulling these resources together into a plan), $_____ may be available, totaling $_____.		

Five Senses Exercise

Sense	Description	Importance
What should customers see?		
What should customers feel?		
What should customers hear?		
What should customers taste?		
What should customers smell?		

Making Self-Employment Work for People with Disabilities by Cary Griffin and David Hammis

Market Positioning Worksheet

Customer demographics or identifiers	Primary customer	Secondary customer(s)
Location of the customers (e.g., city, county, particular part of town, cyberspace)		
Age range		
Male or female?		
Income level (e.g., low, middle, high)		
Educational level		
Career type ("white collar," "blue collar")		
Marital status		
Has children?		

From Griffin, C., Hammis, D., Katz, M., Sperry, C., Flaherty, M., Shelley, R., Snizek, B., & Maxson, N. (2001). *Making the road by taking it: Team and individual exercises for self employment training* (pp. 37–41). Missoula, MT: The Rural Institute; adapted by permission.

Market Positioning Worksheet

Customer demographics or identifiers	Primary customer	Secondary customer(s)
Pet owner?		
Hobbies/interests		
Religious/political traits		
Do potential customers know that they have a need for this product/service?		
Do potential customers need your product/service but not know it?		
Marketing for Business to Business (B2B) Companies		
Type of business to supply		
Specific businesses to supply		
Size of business revenue		

From Griffin, C., Hammis, D., Katz, M., Sperry, C., Flaherty, M., Shelley, R., Snizek, B., & Maxson, N. (2001). *Making the road by taking it: Team and individual exercises for self employment training* (pp. 37–41). Missoula, MT: The Rural Institute; adapted by permission.

Market Positioning Worksheet

Customer demographics or identifiers	Primary customer	Secondary customer(s)
Number of employees		
Location(s)		
Other descriptors		

Sources of Marketing Research Data	
List the pertinent "whos", "whats", "whens", and/or "wheres" discovered from each category.	
Similar businesses	
Related web sites	
Yellow pages and business directories at the public library	
Newspaper business section, classified advertisements, and display advertisements	

From Griffin, C., Hammis, D., Katz, M., Sperry, C., Flaherty, M., Shelley, R., Snizek, B., & Maxson, N. (2001). *Making the road by taking it: Team and individual exercises for self employment training* (pp. 37–41) Missoula, MT: The Rural Institute; adapted by permission.

Market Positioning Worksheet

Sources of Marketing Research Data List the pertinent "whos", "whats", "whens", and/or "wheres" discovered from each category.	
Chamber of commerce and/or local economic development office	
Small Business Development Center (SBDC), local business incubator, and/or Small Business Administration (SBA) programs	
Business and trade schools	
Bankers, investors, and/or financial advisors	
The state's Secretary of State office, Internal Revenue Service, and the state department of revenue	
Vocational Rehabilitation (VR)/One-Stop Centers, employment security, and/or community rehabilitation programs (CRPs)	

From Griffin, C., Hammis, D., Katz, M., Sperry, C., Flaherty, M., Shelley, R., Snizek, B., & Maxson, N. (2001). *Making the road by taking it: Team and individual exercises for self employment training* (pp. 37–41). Missoula, MT: The Rural Institute; adapted by permission.

Market Positioning Worksheet

Sources of Marketing Research Data List the pertinent "whos", "whats", "whens", and/or "wheres" discovered from each category.	
Census data and U.S. Department of Labor and/or U.S. Department of Commerce reports	
Industry associations	
Other sources of information	

From Griffin, C., Hammis, D., Katz, M., Sperry, C., Flaherty, V., Shelley, R., Snizek, B., & Maxson, N. (2001). *Making the road by taking it: Team and individual exercises for self employment training* (pp. 37–41). Missoula, MT: The Rural Institute; adapted by permission.

Places Map

Use this map to list and describe the environments frequented by the prospective business owner (PBO). Include details such as the surroundings, others who are there, the person's major activities in the place, the skills utilized or needed to participate in the environment, the transportation used to get there, the time of day or week that the person goes there, the value of the place to the person and/or his or her family, and so forth. This map often reveals that individuals served in traditional special education or rehabilitation programs desire but have few true community experiences available. Studying the results may help the business design team identify which places the person should spend more time, which people and supports are important in gaining access to such places, and which new or augmented skills or supports are needed for successful participation in these community places. All of these details offer clues to services/products and types of businesses that might be interesting to the PBO.

Home

From Griffin, C.C., & Hammis, D. (1996). *StreetWise guide to person-centered career planning* (p. 9). Denver, CO: Center for Technical Assistance and Training; adapted by permission.

Preferences Map

In the left column, list the situations, materials, people, environments, occasions, experiences, and so forth that make the potential business owner (PBO) happy, successful, and connected. In the right column, list the things that are undesirable for the PBO. Completing this map helps the business design team (BDT) foster the attainment of things that work instead of things that do not work.

What works?	What does not work?

1. *Team members should think of what works in their own lives, consider the importance of these positive aspects, and consider how self-determination in their lives is guided by these preferences.*

2. *Team members should likewise consider what does not work for them and how they personally and professionally act to avoid, control, or minimize these items in their own lives.*

From Griffin, C.C., & Hammis, D. (1996). StreetWise guide to person-centered career planning (p. 12). Denver, CO: Center for Technical Assistance and Training; adapted by permission.

Relationships Map

On this map, list the people (typically, human services staff) who are paid to be with the potential business owner (PBO), family members, and friends from the community. The business design team (BDT) should discuss the quality of relationships, the frequency of contact, and the quality of contact. The BDT should consider methods and opportunities for increasing the types of relationships desired by the PBO. Once the map is completed, the BDT and PBO should consider the questions that follow.

From Griffin, C.C., & Hammis, D. (1996). *StreetWise guide to person-centered career planning* (p. 11). Denver, CO: Center for Technical Assistance and Training; adapted by permission.

1. What does this map indicate regarding personal connectedness?

2. Do others on the BDT or in the community have similarly dominant paid relationships?

3. How will the BDT take action to bring more people into the PBO's personal network?

Skills and Needed Supports

Business skill	I can do this	I need these supports	Who can help (a personal contact or a professional to be hired, such as an accountant)
Bookkeeping			
Managing inventory/ ordering supplies			
Producing the product/service			
Customer service/ managing complaints			
Record keeping			
Sales			
Marketing/promotion			
Establishing and maintaining a consistent work schedule			
Managing cash and checks			
Supervising personnel			
Other:			
Other:			
Other:			

Making Self-Employment Work for People with Disabilities by Cary Griffin and David Hammis

Small Business Benefits Planning Initial Worksheet

Name: _____ SS#: _____ DOB: _____

Are you married?　　Yes　　No

Are you receiving any of the following?

SSI　　　　　Yes　No　If yes, amount received each month _____

SSDI　　　　Yes　No　If yes, amount received each month _____

Are you working or operating your small business (or both) at this time?

If yes, what type of work or business? _____ Hours worked per week _____

Gross monthly salary or income? _____ Supported employment?　Yes　No

Does it appear that you will maintain this work for the next 6 to 12 months?　Yes　No

In what type of home do you live?

Own home? _____　　　Rent? _____　　　Subsidy? _____ If yes to subsidy, what type of subsidy?

Live with family? _____　　　Live with roommate(s)? _____

Other housing arrangement? If yes, please describe:

How much do you pay for rent each month? _____

What is your current total household monthly income?

List all sources of income that your household receives in addition to the social security benefit listed above:

_____ amount received _____ from _____

_____ amount received _____ from _____

_____ amount received _____ from _____

What type of health insurance are you currently receiving? (list all types of insurance you are receiving)

Making Self-Employment Work for People with Disabilities by Cary Griffin and David Hammis
© 2003 Paul H. Brookes Publishing Co., Inc. All rights reserved.

How much do you pay per month to meet your living and medical expenses?

Please attach a copy of your business plan and/or small business income historical information and projections for the next year.

Describe your personal living situation and benefits from any government programs (e.g., SSI, Medicaid, food stamps, Section 8 rent subsidy) and the impact of those benefits on your life. This section should include any and all government benefits information.

Describe your work history since the time you began receiving benefits (e.g., I began receiving SSDI of $1,000 per month after a car accident, have received it for 3 years, and have not worked for pay yet—but I have volunteered). This section needs to include an accurate employment history since the prospective business owner (PBO) first began receiving government benefits. This is often difficult to accomplish with someone that has worked in multiple employment and self-employment situations. If there are information gaps, it may be necessary to contact related government program offices, such as the SSA and Medicaid, to obtain the best possible information available for an accurate small business benefits analysis.

Describe your small business income, or projected income, and include any start-up or expansion funds needed for your business. This section often requires a fairly well-developed business idea or business plan and is often a dynamic interplay between the associated business planning efforts and the benefits analysis.

Please provide any additional information, such as a pending marriage or other income from family members that live with you or will be living with you. This section addresses needed information concerning the interactions of all income and family members in a household and how that income interacts with related government programs.

Please note any self-directed work accommodations that you may need to run your business, such as flexible work hours or personal assistance with some business operations. Accommodations for a small business owner often directly relate to various work incentives available through government programs such as SSI's Blind Work Expense income exclusion and SSDI's self-employment unpaid help and subsidy interactions with NESE.

List any vocational support services you are currently connected with or using (i.e., state Vocational Rehabilitation services, private rehabilitation, workers' compensation, mental health employment supports). This analysis may show gaps in services for which applications could be made. For instance, if the PBO is not working with state Vocational Rehabilitation services, it may be useful to apply for such services for business development, counseling, and funding.

Self-Employment Benefits Analysis

(*Note:* Parts 1, 2 3, and 4 of this final section may require a skilled benefits planner to complete after information is gathered from the first section of this worksheet.)

1. Impact of small business income on Medical coverage

2. Impact of small business income on monthly cash benefits (SSI and/or SSDI)

3. Potential work incentives that apply to this business (e.g., PASS, IRWE, BWE, SEIE, Subsidy, 1619(b), Subsidy, Extended Medicare, Ticket to Work)

4. Action plan from small business benefits analysis recommendations

Steps and rationale for the specified time required to meet completion date

a.

b.

c.

d.

e.

f.

Telephone Survey Worksheet

Use this worksheet to record each call conducted for the business feasibility survey. The form provides space for names and addresses of respondents, if the research necessitates recording this information; otherwise, asking such questions is not recommended because responses typically should be anonymous. One item of note to record is the survey number, a way to keep track of calls that helps establish the response rate and also sets the expectation that the surveyor should attempt a certain number of surveys.

   The surveyor, either the PBO or a member of the BDT, follows the telephone greeting that was scripted by the BDT. In the Response to greeting space, the surveyor records any suspected reasons for the respondent's hesitancy to answer or desire to discontinue the survey. If the conversation continues past the greeting, the surveyor poses the questions in order and briefly records the responses. Immediately following the telephone conversation, the surveyor notes any impressions (e.g., the respondent seemed hostile to the idea or did not understand the business concept). These impressions may help identify strengths and weaknesses in the business design.

Business idea:	Date:	Telephone number:
Respondent address:	Time of call:	Survey number:

Greeting:
Response to greeting:
Question 1:
Response to Question 1:
Surveyor's impressions:
Question 2:
Response to Question 2:

Telephone Survey Worksheet

Surveyor's impressions:

Question 3:

Response to Question 3:

Surveyor's impressions:

Question 4:

Response to Question 4:

Surveyor's impressions:

Is there anything else that you care to tell me about the idea we've discussed?

Response:

May we contact you when we open for business, perhaps to offer a discount?

Response:

Contact information provided by the respondent:

Thank you so much for your time. Have a pleasant evening.

Making Self-Employment Work for People with Disabilities by Cary Griffin and David Hammis

Business Plan

1. Primary product/service

Details:

2. Business goals

Short-term goals include

*
*
*

Long-term goals include

*
*
*

3. Support

4. Other complementary products/services

A.

B.

C.

D.

E.

F.

5. How each complementary product/service listed in #4 adds value

A.

B.

C.

D.

E.

F.

6. What is the anticipated market position for the primary product/service (i.e., high quality/high price, moderate quality/low price)? Are you seeking an upscale, an average, or a discount-seeking buyer? Explain.

7. Business/work hours

8. Who is the likely buyer (e.g., younger/older, male/female, wealthy/restricted income)? Where would the buyer look for this product/service? Explain.

Making Self-Employment Work for People with Disabilities by Cary Griffin and David Hammis
© 2003 Paul H. Brookes Publishing Co., Inc. All rights reserved.

9. Will the buyer need to purchase this product/service more than once? How often? How does this affect the marketing approach, packaging, and volume discounts (e.g., a lawn mowing service gives a $10 discount to customers who sign up for six mowings)? Explain your strategy.

10. Expected wages/pay. Explain the basis for this calculation or forecast.

- Wages

- Rent

- Depreciation/amortization

- Miscellaneous expenses

Total monthly expenses

11. How will you know if your product/service is over- or underpriced? What do similar products/services sell for at other businesses?

12. Where will you sell this product/service (e.g., other people's stores, your own store, door to door, in magazines, over the Internet?). List specific outlets.

13. How will the product be packaged? What will it look like? Explain.

What should customers see?

What should customers hear?

What should customers taste?

What should customers feel?

What should customers smell?

14. Will each package contain multiple products? Will the product(s) be bundled with other complementary products from your company? Will you bundle complementary products from other companies? Explain.

15. What image do you seek for this product/service? That is, is it convenient for customers? Is it cheaper than similar services offered by other businesses? Does it add value to or complement another product/service that the customer is likely to use? Are you pledging high-quality customer service? Does it have "snob appeal," or is it for the "do-it-yourselfer"? Explain.

16. Does this service complement another company's service? What makes your service better? Does the opportunity exist to bundle this service with the product/service of another company? Explain.

17. What is the overall promotional strategy for your product/service? What "look" or image do you want?

18. How will you use advertising? Is this a major part of your marketing strategy? Which advertising outlets will you use? How often will you advertise?

    A.   Print advertising (newspapers, yellow pages):

    B.   Direct mail:

    C.   Television:

    D.   Radio:

    E.   Word of mouth:

    F.   Business cards and brochures:

    G.   Novelties:

    H.   Signage:

Making Self-Employment Work for People with Disabilities by Cary Griffin and David Hammis
© 2003 Paul H. Brookes Publishing Co., Inc. All rights reserved.

I.   Classified advertising:

J.   Telemarketing:

K.   Press releases and public service announcements (PSAs):

L.   Sales staff:

M.   Other:

19. How will you measure the effectiveness of your promotions?

20. How much do you propose to spend monthly on marketing and advertising? How will you know if it is enough or too much?

21. Other issues of product, price, place, and promotion

Appendix B

Internet Resources

BUSINESS FEASIBILITY RESOURCES

The Abilities Fund
http://www.abilitiesfund.org

Information on loan programs, training, and small business development

Association of Small Business Development Centers
http://www.asbdc-us.org/

Information on local resources, training, and loan programs

Entrepreneur.com
http://www.entrepreneur.com

Articles on business trends and operations

FirstGov
http://www.firstgov.com

A portal to all of the government web sites

Forum for Women Entrepreneurs
http://www.fwe.org

Information on local resources, training, and loan programs

Griffin-Hammis Associates, LLC
http://www.griffinhammis.com

Full-service consultancy that develops communities of economic cooperation by providing high-quality training and technical consultation, project development and management services, and inventive service delivery

Inc Magazine
http://www.inc.com

Articles on business trends and operations

Job Accommodation Network
http://www.jan.wvu.edu

Information on small businesses and disability, assistive technology, training programs, and local resources

National Association of Women Business Owners Center
http://www.nawbo.org

Information on local resources, training, and loan programs

Office of Women's Business Ownership
http://www.sba.gov/womeninbusiness

Information on local resources, training, and loan programs

Online Women's Business Center
http://www.onlinewbc.gov

Information on local resources, training, and loan programs

The Rural Institute at the University of Montana
http://ruralinstitute.umt.edu

Information on training events, publications on self-employment and disability, policy information, technical assistance on self-employment and Social Security Administration work incentives, and grant opportunities

The Rural Institute's PASSplan.org
http://www.passplan.org

Plan for Achieving Self-Support (PASS) samples that received the Social Security Administration's approval

Senior Corps of Retired Executives (SCORE)
http://www.score.org

Business articles, how-to information, local mentoring assistance for small business owners

U.S. Department of Agriculture
http://www.usda.gov

Information on business resources, loans, grants, and local resources

U.S. Department of Education
http://www.ed.gov

Information on special education, rehabilitation, grant programs, research findings, and local resources

U.S. Department of Labor
http://www.dol.gov

Information on Workforce Investment Act services, grant programs, and local resources

U.S. Small Business Administration
http://www.sba.gov

Information on small business training, loans, and local resources

WorkSupport.com
http://www.worksupport.com

Information provided by the Virginia Commonwealth University Research and Training Center on Workplace Supports regarding training and technical assistance, best practices in rehabilitation, and current research in rehabilitation

INDUSTRY STANDARD INFORMATION

BizMiner
http://www.bizminer.com

Charges a fee per report on industry information

BizStats.com
http://www.BizStats.com

Services are free but limited to only a few broad industry categories

Creditworthy
http://www.creditworthy.com

Provides links to other sites. It may be especially helpful for PBOs and BDTs to look under "Credit Providers," then under "Industry Research & Reports."

The North American Industry Classification System (NAICS)
http://www.census.gov/epcd/www/naics.html

According to this site, "NAICS has replaced the U.S. Standard Industrial Classification (SIC) system. NAICS was developed jointly by the U.S., Canada, and Mexico to provide new comparability in statistics about business activity across North America."

The Risk Management Association
http://www.rmahq.org

Charges a fee per report on industry information

Small Business Development Center
National Information Clearinghouse
http://sbdcnet.utsa.edu

Provides links to other sites

SPREADSHEET PUBLIC ACCESS FILES

ChamberBiz
http://www.chamberbiz.com

Free Microsoft Excel business plan and finance templates for personal use. Click on the link "BizCenter," then select "Business Forms and Templates."

Microsoft Office Template Gallery
http://officeupdate.microsoft.com/templategallery/

Free Microsoft Excel business plan and finance templates for personal use. Click on the link "Finance and Accounting," then select "Business Plans and Financial Statements."

Service Corps of Retired Executives (SCORE)
http://www.score.org

Links to free business plan and financial software. Click on "Business Resources," then choose from the links provided.

Index